What's Keeping You Broke?

What's Keeping You Broke?

An Illustrated Guide to Financial Freedom by The Simple Sum

WILEY

This edition first published 2025

Registered Office(s)
John Wiley & Sons, Inc., 111 River Street, Hoboken, NJ 07030, USA
John Wiley & Sons Singapore Pte. Ltd, 134 Jurong Gateway Road, #04-307H, Singapore 600134

For details of our global editorial offices, customer services, and more information about Wiley products visit us at www.wiley.com.

Wiley also publishes its books in a variety of electronic formats and by print-on-demand. Some content that appears in standard print versions of this book may not be available in other formats.

Library of Congress Cataloging-in-Publication Data Is Available:

ISBN 9781394268580 (Paperback)
ISBN 9781394268597 (ePub)
ISBN 9781394268603 (ePDF)
ISBN 9781394319367 (Print Replica)

Cover Design and Image: The Simple Sum Pte. Ltd.

Set in 11/15pt Halyard Display Book by Straive™

SKY10086350_100124

CONTENTS

Contents

PREFACE

Why, hello there!

Let us take a guess. Are you living from paycheck to paycheck? Or maybe waiting for a ring buoy to save you from drowning in debt? If you feel frustrated, stressed, and helpless when it comes to money and you can't seem to figure out what's wrong, know this: you are seen.

You are not alone. Millions are in the same boat, struggling with money problems and clueless about building lasting wealth. Often, they blame it on not earning enough. Oh, if only it were that simple! Truth be told, it's more than that. And you picking up this book might just hold the answers to your money questions.

Fact: financial well-being goes beyond just income. Even billionaires find themselves broke, thanks to one bad decision and one too many bad financial habits. What's keeping you broke might not even be a lack of income or resources; could it be the way you think about your finances? Your money management, perhaps?

We won't let you guess. What we will do is help you uncover the not-so-obvious forces that undermine your financial well-being. We'll also let you in on tips on how to better manage your finances and steer your relationship with money in the right direction. Sound good?

What you have in your hands right now is a book that comes in four sections.

The first one puts your money habits on the spot!

We'll start by identifying hidden (and maybe not so good) factors that influence your spending habits. Here, we'll help you uncover the many myths and emotional triggers you don't even know you had that can push you to make financial decisions you'll later regret. Making informed decisions starts by understanding your financial habits and beliefs, you see.

Then there's wanting to do everything perfectly. Setting unrealistic financial plans or expecting complete control can lead to frustration and missed opportunities. It helps to be practical. Life isn't perfect, no one is. So why not cut yourself some slack and allow for some flexibility in managing your finances?

Take control of your money...or something, if not somebody else, will.

With money coming in uninterrupted, like a regular income, it's tempting to buy whatever we want or succumb to whatever we feel can reward us at the moment – we work so hard after all, don't we?

The thing is, if we give in every time, our wallet's bound to get hurt. That's why we'll have you set up some financial boundaries, with clear limits and guidelines that you can follow so you can make choices.

Of course, we'll talk about how you can make your money work for you!

Everybody knows money can do wonders. This can't be more true than if you know how to tap into its potential and make it work for you. Everybody dreams of getting rich, but without the proper wealth-building techniques, dreams are all they will ever be.

The time value of money, debt management, credit and credit scores, and even investing – we'll introduce them to you so you can stop feeling intimidated by them and instead, deal with them confidently. They are just fancy words that can always be broken down into very simple terms.

Lastly, we'll leave it up to you to level up your money game (but with much friendly prodding from us!).

It's your money, so giving it a positive spin is entirely up to you. But there's no need to worry because we'll be here cheering you on! Write yourself a new money story and create a stronger financial road map built to last and weather any curveball that life throws your way.

This book is filled with fun (yes, not boring!) activities, quizzes, and templates you can try your hands (and mind) on!

By the end of this book, you'll have a deeper understanding of the things that make and keep you broke. More than that, you're going to be armed with the knowledge, tools, and mindset to counter them.

The road to financial freedom sure is tough, with twists and turns here and there. But it is absolutely within your reach! This is why we created this book, to cheer you on and support you every step of the way.

Buckle up, 'cause you got this!

Chapter
One

Keeping Up
Is Keeping
You Broke

KEEPING UP IS KEEPING YOU BROKE

When it comes to money, you usually think of ways to make more of it. It's natural and not even a bad thought. The thing is, when you have more money, you also tend to spend more, too. This may mean that even if your earnings increase, your savings do not.

Let's backtrack a bit to the time when you got your latest paycheck. Yes, the one with those extra zeroes that made you starry-eyed with a big smile on your face. The feeling must have been really good that you instantly checked out your online shopping cart. Then you booked that trip to Japan. Of course, you had to match it with the trendiest wardrobe. There's also the celebratory dinner where you ordered steak. Oh, and don't forget it's the *grande* cup for you since then, instead of your usual *tall* coffee fix. Not that many expenses, don't you think?

Hello, lifestyle inflation.

Lifestyle inflation, in simple terms, is when you let your spending balloon alongside your income. It's that feeling of needing a bigger place, a flashier car, or once-in-a-lifetime experiences just because you have a little more cash flow.

The culprit? Often, it's the pressure to keep up with the seemingly amazing lives we see on social media. It's when we feel like everyone's living their "best life," and we're falling behind. What isn't obvious is that this constant comparison comes at the dangerous price of wrecking our financial goals, leaving us stressed, and far from becoming debt-free.

1. The Two Faces of Lifestyle Inflation

Knowing your enemy is your best bet in defeating it, and here, we unmask the two faces of lifestyle inflation so you can quickly recognize it the moment it creeps in:

The Comparison Cheat

Ever find yourself feeling content and happy one minute, only to be miserable the next after a quick scroll through your phone? Everyone else's life seems to be more interesting than yours. Yeah, it happens to us, too. No thanks to the sneaky power of comparison.

Let's break it down further and look at what goes on in our heads when we let this lifestyle creep in:

The Keeping Up with the Joneses Effect

It's that natural urge to see what and how our neighbors are up to, to check whose grass is greener. Don't worry – you're not alone! It helps to remember that this can be an endless spiral, so it is best to focus on yourself.

The Envy Epidemic

When others seem to be "living it up," envy creeps in. This can lead us to believe that material possessions are the key to happiness, making us spend more to feel better. But wait, ever wonder about the stuff you don't see? What if their dream vacation came with a mountain of laundry they'd rather not deal with or if their shiny new car gives them a panic attack every month?

The Fear of Missing Out (FOMO)

We panic if we're not part of the experiences we see online, pressuring us to spend to keep up. Don't let FOMO fool you! There are endless amazing experiences out there, and you don't need the latest console to have fun.

The Highlight Reel

Extravagant parties, designer shoes, perfect smiles. What you see on social media is but a tiny slice of everyone's lives, trimmed to only showcase the best moments. Not everyone posts about their dirty linen, right? Cheer up and remember that reality is a mix of good times and bad, and that is totally okay.

The Self-Worth-Triggered Shopping Spree

Often, we let the things we own and our projected image define our self-worth. This might convince us that we need to spend more so we can feel better about ourselves. But no amount of stuff can ever provide fulfillment. True self-worth comes from within so why not focus on experiences, relationships, and self-growth – these things will surely make you truly happy!

The Upgrade Urge

Social comparison aside, lifestyle inflation still finds its way to you, especially when your bank account gets a bump. Here's how:

Normalizing Higher Expenses

You may not notice it, but your daily lattes, weekend brunches, or subscriptions to all kinds of streaming services can add up faster than you can say "payday!" Little by little, your expenses pile up, draining your savings before you know it.

$15.80

$12.99

$6.50

TOTAL: -$35.29

Upgrading as a Habit

Maybe you switched to a bigger phone plan with features you won't use, a newer car model with a slightly better engine (that will most likely sit in traffic), or a larger apartment with extra rooms you might not need. Whatever it is, you've been led to believe that a higher pay grade needs some serious lifestyle upgrades. It may seem fun but often, the best upgrades are the ones you don't even need!

Rewarding Yourself Mentality

Your hard work does deserve a reward but splurging every time you get a pay raise can mean harm for your finances. Treating yourself every once in a while is fine, as long as you don't make it a habit.

Turning Points in Life

Your priorities might shift over time. You might get into an expensive hobby or decide it's time to start a family and meet adorable mini versions of yourself, both of which entail higher expenses. Fret not, because as long as you plan for these, you can make sure your finances are intact.

7

Story Time: Chris, a coding wiz who thrives on cozy nights in, just got promoted! To celebrate, his coworkers invited him on a multi-destination adventure. Stepping outside his comfort zone, Chris said yes, figuring it could be a fun experience. And it was! Until he saw the travel bill. Between flights, food, accommodation, gas, and all the stuff they had to rent, Chris realized traveling as a new hobby might take some serious budgeting.

Here's why we're wired to want more even without the external pressure to keep up with others:

We Get Used to the Good Stuff Quickly

Also known as hedonic adaptation, our happiness fades fast (the same goes for sadness). Remember how excited you were to get your hands on a new phone?

The thrill didn't last, did it? The next thing you know, you're onto your next exciting purchase just to relive the high. It's a wallet-draining cycle of pursuing happiness through buying stuff.

We Overvalue Things We Own

It's the endowment effect at play: we think that the things we already have are worth more. It's like spending on what you've gotten used to just because you have more money. These unnecessary expenses become your new normal that drains your wallet over time.

We Dislike Losing

We hate losing even small conveniences. That's why upgrading to a pricier service might seem like a small sacrifice compared to sticking with an inconvenient, older version. This fear of losing out on minor comforts, in turn, can easily bloat our budget.

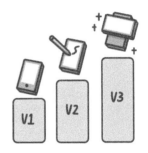

We Are Marketing Fans

There's no escaping ads telling us to get things we don't need. They tell us we need to make new purchases to be happy and influence how we spend our money.

We Try to Keep Up with Ourselves

When we're not busy comparing ourselves to others, we compare ourselves to past versions of us. We see income growth as an added pressure to maintain or even upgrade our lifestyles.

Name Your Struggle

List the times you gave in to social pressure so you'll know better to avoid them next time!

_____

_____

_____

_____

_____

_____

2. The Hidden Costs of Lifestyle Inflation (And How to Avoid Them)

Don't let your spending outpace your savings. When you know your financial habits, you can make them work for you! There are two ways lifestyle inflation can creep in and surprise you, but we've got tips to turn them from challenges to opportunities:

Immediate Hit

Sudden Money Drain: You spend more on your wants than your needs so you end up saving less.

What to do: Become a savings master by tracking your wins, celebrating every dollar you get to save. You'll be surprised to realize how motivating it is to see your progress, no matter how little. Plus, it helps keep you on track. Do not forget to identify your priorities too! Instead of shelling out cash for your daily coffee fix, why not replace it with home-brewed coffee, which means extra budget for that vacation of a lifetime on your bucket list.

Long-term Blow

Plans Derailed: With less money left after spending to keep up, long-term goals like retirement, your dream house, or educational funds for your children get impacted.

Mounting Debt: You end up with more debt due to credit cards or loans. You pay higher interest as you cannot pay in full.

Financial Vulnerability: Your financial security is also on the line, leaving you less protected against emergencies, unexpected expenses, or unemployment.

Investment Blocker: Less money saved means less funds to invest, limiting your potential to grow your wealth.

> *What to do:* When you get a raise, prioritize paying off your debts so you can say goodbye to mounting high interest payments. Imagine sleeping soundly because you are debt-free! Once your savings are secured, you can then look into options for growing your wealth, like investments (which we'll talk about later).

3. Breaking Free from Lifestyle Inflation

This might seem tough at first, but taking action now will have you celebrating your progress in no time! First off, some things need to be set straight.

Money Myths to Bust:

Myth 1: Fancy Things Mean Financial Freedom.

You don't need the trendiest gadgets or the coolest cars to be successful. Financial freedom is about achieving your goals, and not about impressing others.

Myth 2: Keep Up with the Joneses or Fall Behind.

Forget the Joneses. You don't need their or anyone else's approval. You do you. Focus instead on creating connections with people who accept you for who you are and not for the figures in your bank book.

Myth 3: You Don't Deserve to Have Fun.

Says who? Finding balance is key! You can reward yourself every now and then as long as you spend within your means. Delayed gratification is also something you can try!

Shifting Your Mindset to What Truly Matters

It's never too late to deal with lifestyle inflation and prevent the damage it can do to your finances. As much as it's a psychological battle, it's not something that can't be won.

Get Social Media Timeouts

Set time limits on your social media consumption. This way, you avoid seeing things that make you feel less.

Define Wants and Needs

It's sometimes hard to distinguish your needs and desires, especially if you think making a purchase will make you happy. But for how long? Are you buying things that matter or is it just for the sake of appearances? Try sleeping on a purchase to make sure you won't regret it.

Be Grateful

There's a lot to be thankful for. Focusing on your blessings, no matter how big or small, can make you realize how much you truly have. A grateful heart even reduces the urge to buy more.

You Think of You

Focus on yourself and the things that truly bring you joy and fulfillment more than any material possessions ever could – friends, loved ones, personal growth. Ultimately, know that you are enough.

WANTS

NEEDS

MIND

SHIFTER

Gratitude

Practical Financial Tips to Keep Yourself from Keeping Up with Others

Once the mind is taken care of, it's time to work on your game plan.

1. **Track Your Spending:** Zoom in on every expense you make. You might be surprised how much you spend on afternoon lattes or takeaway lunches. Seeing where your money goes can be a real eye-opener. We've included an expense tracker sheet in this chapter to help you get started!

2. **Make Budgeting Your BFF:** Think of a budget as your guide to financial freedom where you split your money between needs, wants, and savings, of course! There are a lot of budgeting methods you can follow. Preparing for a big event? Let us help you plan for it using our budget-friendly party planner!

3. **Sleep on a Purchase:** Delayed gratification is key, especially for big-ticket items. You'll soon realize that your urge to buy fades over time. If it won't matter in a year or two, better put that money into your savings instead!

4. **Take on a Spending Challenge:** "No spend challenges" on things you can do without like dining out, extra clothes, and items you find cute but won't use can be fun to take on. Aside from breaking bad spending habits, it can also help you discover cheap thrills.

5.

Go for Free Fun: Nothing beats free fun! You can always entertain yourself without spending a dime. Explore local activities like museum trips on free-admission days, nature park hikes, or community events. Warm home-cooked meals with loved ones and game nights are more rewarding than expensive outings.

EXPENSE TRACKER

MONTH & YEAR:

Date	Description	Amount	Balance

TOTAL:

NOTES:

What's Your
Monthly Budget?

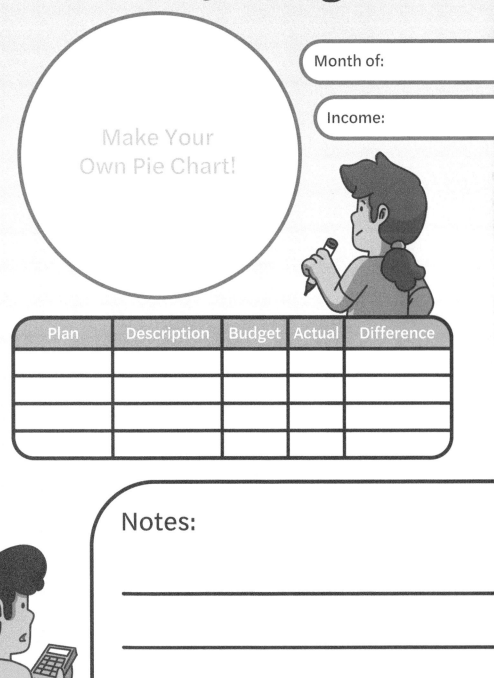

Make Your
Own Pie Chart!

Month of:

Income:

Plan	Description	Budget	Actual	Difference

Notes:

Chapter Takeaways

1. Keeping up appearances is keeping you broke.

2. Lifestyle inflation or the need to constantly spend and upgrade just because you earn a little more is triggered by two factors:

- **The Comparison Cheat**
- **The Upgrade Urge**

3. When you keep up with others or yourself, your finances suffer immediate and long-term blows:

Immediate: high expenses and reduced savings
Long-term: dreams put on hold, debt trap, and financial insecurity

Lifestyle inflation may rob you of your financial dreams but if there's one truth that you should know, it's this: You. Are. In. Control.

Wait no more and take action today! Start by becoming your own financial detective. We challenge you to track your daily spending for the next seven days – every dollar, every penny that goes out of your pocket. There's no better wake-up call than seeing how you spend your hard-earned money in black and white. You'll be surprised how many lattes, fancy dinners, or impulse buys you make in a short time!

Set a clear intention for your goals. Be it a dream house, a secure future, or a worry-free retirement, let it be your financial North Star. Focus on those, clearly define your needs, take a break from social media, and ditch the comparison game.

These may be small acts but it's tiny (and hopefully) consistent steps like these that create discipline in you, helping you to be grateful for what you have and realize that success isn't measured by material possessions. Ultimately, it will help you overcome lifestyle inflation and live life on your terms.

Chapter
Two

Your Splurge Squad Is Keeping You Broke

YOUR SPLURGE SQUAD IS KEEPING YOU BROKE

Ever noticed your lunch routine changing after hanging out with a new group? Maybe you used to frequent fast food chains with colleagues, but since your promotion as a manager, fancy lunch-outs with your co-executives have become a thing. Without you knowing, this "squad upgrade" can definitely impact your spending.

After talking about keeping up with others and keeping up with ourselves in the previous chapter, we now shift our focus and zoom in on those whose company we choose to keep and who can equally influence our financial choices for the good (or the bad) – our friends.

1. Your Squad's Hidden Superpower: How Friends Impact Your Finances

See, our friends influence us in more ways than one. It isn't obvious, but if you pay attention, you'll realize how uncannily similar your habits are. This is because friends' actions and choices subtly seep into each other's.

For instance, once-in-a-while weekend brunches at trendy cafes are harmless, right? Maybe, but not when these occasional treats become regular, expensive splurges.

June is a young professional belonging to a group of friends from college, all of whom are doing well in their careers. They love to live it up with lavish vacations, designer clothes, and fancy dinners. Fearing exclusion, June gives in to the pressure to keep up with her friends even if she cannot afford it.

Sure, she loves spending time with her best friends, but her credit card screams, her bank account protests, and her stress level goes through the roof.

We feel sorry for June, but let's face it: we've all been a June before, and there might still be one in your group right now (we're crossing our fingers it's not you!).

Why? There's a reason our brains work differently when we're around other people. Studies show that we are wired to crave social connection. So much so that hanging out with friends triggers a "return the favor" thinking in our heads, prompting us to make impulsive purchases or overspend to maintain a certain image. Speaking of image, the fear of judgment can make us prioritize looking good or affluent over being financially responsible.

It's not all bad though as this influence can work positively too! As we move along, we explore that and more, plus tips on how to navigate and use the power of peers to your advantage without breaking the bank!

Peer Ripple Effect: A Double-Edged Sword

You might have heard the saying, "You are the company you keep." Well, the same applies to your finances. As mentioned earlier, how your friends spend their money influences your financial choices.

Meet the "peer ripple effect."

Imagine tossing a pebble in a pond. See how one splash creates smaller patterns, affecting everything around it. That initial splash is your friends' spending habits, creating the smaller waves that influence how you spend your money. While social pressure is at play, it helps to know that this is actually rooted in our natural craving for connection and a sense of belonging as humans. To satisfy this, we adjust our spending habits to match our friends'.

How is it a double-edged sword, you ask? The thing is, it's not all bad, you know. This same peer ripple effect can, in fact, be a good thing. If it influences you to spend your money loosely, it can also push you to save and make better financial decisions.

Post-It.

"Sinking" Fund: Save money in this fund over time for your large ticket items, like a dream vacation.

Used in a good way, it can be helpful – goals achieved, savings intact and healthy. On the flip side, it can lead to financial trouble and anxiety. How many stories have you heard of people drowning in debt trying to keep up with a lifestyle they cannot afford? Fitting in alone is intense, and the peer ripple effect only makes it worse.

Takeaways:

It helps to know how our friends can influence our relationship with money to better understand how it can make or break us in our goal of being financially independent.

More in this chapter: Don't worry because as we move along, we'll help you find a balance between squad goals and money goals, and share tips on how to build a financially supportive group of friends!

Why Do We Spend More When Our Friends Do?

Here's a quick look at the factors that set the peer ripple effect in a smooth, almost discreet motion:

Validation is everything. We humans desire acceptance, and let's be honest, we want to be part of the cool group or the *it* group. If achieving this means copying our friends' unhealthy spending habits, then that's what we do, even if it hurts our budget in the long run.

Ask yourself: What is temporary social validation compared to a secure financial future?

We mean to please. The last thing we want is to rock the seemingly smooth sailing boat we share with our peers, so even if a proposed investment seems risky to you, you ignore your gut feeling and invest anyway. The group's going to stay intact that way.

Ask yourself: Is the pressure to keep the group solid and happy stronger than your financial well-being?

It's either you keep up, or you can't sit with us. Ever feel pressured to keep up with your friends, no matter the cost? Whether it's planned activities or spontaneous splurges, you feel like you have to say "yes" to everything. Saying no not only makes you look poor, but it also threatens your very place in the circle.

Ask yourself: Is keeping your status in the group worth all the stress it brings to your mind and your wallet?

It pays to think of yourself, too. Having friends is great but blindly following them can be harmful for your wallet. When everyone's raving about an investment that's too good to pass up, stop yourself from simply jumping in just because your friends are all doing it. Do your own research, and ask them about their experiences. Your needs and goals should come first when making financial decisions and not the groups'.

Make sure to also remember that there is a good kind of peer pressure. It's the one that can actually help you with your finances. Find supportive friends that are there for your financial goals and vice versa. These are the kind of friends you deserve.

Takeaways

We love our friends, but they can significantly impact our financial wellness. Being aware of this can help keep your wallet full and your friendships thriving.

2. Name Your Spend Squad

Knowing who among your peers influences your financial decisions the most is a key step in using the peer ripple effect to your advantage (hello, fat bank account!). Here's a short description of each for you to recognize:

The Unintentional Influencer:

They live a high life and love to show it. They propose and arrange the next fancy group activity without realizing that not everyone has the same budget to spare. They're so enthusiastic they can make you feel like you need to keep up even if you don't have the means to.

The Passive Flaunter:

They're the living, breathing version of lifestyle inflation. Be it designer bags or the coolest cars, they never forget to do everything for the gram. They might not press you to spend, but you might feel compelled to keep up with their lavish lifestyle even if it hurts your wallet.

The Competitive Spender:

Nothing excites them more than a good spending challenge. As YOLO (you only live once) believers, they never turn down a pricey night out or a spontaneous luxury shopping spree. They expect you to keep up and silently judge you if you don't.

3. Navigating the Waves of Peer Pressure

Now that we've identified your budget busters, it's time to share with you some secrets on how you can navigate peer pressure without breaking the bank! Never let your guard down though, there are some pretty bad consequences you need to watch out for!

Obstacle 1: Sunken Future Plans.

As fun as night outs or weekend getaways are, they add up fast especially if done regularly. Before you know it, you're putting off long-term plans like a dream vacation, a house, or your retirement in exchange for fleeting thrills.

Obstacle 2: Uncharted Debt.

Although it's easy to swipe your credit card for every fancy meal or wardrobe shopping, it can be very tough to get out of the unpredictably dangerous sea of debt brought about by keeping up with your friends. We haven't even talked about interest rates yet – the whirlpool to your savings.

Obstacle 3: The Friendship Kraken.

The constant pressure to match your friends' spending can make you feel burnt out and anxious. It distracts you from focusing on your goals and feeds on your peace of mind.

Lifeline 1: Imagine Your Treasure Chest.

Fix your eyes on the prize: a dream home, an adventure across the globe, a stable future. When you are in control of your finances, these goals are within reach!

Lifeline 2: Build Bridges, Not Debt.

Say goodbye to the endless game of catch-up. Forget swiping that card and think of fun, creative ways you and your friends can enjoy together like game and movie nights at home. Note: real friends value you more than your gold!

Lifeline 3: Come Clean to Your Crew.

As tricky a topic as money is, nothing beats an open and honest conversation. You might be surprised that you share the same issues with cash and keeping up. Your friends will also appreciate your honesty, making your bond stronger.

Lifeline 4: Say No and Mean It.

Stop stressing over giving a lengthy explanation for why you can't make it to an expensive dinner. It's perfectly okay to say "no" if your budget is a little tight. Setting boundaries will make you feel comfortable and in control, so practice it. After all, true friends want to spend time with you, not your wallet.

Lifeline 5: Find Common Ground.

Not all your friends will be on the same financial page as you, and that's okay! There's more to friendship than your bank accounts, so go find what made you want to be mates in the first place: Was it humor? A shared pet peeve? Movies? Go rediscover that.

Lifeline 6: Be the Good Captain.

Steer the ship the financially responsible way. Your big spender friends can also learn from you so don't go hard on them or ditch them immediately. Instead, propose fun but cheaper alternatives like a movie marathon at home or potluck lunches.

Warning: If you feel your group requires a minimum wealth to fit in, say goodbye and set sail this instant!

Takeaways

Friendships are a two-way channel. When you take control of your finances and refuse to go with the flow, your wallet will thank you for it and so will your friends.

4. Squad Goals: The Friends You Should Be Keeping and Where to Find Them

Can't wait to get your crew together? Awesome! Again, there's no need to ditch all your friends. Remember, you don't have to be at the same financial level to help each other out – it's all about wanting the same freedom and security that financial independence gives. Here are those you'd want on your team to help you get started:

Financially Fierce Fiona. She's got her money under control. She knows her budget, plans around it and responsibly sticks to it. She also avoids debt as much as she can.

Creative Spender Chris. For him, experience trumps material possessions. He knows how to have fun without breaking the bank. You'll be amazed at how far your dollar can go when you spend time with Chris who has all the best deals and money hacks memorized.

Disciplined Donna. Nothing you or others can say will make her give in to impulse spending. Her no means no. She's firm like that. You can also count on her to check your financial goal progress and hold you accountable for your every move. Strict as she is, you can expect support and encouragement from her when the going gets tough.

Goal Getter George. He has his retirement all planned out and hustling is his game. Armed with a "make it happen" attitude, everything he does is motivated by a clear vision of his financial future.

In case you're wondering if there are qualities all of them share, the answer is yes. They see money not as a source of anxiety but as a tool to unlock their dreams. They have this shared value of striving for financial freedom and take it upon themselves to inspire others to do the same. Ultimately, they are friends who will never use your spending habits against you nor judge you for them. It isn't pressure that their ripple effect creates but understanding, support, and motivation.

When you find yourself surrounded by friends like these who have your well-being in mind, who celebrate your financial goals and success and help you out in the humps and bumps, and who know that a great time need not drain your wallet, then you've just found your squad for keeps!

Appendix

Fund for emergencies or "Emergency Fund"

Setting aside funds for a rainy day. It could be for an unexpected retrenchment or when you fall sick. It provides a safety net for you to rely on when there are emergencies in life, because don't we all know that life is full of surprises.

Here are some key characteristics of an emergency fund:

Purpose: It provides you with security and shelters you from sudden shocks such as a retrenchment, if you fall ill and cannot afford to go to work, and sudden home repairs.

Accessibility: It's essential to choose a bank account or savings product with no withdrawal restrictions or penalties to ensure funds can be accessed quickly and easily in emergencies.

Size: Common guideline is to aim for enough savings to cover three to six months' worth of living expenses. However, some financial experts recommend saving even more, particularly for individuals with variable income or high-risk factors.

Simple reasons why you need an emergency fund:

Job Loss: An emergency fund can help cover your living expenses, such as rent or mortgage payments, utilities, groceries, and other essentials, while you search for new employment.

Medical Emergencies: Tap on the fund to cover medical bills and expenses. You have already set aside a sum that is beyond your daily spending. This provides you peace of mind.

Car Repairs: Vehicle issues can occur at any time, leading to costly repairs or even the need for a replacement.

Home Repairs: Home maintenance issues, such as a leaking roof, malfunctioning HVAC system, or plumbing problems, can arise unexpectedly and require immediate attention.

Unexpected Travel Expenses: Emergencies or unforeseen circumstances may require last-minute travel, such as attending a family member's funeral or dealing with a personal crisis. An emergency fund can cover the costs of airfare, lodging, transportation, and other travel-related expenses.

Natural Disasters: An emergency fund can help cover evacuation expenses, temporary lodging, emergency supplies, and repairs to your home or property.

Loss of Income Due to Disability or Illness: If you become temporarily disabled, you may experience a loss of income during your recovery period. An emergency fund can help bridge the gap until you're able to return to work or access disability benefits.

Family Emergencies: Unexpected family emergencies, such as providing financial assistance to a family member in need or covering expenses related to a family crisis, can arise unexpectedly. An emergency fund can provide the funds needed to support your loved ones during difficult times.

Unforeseen Expenses: An emergency fund provides financial flexibility to handle these unexpected expenses without relying on credit cards or loans.

Examples include legal fees, veterinary bills, and unforeseen taxes. By having an emergency fund in place, you can better withstand unforeseen circumstances and protect yourself against financial setbacks.

What are the dos and don'ts of having a fund for emergencies?

Dos:

Establish Clear Goals: Assess your financial needs based on your monthly expenses and personal risk factors. Set precise targets for your emergency fund to cover three to six months of living expenses, ensuring you're prepared for the unexpected.

Prioritize Consistent Savings: Be committed to saving! You can set up automated savings if your bank has that tool to help you save up with discipline.

Keep It Accessible: Don't lock in your savings in funds that will incur penalties if you withdraw your funds early.

Review and Adjust: When you journey in life, your needs change. There are also moments when you may not be able to save as much money. Take note to adjust your savings strategy as necessary.

Don'ts:

Don't Use it for Non-emergencies: Only use it when there is a real emergency.

Don't Risk Your Savings: Keep them safe from investments that are risky. Prioritize capital preservation and accessibility over potential returns for your emergency fund.

Don't Panic During Emergencies: In the event of a financial emergency, stay calm and use your emergency fund as intended to cover necessary expenses.

Don't Neglect Other Financial Goals: Create separate funds for retirement and investing.

Chapter
Three

Keeping Quiet
Is Keeping
You Broke

KEEPING QUIET IS KEEPING YOU BROKE

1. Breaking the Money Silence

Imagine you and your best friend Lily finally decide to make your dream vacation come true and visit France. You've been planning it for months, checking out aesthetic apartments and dreaming of freshly baked pastries as you stroll the streets of Paris in low-key local fashion.

The thing is, you naturally assume everything will be split between the two of you, just like your regular catch-ups over coffee or dinner. Because it has been your dream since you can't even remember when.

Lily, for her part, finds herself a bit short on money for a few weeks now and was too shy to tell you, careful not to dampen the mood. She believes it'll be no problem if she pays you back later, with you both being best friends and all.

You flew to France. You didn't mind paying for the charming Parisian apartment while Lily tried to look away. Your itinerary seems to have changed, though, with fine dining replaced by budget restaurants and reservation-only experiences with free attractions. You begin to notice something is wrong.

To end the awkward silence during a meal, Lily finally opens up about her financial issues. With the cat out of the bag, you both feel bad. You thought you always told each other everything. Apparently, not when it is about money. If only you had the chance to talk honestly about each other's financial situation, this could've easily been avoided. If not scheduling the trip to a later date, a cheaper apartment could have been booked or perhaps, a closer destination.

Money talk may be awkward, but it can actually strengthen ties and prevent financial stress.

You know how, when faced with a certain situation, you feel that it is better not to say anything because you think it won't harm you, let alone financially. Like the saying "ignorance is bliss," staying quiet about money can feel easier.

This is because we've always been led to believe that money is a sensitive topic. Talking about it is taboo. We feel uneasy, even uncomfortable, when it is brought up. We bet you shy away from discussing your financial situation openly, whether with family members, partners, or colleagues. We often fear judgment, embarrassment, or simply lack the confidence to dare raise the topic. That's why, in most cases, we choose to stay "financially muted."

Consider this: What if this silence costs us more than we realize?

Not everyone knows that silence is often a hidden thief that quietly drains our finances, steals our progress, and makes it harder for us to be financially independent.

How many times have you clammed up when asked about your salary, debt, or simply how much is in your wallet? We tend to dodge every discussion and choose to keep mum about our financial situation even to those closest to us.

We stay silent and think it's better that way when it actually holds us back, creating more problems. Keeping quiet can lead to misunderstandings, hurt feelings, missed opportunities, or even being taken advantage of. Who knows, you might be stuck in a job that does not pay fairly simply because you won't talk about it.

How about we break the silence and start opening up about money? A simple conversation can be the jumpstart to a bright financial future.

2. Why We Need to Talk About Money

One way or another, you have surely found yourself in a conversation that awkwardly fell silent the moment it involved talking about money. To help you remember, we listed some familiar situations when you seem to have "lost" your financial voice. As a bonus, we've included some tips on how to address them:

Among Friends

Splitting the Bills. Remember Lily earlier? We've all been there – fun dinners, outings, or trips that end sour because of bill-splitting issues. To save yourself and your friends from conflict or discomfort, why not figure out early on who pays for what? This way, you can enjoy and everybody's good.

Borrowing and Lending. It can be tricky to loan a friend some cash, resulting in awkwardness or resentment, if things go wrong. By setting clear expectations and agreeing on terms and repayment plans at the onset, you can save your wallet and your friendship.

Choosing Social Activities. Friends may propose a posh weekend getaway or a fancy dinner that does not exactly fit your budget. You hesitate to discuss it to avoid discomfort or be seen as insensitive (or worse, no fun). Instead of eating instant noodles for the next month, try speaking up. There are lots of awesome activities you can try without busting your budget. It's easier to decide on activities that work best for everyone by letting them know what you can and cannot afford.

Among Family, Spouses, and Partners

Financial Goals. Couples steer clear of talking about money to avoid conflicts or being judged. Particularly for new couples who haven't had the chance to discuss their take on savings, investments, and spending habits, thinking it's rude to bring it up so early in the relationship. The downside is that they may find themselves at odds with each other's financial aspirations somewhere along the way, leading to arguments and financial strain. Talking about these things early on will not only familiarize you with each other's financial outlook but will also help you in working toward your goals together!

Priorities and Lifestyle Choices. You were very much in love and got married instantly, figuring you have a lifetime ahead of you to get to know each other better. Over breakfast, your spouse mentioned having kids soon – something you don't see in the immediate future. You wanted to focus on your career, make a name for yourself, and rack up on properties before having little ones. Misaligned visions and priorities for the future are a recipe for marital trouble, so it's best to talk about these things openly before making a lifelong commitment.

Financial Contributions and Responsibilities. Say you make more money than your partner or your sibling. It can be awkward to discuss differences in household financial contributions or responsibilities, especially if everyone expects the highest earner to take care of the largest share. You should always strive for fairness in finances to avoid ill feelings and build a strong financial foundation.

Financial Hiccups. Job loss, unexpected bills, budget-blowing purchases, or mounting debt/financial obligations are life bumps that can happen. To avoid confrontation or disappointing our family members, we choose to keep these from them, shaking the foundation of our relationships that should be built on trust, transparency, and mutual respect. An honest conversation with your partner or family about these challenges can help you come up with solutions and let you support one another in these difficult times.

Retirement Planning. You might brush off the topic of getting older, thinking it is unappealing and too far ahead for you to be concerned about. We suggest that you give it another thought and as early as you can, discuss retirement plans with your spouse or your parents even to ensure a secure and happy future you can all enjoy.

Among Colleagues

Salary Talk. Whether you're concerned about being underpaid or simply need to know how to negotiate for a raise, you're often left wondering if it's right to even ask. Take charge of your career growth by speaking up about it. Research average market rates for your position, and set a meeting with your boss to discuss your performance and salary expectations.

Lunch-Out Dynamics. It's great to have regular group lunches as long as you're not always taking care of the bill. Try suggesting payment options that are fair for everyone, like taking turns paying, going Dutch, or splitting the bill.

Gift-Giving. Whether for a birthday, a wedding, or a farewell party, giving gifts that are way beyond your budget can be a problem. Sit down with your colleagues and share your honest thoughts about not having enough in your wallet for the gift. You can also propose more affordable yet equally fun gift ideas.

Story Time: Secret spending leads to trouble for married couple, Chelsea and Rob. While living comfortably on one income, they both craved upgrades: Rob for his wardrobe, and Chelsea for a laptop. They agreed on a new tablet for Chelsea, but she secretly bought both. The hidden purchase caused guilt, which later led to a fight and a hit on their finances. Things would not have gotten out of hand if they had been more open and honest in communicating.

Takeaways:

When it comes to your finances, open communication goes a long way, whether with friends, family, or colleagues. It fosters stronger relationships and helps everyone make their financial journey smoother.

Post-It.

Going Dutch. A common term used when everyone in a group pays for their own share of an activity, like a meal or movie ticket. It means "You pay for yours, and I'll pay for mine."

Silence Is Pricey

Keep your wallet (and yourself) happy by watching out for these money mistakes that make you want to "zip it":

Peer Pressure and "Everyone's Living Their Best Life But Me" Mentality.

Who doesn't want nice things? We all do, especially if we see others enjoying them. But often, they break the bank and leave us swimming in debt, making our dream of financial independence too far to reach. Opening up to your friends about your financial situation can make your friendship stronger.

Family First, Your Future Second...or Last?

Helping your loved ones is important, but if it comes at the expense of setting aside, if not neglecting your personal financial needs and goals altogether, you might end up with an empty wallet and zero savings. Think of yourself too and voice your personal concerns and needs. Together, you can come up with a creative solution to take care of each other.

Signing Without Reading the Fine Print.

Before signing any contract for a job or a loan, read the terms and conditions thoroughly. You wouldn't want to be underpaid or, worse, stuck in a job or commitment that will drain you and your finances. Learn and choose to speak up as it concerns your finances and your future.

Fast Talkers.

Social media, advertising, and even smooth-talking salespeople can make you buy something you can live without. It helps to look up the products they sell before putting your money down. Ask around and read reviews. You might just save yourself from debt and financial stress.

Open Communication Is Priceless

Believe it or not, money talks hold the key to stronger relationships, deeper connections, and a bright financial future.

Trust is built and nourished when we talk about money. Let's put it this way: keeping your finances a secret is like hiding a part of yourself. It keeps you from trusting anybody. But when you speak of your financial aspirations and share your challenges, you open yourself up which means you are learning how to trust. You are not on your own now, you have others who share your financial journey with you. A safe space is created where you can be yourself and where honest conversations can take place, even outside of money.

You should communicate with them

This safe space, in turn, leads to collaboration. It's when your personal worries become shared within a circle you trust, whether family, friends, or colleagues. Overcoming financial anxieties becomes a collaborative effort. You set goals and work toward achieving your financial dreams together. Best of all, you learn from each other's experiences and face financial challenges as a team.

Finances may have been the primary topic, but you'll be surprised to know how far it can go: deeper connections beyond the figures. Once you talk about money, you also open the door to discussing things that matter most to you: life, values, priorities, and even dreams. Empathy and understanding come in, where sharing your student loan worries or the satisfaction of finally buying your dream house becomes second nature. Beyond the practical, open communication also shapes emotional bonds.

With such benefits, how can you keep quiet about money? Financial conversations don't have to be scary. You can start with common topics like tracking expenses or setting a monthly budget. Watch how your relationships and finances grow from there. Remember, open communication is priceless. It's like investing in your financial wellness all the while creating and fostering connections you'll keep for life.

3. Building Your Financial Voice

Why We Stay Silent

Facing financial conversations can be daunting, and people often stay quiet about financial matters, leading to negative outcomes. Let's try to understand the need to keep it under wraps and why talking about it is key to a fuller financial life.

Money Hush-Hush

Talking openly about our finances is difficult because we feel embarrassed and worried about being judged. We don't want to be seen as show-offs or feel we are not good enough.

Financial Fog

Some of us are unsure about saving, investing, or budgeting. Because of this, we avoid financial topics because it is scary.

Fight Fright

Money can be a touchy subject, and most of us worry that talking about it might only cause disagreements or hurt feelings, so we avoid the conversation altogether. Tell you what, open communication actually prevents arguments!

Culture Clash

Depending on where you're from, there may be unwritten rules about discussing money. In some cultures, talking about it is a no-no – they see it as a sensitive topic; while others talk about it more openly.

Privacy Concerns

Keeping financial matters private is totally fine especially if you don't want everyone knowing too much about your money. Don't let it stop you from talking to people you trust about it, though.

Bad Money Memories

Past financial struggles, like debt or losing money in investments, can make us hesitant to talk about it to avoid reliving those experiences or feeling judged. It helps to know that speaking up can heal us so we can move forward.

Don't worry if you're not sure how to talk about money. There really isn't a right or wrong way to do it, you just have to take the first step. We all have to start somewhere, right? So, start building bridges instead of walls. Speak up and tear down these communication barriers for the sake of your finances.

Breaking the Cold Ice of Silence

Are you ready to speak up and break free from the financial silence that's holding you back? Start small and follow these easy and practical talking points as your conversation starters:

Naming apps and tools make for jumping-off points to find something

"Hey, I discovered this budgeting app called [app] and it's been really helpful! Have you tried looking up budgeting apps, too?"

"You know what, I read an interesting article about [financial topic]. Did you also hear about it?"

Sharing dreams and aspirations tells our families and friends they are also welcome to share theirs without getting into specifics.

"Someone talked to me about [financial product/service]? I'm curious if it can help us reach our goals."

"Lately, I find myself thinking about [financial goals like saving for a place or paying off student loans]. Can you share with me some of your financial goals?"

Discussing trends and events can lead to a personal finance conversation.

"Did you hear about the [financial news]? Can you believe it? It reminded me of…"

"I came across this [funny financial meme] that made me laugh. Somehow, it got me thinking about…"

Sharing experiences and tips are great starters that encourage opening up.

"Guess what? I am finally debt-free! I managed to pay off my [debt type]! Can you share some tips on how to handle debt better?"

"I am trying to learn more about [financial topic]. Did you know that [interesting fact]? I figure it might help us in…"

Lighthearted topics prove to be engaging and can be a fun way to interact.

"How do you keep yourself from spending more than you have to when grocery shopping?"

"I saw this no-spend weekend challenge online. I plan to try it for a month. Want to join me?"

Open-ended questions can lead to deeper conversations.

"I'm wondering, what's your take on [financial topic]?"

"Have you ever been in a [financial scenario]?" You can follow it up with, "How did you handle it?"

Walking the Talk

Have a "we" approach instead of a "me" approach to your finances. A shared vision helps you keep each other's financial journey in check.

- **Teamwork Makes the Dream Work.** Approach financial discussions with family, a partner, or friends with a willingness to find solutions that work well for everyone. Give and take is how you do it.

- **Define What Matters Most.** What are your financial dreams? To see the world or to retire in the south of France? Think hard about your values and goals, and focus on your journey. Ignore the noise that comes from social expectations.

- **Set Limits.** Boundaries are not your enemies! Stand by your financial decisions and be firm in your financial beliefs.

- **Find Your Squad.** Seek out people who strive for financial independence just like you.

- **Talk It Out.** Don't keep things to yourself. Fight feelings of shame and loneliness by talking to your partner or to friends and family you trust. You can also explore support groups! You don't have to deal with things alone. Sharing them can make you feel better and empowered too!

4. Financial Freedom and Stronger Relationships: It's Worth the Talk

Imagine how it feels like to be on the same (financial) page with your loved ones, friends, and even colleagues. There's no more hiding behind closed doors as you freely discuss your budget, spending habits, priorities, and goals. If you think it's good for your wallet, you're right, but it doesn't end there as we've discussed in this chapter: it also makes for a truly solid relationship.

To recap, here's why you should start using your financial voice:

Clear Vision, Shared Goals. Open communication helps you create a financial road map you can share together. Whether it's a dream house, debt repayment, or retirement plans, these conversations help you prioritize and work toward a shared dream while upholding accountability.

No More Guessing. When you keep your communication lines open, financial surprises become a thing of the past. Because trust is built and fostered, there's no room for guessing where your money went or where it's going. Honesty creates a safe space, holding your relationships together.

Connections Built to Last. Knowing you're not weathering financial challenges alone means a lot. Opening up and sharing your experiences solidifies your support system. This time, you know you're facing them together which can be nothing short of empowering!

Story Time: A family of four, the Millers, struggle to stick to a budget. The parents fear they might be setting a bad example for their kids, so they sat down and talked it out. After careful analysis of their spending habits, they realized they've been making unnecessary (and mostly impulse) purchases that take a toll on their budget, delaying their plans of saving up for a family vacation. Resolved on starting anew, they started dedicating a "fun fund" with a limit, giving them some wiggle room while staying on track. As a bonus, they get to involve the kids and teach them about saving too!

Your Turn to Thrive. Make yourself ready for your first money conversation. Here are a few tips to get you started:

- Schedule a regular "money huddle." Find a common time when everyone is available and stick to it.

- Begin with a positive and supportive tone. Highlight solutions and focus on working together.

- Remember to be honest. Share your goals and concerns (if any) openly.

- Listen well. Make your loved ones feel that you value their sentiments and inputs.

Communicate openly and discover how being open can support you on your journey to financial freedom!

Appendix

Sinking Fund

Ever find yourself scrambling to cover the cost of a yearly insurance premium, or wishing you could go on a vacation without maxing out your credit card? Here's where a sinking fund steps in – not just as any savings plan, but as your proactive strategy to manage finances for specific, anticipated expenses. It's about saving smart, not hard, and preparing for future costs systematically to maintain your financial peace.

Sinking Fund: Saving for planned expenses.

Unlike an emergency fund, which is reserved for unexpected situations, a sinking fund is designed for planned expenses that are foreseen yet don't happen regularly. The beauty of a sinking fund lies in its ability to help you accumulate money over time, readying you for when that expense rolls around. This means you can avoid the financial strain that often comes with large, infrequent costs.

Here are some key characteristics of a sinking fund:

Specific Purpose: Each sinking fund has a mission. The fund's purpose drives its funding strategy, influencing how much and how often you need to save.

Gradual Accumulation: Like a slow and steady drip fills a bucket, regular contributions from your income fill up your sinking fund. This methodical approach allows you to build up the necessary funds gradually, ensuring you have enough saved when you need it.

Predictable Expenses: Think of expenses that come around every so often – like vehicle maintenance or holiday gifts. These costs are perfect candidates for a sinking fund because you know they're coming and can plan for them without dipping into your regular budget.

What is a sinking fund used for?

Whether it's for annual insurance premiums or the family vacation of your dreams, a sinking fund makes saving for these expenses manageable and stress-free. Here's a closer look at some common expenses you might use a sinking fund for, ensuring you can enjoy life's moments and milestones without financial worry:

Vehicle Maintenance and Repairs: From routine oil changes to unexpected repairs, cars can be expensive. A sinking fund for your vehicle helps keep your car running smoothly without unbalancing your monthly budget.

Home Repairs and Maintenance: Whether it's fixing a leaky roof or updating an old HVAC system, you tap on the fund for planned maintenance costs.

Annual Insurance Premiums: Insurance is essential, but those annual premiums can be hefty. By contributing to a sinking fund throughout the year, you're ready when those big bills land in your mailbox.

Property Taxes: Property taxes come due every year. Regular contributions to a sinking fund help you meet these obligations without stress.

Vacations and Travel: Dreaming of sandy beaches or a European adventure? Planning and saving for your travel expenses ahead of time means you can embark on your getaway without financial guilt or debt.

Holiday and Gift Expenses: The holiday season should be joyful, not stressful. Save for gifts and festivities throughout the year, and you won't be short of cash during holiday periods.

Education Expenses: A sinking fund can help you manage the costs of tuition, books, and supplies, paving the way for academic success without financial strain.

Major Purchases: Looking to buy new furniture or upgrade your tech? Save up with a sinking fund and pay in cash, avoiding the high interest rates of credit cards or loans.

Healthcare Costs: From routine check-ups to unexpected medical needs, healthcare costs add up quickly. A sinking fund for health expenses ensures you can care for your well-being without financial worry.

Special Occasions and Milestones: Life's special moments – weddings, anniversaries, and birthdays – deserve celebration. By planning and saving for these events, you can enjoy them to the fullest, free from the burden of debt.

A sinking fund does more than just cover upcoming expenses; it builds your confidence in handling money and planning for the future. Empower yourself to manage money proactively, ensuring you're ready for the future, whatever it may hold.

What are the differences between an emergency fund and a sinking fund?

Purpose

Emergency Fund: Its primary purpose is to provide financial security and stability during unforeseen circumstances.

Sinking Fund: It helps you gradually accumulate funds over time to cover specific expenses, such as vehicle maintenance, property taxes, vacations, or home renovations.

Timing of Expenses

Emergency Fund: Uses are spontaneous and urgent. This fund is designed to be tapped into at a moment's notice, providing quick access to funds when the unforeseen strikes.

Sinking Fund: Uses are anticipated. You know these expenses are coming and when they'll hit, so you can save at a pace that matches the timing of the future expense.

Frequency of Contributions:

Emergency Fund: Contributions are made regularly to build and maintain a financial safety net. The goal is to have enough savings to cover several months' worth of living expenses.

Sinking Fund: Contributions are made regularly to save for specific expenses or financial goals. The amount and frequency of contributions depend on the timeline for the expense and the desired savings goal.

Accessibility of Funds:

Emergency Fund: Funds are easily accessible and liquid, allowing you to withdraw them quickly when needed. The focus is on providing immediate financial relief during emergencies.

Sinking Fund: Funds are also accessible but may be less liquid depending on the timing of the expense. While you can access the funds when needed, the focus is on saving gradually to cover a future expense.

Types of Expenses Covered:

Emergency Fund: Sudden job loss, accidents, emergencies or urgent payments that occurred unexpectedly.

Sinking Fund: A sinking fund covers specific planned expenses or financial goals that are anticipated but occur irregularly. These may include vehicle maintenance, property taxes, insurance premiums, vacations, or home renovations.

By distinguishing between these two crucial types of savings, you set the stage for a more secure financial foundation. An emergency fund keeps you safe from unexpected downturns, while a sinking fund ensures you're prepared for the expected, making large expenses manageable and predictable. Together, they provide a comprehensive buffer that protects your financial well-being, helping you navigate both calm and turbulent financial waters with confidence.

But to achieve it, you'll need to understand where you stand. In Grant Sabatier's book*, he lists 7 levels of financial freedom.

LVL 7
LVL 6
LVL 5
LVL 4
LVL 3
LVL 2
LVL 1

Which level are you?

*Financial Freedom: A Proven Path to All the Money You'll Ever Need

Level 1: Clarity

You know how much money you have, how much you owe, and what your goals are.

GOAL : MOVE OUT!
EXPENSES   BUDGET

Chapter
Four

Staying Still
Is Keeping
You Broke

STAYING STILL IS KEEPING YOU BROKE

We all have dreams of making it big one day, or at least to be free from worries when it comes to our finances. We also know that to get there, we need to do something. The thing is, we're quite comfortable where we are right now that any change might be risky. We're running on autopilot mode and we think we're okay. But are we, really?

Investing looks scary...I'll just stick to saving money.

What if we tell you there's so much more you can achieve outside the seemingly steady state of your finances? Name your destination and know exactly how to get there. Time to take control of your financial future!

1. Shift Gears and Take Control

Meet Olivia. She's a talented graphic designer who dreams of someday starting her own business. She's been putting it off, thinking a fixed paycheck from her day job meant security. It has been years, and still, her dreams have remained just that – dreams. She's stuck in an autopilot state that keeps her from fulfilling her goals.

Like Olivia, we all have dreams – that perfect vacation, a comfy retirement, or maybe owning a home someday. Now, it's either we work through that or let a sly force called financial inertia hold us back. Inertia what? Don't worry, we'll break it down for you. Financial inertia is like hitting snooze on your financial alarm – you know you should be saving, but taking action feels challenging, so you put it off for as long as possible.

Who can relate?

Financial inertia or stagnation can also be likened to sleepwalking, but instead of your place, you walk aimlessly and unconsciously through your finances. You read articles about saving and investing, but the steps overwhelm you, and you can't wrap your head around them. Instead of learning more and trying it, you decide it's easier to stick with what you're used to. Your dreams can wait, can't they?

Then there's fear. It steals your dreams by making you feel like you're making the wrong decision just when you're about to try something new, like changing banks or different budgeting methods. Fear keeps you stuck, making you miss out on opportunities.

That's when we know that doing nothing costs us, too.

Keeping Still = Complacency

Financial inertia often starts subtly. You set up a budget, stick to it religiously, and develop comfortable spending and saving habits. Because these familiar routines seem to work just fine, it creates a false sense of security. You've become too comfortable with it to notice that it's a trap called complacency.

You've gone on full autopilot mode with a set destination, but are you reaching your full potential to get there fast?

Complacency can hold you back in many ways:

- **Missing out on more.** Life surprises you with many things: promotions, raises, and career shifts. Believing you're good where you are, you pass up on chances to boost your savings and level up.

- **Playing it too safe.** Turning down all opportunities because you think they're risky and outside your comfort zone.

- **Losing to inflation.** Your income is stagnant and the cost of living continues to rise. You can't keep up and live paycheck to paycheck forever. You may be sticking with a practical spending habit, but your buying power shrinks over time.

Post-It.

Inflation. Did you notice your wallet shrinking? For example, that burger used to cost less but now it costs more. Over a period of time, when the price of goods and services rise and impact your spending power, that's inflation.

These seemingly small choices add up over time; you are stuck in a financial rut before you know it. Yes, the familiar feels safe, but you also allow no room for growth. Settling for short-term comfort can mean danger to your long-term goals.

It's not all bad news, though. It's quite common and happens to most of us, so you are not alone. The best part is we can help you free yourself from financial stagnation.

In this chapter, we'll help you:

- Expose the hidden costs of financial inertia and how it steals from you a promising future.

- Smash the mental blocks and create an empowering mindset that leaves little-to-no room for fear and doubt.

- Create a clear road map by providing a step-by-step plan on how to take charge of your finances.

- Make things happen and show you how to build a future of "I cans," and not "what ifs."

Are you ready to finally control your money? Then it's time to ditch hitting the snooze button on your finances, switch off autopilot mode and steer toward maximizing your financial potential.

2. Diagnosing Financial Stagnation

Signs and Symptoms of Financial Inertia

Just because you are comfortable where you are doesn't mean you're getting the best of what life offers. This comfort comes with a price that could derail your financial goals. To avoid this, we must check for signs and symptoms that tell us we may be experiencing financial inertia:

Living for today.
With everything going on in the present, it's easy to neglect the future. You might be getting too fixated on today when you:

- **Delay decision-making.** Hitting snooze on important things like budgeting, investing, or retirement planning because they feel overwhelming to tackle. Do know that the earlier you deal with them, the easier they'll get. Preparation is key!

- **Prioritize wants over needs.** Life gets stressful at times and you reward yourself to feel better. Doing this regularly eats away your funds that could be used for bigger goals instead. Try setting aside a "fun fund" to make sure you get to treat yourself and save for the future at the same time.

- **Deal with adulting issues later.** Thinking that insurance and retirement are not urgent matters to address immediately, you put them off for later.

Fearing change, uncertainty, and missteps.
There's obvious resistance to change when faced with anything unfamiliar, like financial plans or investments or new budgeting apps or trends, even if they can help you grow your money. Choosing to be conservative always trumps taking a risk. You also:

- **Constantly need reassurance.** Unable to decide on your own, you tend to ask friends, family, or other sources for financial advice. This usually ends up with having information overload leaving you with decision paralysis.

- **Play it overly safe.** You hoard cash or keep most of your money in low-interest accounts because you worry about the stock market or the economy crashing.

- **Avoid responsibility.** When things go wrong, you tend to blame everything else rather than holding yourself accountable and trying to learn from your mistakes.

Sticking with the familiar.

Even if there are better options to choose from, you stick with what you're used to, like the same bank, financial advisor, or budgeting method, even if they don't really work for you anymore. Your comfort zone makes you:

- **Live on auto-renew.** Instead of regularly reviewing your subscriptions, you keep on paying for them even if you barely use them. Not only is it a waste of money, but you might also be missing out on better deals.

- **Settle for the bare minimum.** You're okay with what's good enough as long as it works like low-return investments instead of exploring other options that can give your money a boost.

- **Assume everything's under control.** Just because things have been working out well today doesn't mean they'll stay that way forever. You might be okay with your income today but will it be enough to cover emergencies or unexpected expenses?

- **Resist any changes.** You reject new financial strategies or options simply because "this is how we've always done it" or "it's worked fine so far." New tools and apps pop up all the time and they might just be a perfect fit for you!

- **Second-guess yourself.** You doubt your ability to make good financial choices, making you run to everybody else for advice or, worse, let someone else make the decision for you. While it's okay to ask for help, you must trust yourself, it's the best decision you can make.

- **Live in the past.** Sure, you made money mistakes, but it doesn't mean you lack the skills to make good financial choices. Nobody's perfect, and everybody makes mistakes. Learn from the past and face the future boldly.

Whether you are experiencing one or all of these symptoms does not mean you are hopeless. Staying still won't get you nearer to a bright financial future, so it's best to take action now.

Financially Stuck Scenarios

To convince you, here are some everyday examples of financial inertia with some tips on how to break free from it:

Career on Autopilot: John is a video editor who loves his job. He is comfortable career-wise, but there's not much room for growth. He has stopped updating his resume for a long time now and hasn't worked on upgrading his skills or expanding his network. John might be missing out on better-paying opportunities out there!

What to do: John can choose from tons of online courses he can take, as well as attend conferences or conventions where he can connect with other like-minded peers and professionals to learn new skills and explore higher-paying options.

Lost After College: Jesse graduated with an English degree but is unsure of what to do next. Everything's a blur – she has no idea if she wants to become a writer, an editor, or anything else. This keeps her from building her resume and looking for work opportunities.

What to do: Researching career paths in her field can help her find a job she likes. Jesse can also volunteer or try internships at related companies for more options. Consulting a career coach can also be a way to find her dream job.

Saving Money Blunders: Inflation is eating away at Sam's purchasing power without him knowing because he chose to keep all his money in a low-interest bank account. Unaware of other options that can increase his savings, he does nothing about it.

What to do: Sam could look up investment accounts that offer higher returns, which would help him grow his wealth and stay ahead of inflation.

Stagnant Savings: Lisa just got promoted. With a significant raise, she hasn't increased her retirement savings contributions. This means she's saving a smaller portion of her income, slowing down her progress toward her retirement goals.

What to do: A budget review could help Lisa decide to adjust her retirement savings contributions. This way, her higher salary is put to better use, helping her save more and achieve her dream retirement.

Gaps in Knowledge and Planning: Overwhelmed with financial jargon, Matt puts off learning about investing or managing his taxes. As much as he wants to make good financial decisions, he thinks he lacks the proper knowledge to do so.

What to do: Many free resources are available online or at libraries to help people understand personal finance. Signing up for classes on investment basics can help empower Matt to take charge of his money.

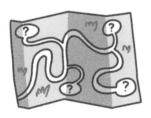

Aiming Without a Goal: Claire and Leo are a couple with high-paying jobs but haven't set any financial goals. They follow a carefree spending style, often without a budget. They talk about a house and retirement but haven't gotten around to starting to save for them.

What to do: Financial goal setting is especially important when buying a house or saving for retirement. Doing so will help the couple analyze their spending habits, define their priorities and targets, and start saving for the future.

Like them, there are things you can do to avoid getting stuck in a financial rut. In the next section, we'll look at the different triggers that cause our minds to choose to do nothing instead of taking action.

3. From Complacency to Continuous Growth

Your Mind and the Convenience of the Autopilot Shift

Do you ever feel like your finances are going nowhere fast? Many people, like you (yes, you are not alone!), get stuck, not knowing what to do, or are convinced they're doing just fine. Let's explore the reasons behind this and why it seems easier to stay still, going on autopilot, instead of proactively dealing with our finances.

Here's why it's easy to press the autopilot button:

We naturally fear change: We mean, who doesn't? Change often comes with risks and uncertainties, clouding our minds with thoughts about failure and mistakes, breaking our comfortable routine. The downside is, this same fear holds us back from better career opportunities, keeping us stuck in a job we hate or afraid to negotiate a raise. We hesitate to dabble in investments or anything that promises financial growth because we love to cling to the familiar, which is not scary and even comfy, no matter how unfulfilling. It helps to remember that small steps can lead to big changes!

We lack confidence: You bet self-doubt is a major roadblock. Maybe we don't believe we can negotiate a raise, start a business, or learn new skills to help improve ourselves financially. This mindset can prevent us from seeking better opportunities or negotiating for what we deserve. Guess what? There are plenty of self-confidence-building resources out there, as well as on financial topics. Start building your confidence by discovering and developing your strengths.

We live in the present: If not today, then when? Instant gratification often defeats long-term goals. This makes us skip saving up for retirement, education, or insurance, especially when we look only at the upfront costs. It's easier to just splurge on things we want today instead of sparing some funds for the future. We must remind ourselves that a week of comfort today can mean months (hopefully not years!) of financial problems in the future.

We are obsessed with scarcity: We feel like there will never be enough money or time, that we can't bring ourselves to think about anything else but to keep them. We reject any thought or pass up on investment opportunities if we think it risks us losing our money. Hear us out: Abundance is real and there are a lot of people who speak of their financial freedom experience that can serve as our inspiration to try and loosen our grasp on our money.

We are too comfortable where we are: Comfort makes us complacent. Used to our daily routines, we find it difficult to adjust once a disruption comes. A sacrifice is so hard to make that we can't give something up even if it means a step toward financial freedom. Find areas for improvement. It's never too late to live intentionally!

Breaking the Myths of Keeping Still

By now, you might have realized that most of your financial woes are triggered by myths that trap us helplessly. Our financial goals seem so distant that we give in to our old habits, pulling us back. Let's break the cycle and expose these myths that trick us into staying stagnant for the sake of our finances, shall we?

Myth 1: Stability is King! We aim for stability, yes, but if it hampers our growth, it may be best to move on and explore the other side of the fence! Many amazing opportunities are only waiting to be discovered if we take the chance.

Myth 2: I Can Only Earn This Much. Says who? You are the limit to what you can achieve, and only you can decide how far you can go. Break out of the income ceiling idea, and with a little effort, arm yourself with new skills to smash those limitations and reach for your financial dream!

Myth 3: My Job Defines Me. No one should be defined by their jobs. Or their bank accounts even. If you believe you should be earning more, go ahead and put yourself out there, explore other options! Life is too short to spend doing something you don't love. The world offers endless possibilities, and you deserve a career that fulfills you!

Myth 4: I'm Too Old to Start Over. Age is but a number. Many successful and wealthy people have started careers or businesses later in life. Learning and growing are never-ending processes. There's always room to train yourself to acquire new skills and discover hobbies. Never let age hold you back from pursuing your dreams.

Myth 5: Sacrifices Do Not Pay Off. Yes, they do, and they almost always change you for the better. The sacrifices you make today, small or big, can lead to greater things tomorrow. Think of it like growing your own financial garden – a little effort now and some tender, loving care can lead to a beautiful landscape tomorrow!

Myth 6: I Can Start Later. Procrastination is the enemy of progress! Your dreams don't deserve to be set aside – they deserve action and they deserve it now. Start today, even with small steps, and watch your future blossom.

Myth 7: Happiness is Where I Am. Maybe yes, maybe not. Can you honestly say your happiness means comfort? Stepping outside your comfort zone may be scary, but it also gives you the chance to change and grow to realize your full potential.

Have we convinced you to stop keeping still yet? Unlearn these myths that hold you back and prepare to chase your financial dreams!

4. Embrace the Power of Change

We keep talking about pulling yourself out of the financial rut you're in, asking you to please take that first step out of your comfort zone. As comfortable and as peaceful as keeping still may be working out for you, you're wasting your chance to build an abundant future, and we won't stop reminding you.

So that you can appreciate how it can help you, here's why stepping outside your comfort zone is your best bet to keeping yourself from being broke:

Level Up!: You welcome growth by challenging yourself. Trying new things gives you fresh ideas and opens up opportunities to help you diversify your skills, build your confidence, and even discover hidden talents!

Fail Forward: It teaches you that it's okay to mess up, it happens to the best of us. Failing doesn't mean it's the end! Think of failure not as a roadblock but as a learning experience. Every mistake is a chance to learn, rethink your approach, and return stronger. View them as practice for your future financial victories!

Growth Mindset: A "growth mindset" means there's no stopping you from learning and growing. You don't fear challenges but view them as stepping stones and opportunities to improve. This mindset helps you to welcome obstacles, seek feedback, and continue learning, setting you up to become more financially able!

Calculated Risks for Bigger Returns: Playing it safe can be nice but it can also be limiting. Taking well-thought-out risks can lead to bigger rewards along the way. Take investments, for example. With the right amount of research and carefully considered options, who knows, you might surprise yourself one day with how far you've come!

Embracing change can be a bit uncomfortable but it sure can help you in your journey to achieving financial success.

5. No Longer Keeping Still: Your Step-by-Step Guide to Growth

If you're tired of living paycheck to paycheck or daydreaming about a brighter financial future but still unsure of what to do, we have some good news. Here are a few easy-to-follow steps to get you started so you can finally stop hitting snooze on your financial wake-up calls:

Do a Financial Spring Cleaning!

Instead of letting all your bank statements, bills, wallet, and everything else money-related gather dust and take up space at home, gather them all up! This will help you figure out what to keep and what to let go of.

Think and Reflect: Why Are You Stuck?

Honesty is key here. Face yourself and ask what's holding you back. Is it fear of change? Does not knowing where to start make you anxious? Or maybe you feel like you are not financially literate? Write down every single thing that comes to mind. When you identify and understand these reasons, it will be easier to overcome them.

Unlearn Money Myths

Our minds are powerful; they can make or stop us from doing things. Feeding your mind with baseless (and limiting) myths can hold you back. Unlearn them by using challenging thoughts like "I wouldn't know until I try it" or "There is no stopping me from learning."

Spend Smart, Save More

Try budgeting hacks, cheap thrills, free activities, and saving trends. A little goes a long way when it comes to saving.

Goal Setting

Imagine what financial wellness looks like. Is it a dream vacation, a beachfront property when you retire, or a small business? Write each one of them and craft a plan with smaller, realistic steps you can take so you can see progress along the way. Make a vision board out of them to motivate you!

Take Baby Steps

Take things one step at a time. Nothing great can be achieved overnight. It takes small, achievable steps you can commit to taking. You can start by setting up automatic transfers for your bank accounts. These small changes lead to big results over time!

Invest in Your Future!

Figure out your investing appetite and what type of investments are the ones for you. (We have an entire chapter about it!). You can also try asking for professional advice.

Bounce Back from Setbacks!

Fail and move forward. Don't dwell on past mistakes and do your best not to repeat them. Make sure you learn from them.

> **Bonus Step: Don't Keep Still but Keep Learning!**
>
> Be always open to learning new things and satisfy your curiosity by feeding your mind. The world of finance is constantly changing, and tons of resources are available to help expand your knowledge. Make sure to apply what you learn to your finances!

6. Get a Move On!

We've uncovered how staying still or financial inertia holds you back from achieving your financial goals. Like a small leak in your financial tank, it silently drains your potential to earn more and save more. It keeps you stuck in autopilot mode, drifting steadily in a "good enough" cycle, but never reaching the maximum potential. Staying still only makes your dream house or your comfortable retirement a distant aspiration.

But they don't have to be because you can choose to act now and break free! By taking charge of your finances, you switch from being a passive observer to an active captain of your financial future.

Financial success requires proactive financial management to help you set clear goals, navigate challenges, and make wiser decisions. Countless people found themselves at the same starting point and have decided to step out of their comfort zones to enjoy financial independence. What's stopping you from doing the same?

Say goodbye to staying still and don't wait for tomorrow! We encourage you to take the first step to a brighter financial future today:

Get "active" with a supportive friend or family member! You can also join our online community or visit our website (www.thesimplesum .com) for the latest financial tips.

Remember, we're with you in your quest to break free from financial inertia. Cheers to your financial wellness journey!

Appendix

Insurance Coverage

Insurance covers car accidents, house fires, or health issues. It helps you manage the risk of significant expenses from these events by transferring the financial burden from you to the insurer.

Safeguarding Your Financial Future Through Insurance

Insurance isn't just another expense – it's crucial as life's unexpected turns can pose serious financial risks. Without proper coverage, these events can quickly drain your savings and derail your financial plans.

Key Components of Your Insurance Policy

Policy: Think of your insurance policy as the rule book in your game of risk management. It spells out what's covered, what's not, what you pay, and what you get. It sets the stage for the entire relationship between you (the insured) and the insurance company (the insurer).

Premium: This is the price you pay for protection. Whether it's paid monthly, quarterly, or annually, the premium amount is influenced by how much coverage you need, the likelihood of you making a claim, and other personal factors.

Coverage: This term describes the types of incidents or events your policy covers. Depending on your specific policy, this could range from minor accidents right up to major disasters or life-altering events.

Claim: If the unexpected happens, you file a claim. It's a formal request to the insurance company for payment based on your policy agreement. Once your claim is approved, the insurance will help cover the costs as detailed in your policy.

Deductible: This is the part of the bill you agree to pay for before insurance is applied.

Underwriting: This process is all about risk. Insurance companies use underwriting to decide if they should insure you and how much to charge. They look at factors like your age, lifestyle, health, and job to determine how likely you are to need your insurance.

Why Do You Need Insurance?

Understanding Its Critical Role in Your Financial Well-Being

Financial Protection Against Losses: At its core, insurance is about protection. Insurance steps in to cover risks and sudden expenses, helping you manage the unexpected without draining your finances.

Legal Compliance: In many situations, having insurance isn't just a good idea – it's the law. For instance, driving a car without auto insurance is illegal in most places. Similarly, businesses are often required to have workers' compensation and liability insurance not just to comply with regulations but also to protect their employees and operations.

Protection of Assets and Investments: Whether it's a family home, a cherished car, or a business facility, insurance protects your assets from unforeseen events.

This layer of security means that in the event of a disaster or theft, you have the support needed to recover and rebuild without the overwhelming financial strain.

Healthcare Coverage: Health insurance is essential for accessing necessary medical treatments without facing crippling bills. It covers everything from routine doctor's visits and hospital stays to prescriptions and preventative care, ensuring you and your family can maintain your health without financial distress.

Investment and Loan Requirements: When you're taking out a loan, such as a mortgage, insurance is usually required as a cover against risks.

Understanding the Different Types of Insurance

Protecting Your Future

Here are the different insurance types that safeguard your future and assets from the unexpected.

Auto Insurance: Damages to your vehicle or road accidents that occur to you are covered.

Insurance for Homeowners or Renters: Homeowners insurance protects the physical structure of your home and everything in it from events like fires or storms, while renters insurance covers your personal possessions and any potential liabilities within your rented space.

Insurance for Health: Your medical expenses, from doctor visits and hospital stays to prescription meds. Health insurance ensures that an illness or injury doesn't derail your finances, providing necessary care without the crippling costs.

Life Insurance: Think of life insurance as your financial legacy. It provides a death benefit to your beneficiaries after you pass away, helping to replace lost income, cover funeral costs, pay off debts, or simply ensure your family's financial comfort moving forward.

Disability Insurance: If illness or injury keeps you from working, disability insurance steps in to replace some of your earnings.

Liability Insurance: This insurance is often included in auto, homeowners, renters, and business policies and protects you against payment for unintentional damages and injuries caused.

With each of these types of insurance, the goal is the same: to mitigate financial risks and provide compensation for losses or claims.

What to Know Before Committing to an Insurance Policy

Making Informed Choices

Read the fine print on your policies. You also need to find the best insurance that suits you. Here are some checklists:

1. Assessing Your Coverage Needs: Consider what you're protecting against. Are you a new homeowner, a car owner, or a parent? Each scenario has different risks. Evaluate your lifestyle, financial situation, and the value of your assets. This will guide you in determining how much and what kind of coverage you need.

2. Exploring Coverage Options: Does your car insurance cover only collisions, or does it include theft and natural disasters? This knowledge is crucial, especially if you live in areas prone to specific risks like floods or wildfires.

3. Choosing the Right Type of Insurance: Find out which is most suitable and match the type to your most pressing needs. This ensures you're not paying for unnecessary coverage.

4. Understanding Policy Details: Dive into the policy specifics – what's covered, the limits, the exclusions, and any optional extras. It's all in the details. For example, if you're getting liability insurance, know the maximum it pays out; this helps avoid out-of-pocket surprises in case of major claims.

5. Exclusions and Limitations: Every policy has its boundaries. Some might not cover natural disasters or specific valuables. Knowing these can save you from unexpected denials if you ever need to claim.

6. Considering Deductibles and Costs: Higher deductibles usually mean lower premiums, but more out-of-pocket costs when you make a claim. Balance is key. Understand all costs involved – premiums, deductibles, and any other fees to find a policy that fits your financial situation.

7. The Insurer's Financial Health: The stability of your insurance company matters. Check independent ratings to ensure they can pay out claims, even in economic downturns.

8. Navigating the Claims Process: Know the steps to file a claim, the required documentation, and the expected timelines. This knowledge is crucial for a smooth claims process should you ever need to use your insurance.

9. Evaluating Customer Service: Check how the company handles inquiries and claims. Responsive and accessible customer service can make all the difference.

10. Seeking Reviews and Recommendations: Sometimes, the best insight comes from other customers. Look up reviews, ask friends, or seek professional advice.

Navigating Insurance

Essential Dos and Don'ts to Ensure Optimal Coverage

When it comes to securing insurance, knowing the right steps to take and pitfalls to avoid can make all the difference.

Dos:

- *Do Figure Out Your Needs:* What's your budget, and can your lifestyle afford additional insurance costs? Do you have a risky job?

- *Do Shop Around:* Prices and terms can vary widely, so comparison shopping is key.

- *Do Understand Your Policy:* Make sure you thoroughly read and understand all aspects of your policy, including what's covered, the limits, exclusions, and any additional options that might be available.

- *Do Ask Questions:* If anything in your policy is unclear, don't hesitate to ask your insurance agent for clarification. It's crucial that you fully understand what you are committing to.

- *Do Bundle Your Policies:* Consider consolidating various insurance policies with the same provider. This can often lead to discounts and simplify your administrative processes.

- *Do Keep Good Records:* Maintain detailed records of all your insurance documents, payments, and any communications with your insurer. Well-organized records can be invaluable in the event of a claim.

- *Do Maintain Good Credit:* Credit scores influence how insurers will price premiums. A good score keeps rates low.

Don'ts:

- *Don't Underinsure:* Skimping on coverage can leave you vulnerable. Ensure your insurance adequately covers your potential risks to avoid significant financial burdens later.

- *Don't Overlook Discounts:* Always inquire about possible discounts. Many insurers offer reduced rates for things like safety features in your home, a good driving record, or multiple bundled policies.

- *Don't Make Assumptions:* Insurance policies can be complex. Never assume coverage. Always check the specifics of your policy and consult with your insurer to clear up any misunderstandings.

- *Don't Ignore Policy Exclusions:* Be keenly aware of what your policy does not cover. Understanding exclusions is crucial to ensuring you're not caught off guard when you need to make a claim.

- *Don't Miss Payments:* Missing payments can lead to a lapse in coverage, leaving you unprotected. Always ensure your premiums are paid on time.

- *Don't Forget to Review Annually:* Conditions change, and so should your policy. When your insurance no longer matches your requirements, revise it, particularly after significant changes in your life or assets.

- *Don't Settle for Poor Service:* Don't tolerate poor service from your insurer. If you're unhappy with their customer support or claims process, consider looking for a new provider who values your business.

By adhering to these dos and don'ts, you can more effectively manage your insurance needs.

How to Get Insurance: A Simple Step-by-Step Guide

Securing the right insurance is a critical step in managing your financial risks and ensuring peace of mind. Here's a straightforward guide to navigating the process of obtaining insurance that fits your needs:

Step 1: Assess Your Coverage Needs
Start by evaluating what you need to protect. This could be your home, car, health, or even your business. Consider your assets, liabilities, lifestyle, and potential risks.

Step 2: Research Insurance Companies
Look into different insurers that offer the coverage you need. Check their financial stability, customer reviews, and ratings from reputable agencies. This step is crucial to ensure you're dealing with a reliable provider.

Step 3: Gather Quotes
Collect quotes from several insurers to compare prices and what's included in the coverage. You can do this online, over the phone, or through an insurance agent or broker, whichever suits you best.

Step 4: Compare Coverage Options

Examine each quote in detail. Look at what events are covered, the coverage limits, what's excluded, and the deductibles. This comparison is vital to finding the best policy for your needs.

Step 5: Check for Discounts and Savings

Don't miss out on potential savings. Many insurers offer discounts for things like bundling multiple policies, installing security devices, or maintaining a good driving record. Always ask what discounts are available.

Step 6: Consult with Insurance Professionals

Advisors can give you the information you require and tailor the products according to your needs. A tip is to find someone through word of mouth.

Step 7: Clarify Your Doubts

If any part of the policy remains unclear, ask questions. It's important that you fully understand the terms, the coverage scope, and any obligations you might have.

Step 8: Review the Policy Terms

Pay attention to the policy terms and seek clarifications when needed.

Step 9: Complete the Application

Fill out the insurance application accurately and honestly. This includes providing any required documentation that the insurer needs to process your policy.

Step 10: Make the Payment

Once you've chosen your policy, pay the initial premium to start your coverage. Payment options often include monthly, quarterly, or yearly installments.

Step 11: Receive Your Policy Documents

After your payment, you'll receive your policy documents. Review them once more to ensure everything is correct and store them in a safe place.

Step 12: Regularly Review Your Policy

Some policies may not be as important in different seasons of life. Take the time to review them regularly.

Debunking Common Myths About Insurance
The Truths You Need to Know

Insurance is often misunderstood, leading to widespread myths that can prevent people from making informed decisions about their coverage. Here's the truth behind some of the most common insurance myths.

Myth: Insurance is a Waste of Money

Truth: While it's true that you might not use your insurance every day, the purpose of insurance is to provide financial safety when you do need it. It's a critical tool for mitigating the impact of unexpected events that could otherwise cause significant financial hardship.

Myth: Insurance Companies Always Deny Claims

Truth: Insurance companies are in the business of assessing claims against the policy terms. Valid claims are generally settled promptly and fairly. Claim denials usually occur due to policy exclusions, misrepresentation, or failure to meet policy conditions.

Myth: Insurance Companies Are Only Interested in Profits

Truth: While insurance companies do operate to make a profit, they also have strict regulatory obligations to act in good faith by fulfilling their policy agreements. This balance helps ensure they provide fair service while maintaining business viability.

Myth: You Don't Need Insurance if You're Young and Healthy

Truth: Life is unpredictable. Young and healthy individuals are not immune to accidents or unexpected incidents. Having insurance is crucial, regardless of age or health, to protect against unforeseen liabilities and expenses.

Myth: You Only Need the Minimum Required Coverage

Truth: Minimum coverage may keep you legal, but it might not cover all potential expenses in an event. Evaluating your personal risk and asset value is crucial to determining the appropriate coverage level to adequately protect yourself.

Myth: Insurance is Too Expensive

Truth: The cost of being uninsured can far exceed the cost of premiums, especially if faced with major expenses from accidents or lawsuits. Most insurance plans can be tailored with varying deductibles and limits to fit within a budget.

Myth: Your Insurance Policy Covers Everything

Truth: No insurance policy is all-encompassing. Policies have specific limits and exclusions. Understanding what your policy covers – and what it doesn't – is essential to avoiding unexpected gaps in coverage.

Myth: Insurance Agents Always Have Your Best Interests in Mind

Truth: Many insurance agents do work with your interests at heart, but they may also have sales targets or prefer certain products. Always research independently, ask critical questions, and ensure the recommended policies meet your specific needs.

Myth: Insurance Isn't Necessary for Renters

Truth: Renters insurance is just as crucial as homeowners insurance. It covers personal property, liability, and additional living expenses that can be lifesaving financially in cases of theft, damage, or accidents within rented properties.

Myth: Insurance Companies Always Raise Premiums After a Claim

Truth: Premium increases after a claim are not a given. Factors like the nature of the claim, claims history, and overall risk assessment are considered. Some insurers offer no-claim bonuses or discounts that can offset potential increases.

Effective insurance coverage is key to managing financial risks and protecting your assets. Make adequate choices by understanding insurance better to future-proof your financial future.

Chapter
Five

Aiming for Perfection Is Keeping You Broke

AIMING FOR PERFECTION IS KEEPING YOU BROKE

1. Caught in the Eye of the 'Perfect' Storm

Do you ever find yourself endlessly tweaking a project, convinced it's not quite "there" yet? Maybe you want to start a new hobby but keep waiting for the right time. The sky is clear, it's warm and dry, and nothing's stopping you from sailing. Only you've read that the ideal wind condition for sailing is between 5 to 15 knots. And until you get that perfect balance of moderate and strong, you won't set sail.

Quite the perfectionist, are you not?

Having standards and holding yourself to them is good – to an extent. The ideal is good, but if you're after flawlessness and perfectionism at its finest, we have news for you – it can be a major red flag for your finances. Why? Perfectionists become fixated on unrealistic standards, often believing there's a "perfect time" to take action.

While a healthy dose of ambition can set you up for success, the quest for perfection is a whirlpool that will eventually suck you in. When this approach is applied to your finances – say waiting for an imaginary "perfect time" to invest, start a business, or negotiate a raise – how do you know it is the right time? The reality is that conditions are rarely perfect, and by the time something seems ideal, you may already have missed the tide of opportunity.

This chapter dives deep into how perfectionism cripples progress, leaving you stuck in a cycle of being unable to do things and letting opportunities pass you by. It will also be your survival guide from the whirlpool of perfectionism.

WABI SABI

Embrace Imperfection

We'll help you explore how to loosen your grip on (and hopefully let go of) unrealistic standards, develop a healthy tolerance for imperfection, and learn to use mistakes as a favorable wind, propelling you to financial security. Remember, the key to unlocking your financial potential isn't waiting for the perfect moment – it's about showing up, taking action, and embracing the journey of continuous learning and growth.

2. What Is Perfectionism?

Perfectionism is a trait that involves constantly striving for the best, maintaining high (often impossible) standards, and refusing to accept anything less. When everything is measured against greatness, smaller wins may go uncelebrated.

Often, perfectionists worry too much about what others think and usually tie their self-worth to being flawless.

There are two sides to perfectionism:

- *Inner Champion:* This is when you set goals and standards so high that you push yourself too hard to achieve them. Falling short is unacceptable, making you a bit tough on yourself when you do.

- *Outer Critic:* This happens when you feel like everyone around you, your family, friends, and society, expect nothing but perfection from you. It's as if you have to live up to everyone else's standards, even if they're not realistic.

Perfection Every Day

Aiming to be perfect can drive different outcomes. Sometimes it brings productivity and quality work, other times it becomes limiting as you cannot let go of your self-imposed standards.

This endless pursuit of perfection creeps into every aspect of life, from work and relationships to personal achievements and – you guessed it – finances. While aiming for excellence is great, it defeats the purpose when it brings only stress, anxiety, and a constant fear of failure. Perfectionists are usually hard on themselves, especially when they make mistakes. This is when they're most prone to frustration, disappointment, and self-doubt.

3. Your Wallet and the Pressure to Be Perfect

Do you ever feel paralyzed by the pressure to achieve financial perfection? Maybe you spend hours researching investments, terrified of picking the "wrong" one, or tweaking your budget more times than you can count, only to feel intense anxiety at the slightest error. If this is you, you're most likely trapped by financial perfectionism.

It's when you strive for flawless financial outcomes and feel that anything less is a failure. Afraid you might fail, you find yourself endlessly analyzing options, delaying decisions, and feeling crippled by the pressure to achieve an impossible ideal. Financial perfectionism might sound excellent, but the truth is, it can derail your financial dreams in more ways than one.

Your finances miss growth opportunities when you aim for nothing less than perfection. The time you spend overthinking every decision can mean earning potential passing you by. That dream investment you hesitated to get could have yielded significant returns. Imagine the regret of seeing someone else succeed with the exact opportunity you overanalyzed yourself out of!

Remember that taking calculated risks sets you up for growth. If you keep on perfecting every detail, you limit your chances of building your wealth.

Then, there's analysis paralysis. Stuck in research mode for the "perfect plan," you end up never actually taking action. This prevents you from taking essential financial steps, like building a budget, investing, or even starting a business. It's better to take small steps than find yourself stuck in a research loop.

Of course, it can also be emotionally damaging. Who wouldn't be exhausted by the constant pressure to be perfect with money matters? Financial perfectionism breeds stress, anxiety, and even burnout, which clouds judgment and leads to poor financial decisions. Hey, financial planning should be empowering, not stressful!

The desire for picture-perfect finances can ironically lead to overspending. When you try to keep up to look financially able without a flaw, splurging on luxury items you don't need comes easily, draining your wallet and stopping you from saving or investing instead.

Here's a fact: you don't need to be perfect to be successful with your finances. It's progress you should be after, not perfection. Know that each step, even small ones, takes you closer to your goals. Why don't you stop worrying about being perfect and start building your financial dreams?

4. Financial Perfectionism Versus Financial Inertia

Let's break down these roadblocks to your progress money-wise so you'll know how to address them:

Financial perfectionism is when one sets unrealistically high standards for one's financial goals, never settling for anything but the best. It makes you:

Overanalyze decisions: researching the perfect solution takes up most of your time that you get overwhelmed and end up not deciding at all

Fear mistakes: worrying about making a mistake, thinking it's not the best solution just yet

Set unrealistic goals: drawing up financial goals that are difficult or impossible to attain, like aiming for an unreasonably high rate of return on investments

Financial inertia is the tendency to stick with what's familiar even when it's not working for you anymore. This is when you:

Keep your money in the same bank account from ages ago: even if there are better options available, or even if bonds and stocks may yield higher returns, you go with what's comfortable – it doesn't matter that it's a low-interest savings account

Delay financial planning: hitting snooze on important financial tasks like creating a budget, setting up a retirement account, or buying insurance

Key Differences

Mindset: Financial inertia is the reluctance to make changes or take action, while financial perfectionism is the desire for perfect outcomes.

Action versus Inaction: Financial inertia often results in inaction or sticking with the old ways, whereas financial perfectionism may involve taking action but with perfection as the main driver.

One thing they have in common is that they negatively affect your financial well-being. As we go along, we'll explore some ways we can overcome these roadblocks for a smoother financial journey.

5. Decoding Perfection: Factors at Play

From societal norms to personal experiences, some influences shape our standards of perfection as humans. By extension, our finances are influenced in the same way. Let's walk through them together:

Personal Experiences and Trauma

The good, the bad, the ugly. Be they trauma or wins, they influence our ideas about what financially "perfect" looks like. For one, people who survived traumatic experiences may lead them to develop a strong desire for financial security and control.

Story Time: Darla lost her husband. Jobless, she had to fend for herself and her three kids. They had to make ends meet. Years passed and her children now have high-earning jobs. The tough time they went through made Darla so focused on saving. She's become so frugal to the point of depriving herself because she wants to be in control of her money to avoid getting into a similar situation again.

On the flip side, a large amount of money could make you feel like you should always have more, which could lead to a lot of pressure.

Effect of Financial Perfection

- *Savings:* Traumatic financial experiences, such as bankruptcy or job loss, can make us fear financial instability and prioritize savings to achieve financial perfection.

- *Investing:* A bad investment can prompt us to be overly cautious, and avoid risks altogether.

- *Spending:* Rough financial spots in the past taught us to hold on to our money tighter than we ought to. We've become so frugal we don't get to enjoy anymore.

Overcoming Strategies

- *Talk to someone:* Therapy or counseling might help address and process past financial traumas or challenges and develop coping strategies we can try.

- *Learn more:* Let's educate ourselves by reading books or articles on how past experiences might be affecting our lives and how we make decisions today.

- *Train your mind:* Practice mindfulness and self-care to manage stress and anxiety related to past financial experiences and help develop a positive money outlook.

- *Peer support:* Connect with peers, friends, or support groups that have also faced financial challenges.

Personality Traits

We all have different traits when it comes to money. Some are very disciplined, tracking every penny. Others are more carefree, spending without worrying too much. No matter our personalities, they say a lot about how we see financial perfection.

Take Jenny, for example. She is a perfectionist who meticulously tracks her expenses down to the last cent and sets ambitious financial goals. A slight error easily makes her anxious, and when plans don't go her way, she gets depressed, blaming herself for not thinking things through.

Effect of Financial Perfection

- *Savings:* Perfectionistic tendencies may lead us to set ambitious savings goals and be so super organized when tracking our spending, we forget to pause and appreciate the little things in life.

- *Investing:* Risk-averse individuals may play it safe and prefer conservative investment strategies to maintain a sense of financial security and perfection.

- *Spending:* Imperfect money habits tick perfectionists off. They punish themselves by choosing to be more strict on their spending, avoiding discretionary expenses.

Overcoming Strategies

- *Know yourself:* Reflect on your money management strengths and weaknesses to better understand how to make changes, if needed.

- *Set realistic goals:* Don't overwhelm yourself with targets and benchmark your life according to other people's achievements.

- *Be kind to yourself:* Surprise, nobody's perfect, we all have our fair share of mistakes, so let's not beat ourselves up about it. Instead, we should learn from them and do better next time.

Idealism and Expectations

Our idealistic tendencies push us to set sky-high standards and expectations for our financial goals that we sometimes forget to stay grounded in reality.

Jane has her future laid out. A junior writer in a publishing company, she plans on retiring before 40, buying a property in The Hamptons, and hiring a private chef. She's set ambitious financial goals, and won't settle for less. While it's great that her vision board's all set up, she got laid off, and her dreams came crashing down, leaving her hurt and angry. **Alas,** Jane's made unrealistic expectations and her vision is not grounded in reality.

Effect of Financial Perfection

- *Savings:* Overambitious goals motivate us to strive for perfection to achieve long-term financial security and independence. While it inspires us to move, disappointment runs high when our plans are unrealized.

- *Investing:* Hoping to "get there" quickly, we choose high-risk investments as the perfect strategy to meet our (unrealistic) expectations. Sadly, we risk financial stability in hopes of achieving extraordinary gains.

- *Spending:* Material possessions mean wealth and luxury. This belief leads to overspending on discretionary expenses just so we can paint our own picture of financial perfection.

- *Other areas:* Unrealistic expectations about debt management, retirement planning, and wealth accumulation also shape our view of financial perfection and influence how we manage our money.

Overcoming Strategies

- *Set SMART (Specific, Measurable, Attainable, Realistic, Timely) goals:* Getting rich doesn't usually happen overnight. It takes consistent, baby steps to get there.

- *Be flexible:* As the saying goes, "When life gives you lemons, make lemonade." Things won't always go our way, so we need to be agile enough to cope.

- *Learn self-compassion:* When we accept that we are not perfect and that nothing or no one is, it's easier to forgive ourselves when we fail. Our financial journey, like life, is marked by progress and growth rather than flawless execution.

- *Trust the process:* Shift your focus from achieving perfect outcomes to the process of learning and growth, and celebrate small victories and milestones along the way.

Cultural and Societal Norms

Every culture and society has its own version of what is financially perfect. It can be having a property under your name or a well-published career. No matter what it is, it influences one's meaning of financial success, status symbols, and acceptable money habits.

These norms can also lead individuals to strive for unattainable ideals of financial perfection, often at the expense of their long-term financial well-being. It can work the other way around, too: in a culture that values frugality and modesty, financial perfection may be associated with living within one's means, saving diligently, and avoiding debt.

Effect of Financial Perfection

- *Savings:* In cultures that prioritize status symbols and grand displays of wealth, one may feel the pressure to spend lavishly to maintain social standing, leaving little room for savings.

- *Investing:* We might find ourselves prone to choosing risky investments or stuck in a job we don't love simply because our culture dictates that having a lot of money means success.

- *Spending:* Social pressures to meet our community's expectations may result in overspending on luxury goods or experiences.

- *Other areas:* Cultural attitudes toward debt, inheritance, and family obligations can also impact financial decisions.

Some cultures go big on weddings. The grander, the better. The more guests, the more your social status is affirmed. This compels people to spend beyond their means on wedding expenses, upholding societal expectations of financial perfection over long-term financial well-being.

Overcoming Strategies

- *Keep values in check:* What matters to you should be more important than what the people around you say or believe. Your future and your finances are at stake!

- *Vibe with the right tribe:* Surround yourself with people who promote healthy financial attitudes and habits, and who share similar values.

- *Be the change you want to see:* Don't hesitate to stand up and fight for what you believe is right, especially if it can influence your community. Push for healthier financial habits and ditch unrealistic standards of financial perfection.

Family and Peer Influences

Family and friends significantly influence how we handle money. Beliefs and practices are often passed down through generations and reinforced within social circles, shaping one's financial decisions and aspirations.

Maybe you grew up in a family where financial success meant high-paying careers and material possessions. This may impress upon others the idea of striving for similar standards because that's what financial perfection is to them. The same goes for social circles that promote lavish spending and materialism, further reinforcing these ideals and creating the pressure to keep up.

Effect of Financial Perfection

- *Savings:* We listen to only familiar advice and end up not taking risks in trying new financial products that can help us save money.

- *Investing:* We tend to follow practices or investment strategies that work for our "successful" family members or friends without considering our own risk tolerance.

- *Spending:* Peer pressure to keep up with friends' spending habits or family expectations of financial support can lead to excessive spending and financial strain.

- *Other areas:* Family dynamics, such as inheritance expectations or financial responsibilities as part of the sandwich generation, can stress us out and leave us broke.

Overcoming Strategies

- *Communicate openly:* Talk to your family and friends about your financial goals and values. Help them understand what matters most to you and what your priorities are.

- *Set boundaries:* Establish limits, and don't be afraid to say no when asked to do something beyond your comfort zone. Your financial well-being trumps external pressures or obligations.

- *Find support:* Seek guidance and support from trusted advisors, mentors, or financial professionals to navigate family and peer influences and develop personalized strategies for financial success.

Gender Expectations

Even gender roles play a crucial part in setting standards of financial perfection, influencing how men and women perceive and pursue financial success. Gender-biased thinking that's based on outdated ideas about how men and women should handle money continues to affect our financial decisions.

Men may feel pressured to excel in high-paying careers, take financial risks, and accumulate wealth to be seen as financially successful. Women, on the other hand, may be expected to prioritize family needs, maintain financial stability, and balance taking care of everyone.

Effect of Financial Perfection

- *Savings*: We fall into stereotypes on how a certain gender can save more than the other.

- *Investing:* Men are perceived to be more inclined toward risk-taking invest-ments, while women may opt for safer, more conservative options.

- *Spending:* Men are encouraged to spend on status symbols like fancy cars and luxury items to project financial success, while women are expected to prioritize spending on family and household expenses, aligning with traditional gender roles.

- *Other areas:* Expectations around financial responsibility, earning potential, and career advancement are also topics of interest regarding gender influence.

Overcoming Strategies

- *Stand for equality:* Support efforts pushing for a level playing field in the workplace and financial institutions and challenge discriminatory practices and policies.

- *Educate yourself:* Read up and research on how to financially empower yourself, regardless of your gender.

- *Collaborate:* Normalize talking about money and making decisions together.

- *Be a role model:* Inspire others to break out of gender stereotypes and expectations and show them that financial success is not based on gender.

Mass Media, Advertising, and the World of Socials

Mass media, including television, films, magazines, and social media platforms all shape our ideals and standards of perfection, with a distinct portrayal of wealth and success.

Everywhere we look, we are constantly confronted with a barrage of advertisements featuring glamorous lifestyles; online series, TV shows, or social media posts showcasing unrealistic standards of success representing financial perfection. This seemingly perfect world is achieved only through excessive consumption and materialism. We are left to believe what we see, and pressure ourselves to adopt the same lifestyles, even if it means sacrificing our financial well-being.

Effect of Financial Perfection

- *Savings:* Influenced by media portrayals of success, we may prioritize lifestyle upgrades to feel like we belong.

- *Investing:* Media hype or celebrity endorsements can influence us to make investment decisions without careful thought, basing our decisions only on trends and perceived glamour.

- *Spending:* We might fall victim to impulsive spending habits, convinced by ads that we can attain the lifestyle portrayed in social media as a symbol of financial perfection.

Just because social media influencers say luxury travel destinations are within arm's reach and that you only live once, doesn't mean it's wise for us to book extravagant vacations to match the glamorous lifestyles depicted online, draining our wallets and sacrificing our financial goals.

Overcoming Strategies

- *Push for media literacy:* Let's learn to be critical of what the media tells us, looking for underlying motives and biases.

- *Choose your exposure:* Hitting the unfollow button is okay, especially if it means limited exposure to content promoting unrealistic financial success and perfection standards. Of course, we can follow pages that serve us in terms of financial education and empowerment.

- *Go for media balance:* Maintain a balanced media diet that includes diverse perspectives and voices that resonate with our personal values and goals.

- *Try digital detox:* Take breaks from social media to reduce exposure to idealized online portrayals of financial success, and use the time to work on personal goals and achievements.

- *Do regular reality checks:* Remember that financial success is subjective and true fulfillment goes beyond material possessions. Checking in on reality from time to time will help keep our priorities straight.

The Ideal 'Perfect Time and the Perfect Place'

Who doesn't want perfect timing? When it comes to money, timing can be everything. But waiting for things to go according to plan before taking action can be a financial perfection symptom.

Will delays investing in the stock market because he's waiting for the best economic conditions to ensure he's doing things correctly. He wants everything to be perfect, down to the last detail. The market peaked, and he didn't take his chance. Now prices are falling, and it's too late for Will to buy. His overthinking led to inaction, making him miss out on a possible gain.

This desire for perfection in timing and circumstances reflects a belief that success can only be achieved under ideal conditions, leading to missed opportunities and unrealized potential.

Effect of Financial Perfection

- *Savings:* Waiting for the perfect timing or circumstances to save can delay our progress toward achieving our financial goals. The earlier we save, no matter the amount, the quicker we can grow our money.

- *Investing:* Like Will, waiting for the perfect market conditions and fearing to make the wrong move prevent us from investing and taking risks, and we end up missing out on opportunities.

- *Spending:* We hold off spending for our wants because we believe there's a perfect moment to spend our money. This makes us feel deprived, for we don't know when the perfect time will come.

- *Other areas:* Procrastination and indecision in financial planning and decision-making can result from the pursuit of perfection in timing and circumstances, leading to missed opportunities and stagnation in achieving financial goals.

Overcoming Strategies

- *Act now:* To avoid missing out on opportunities and risk stagnation, we need to act now and break free from our decision paralysis.

- *Manage risks:* Review potential risks and rewards carefully, remembering that any financial plan involves taking calculated risks.

- *Take baby steps:* Focus on making progress, no matter how small. Each step you take, even amidst unfavorable conditions, brings you closer to your financial goals.

- *Learn from mistakes:* Embrace failures and setbacks as opportunities for learning and growth. Remember that taking one imperfect action is often more productive than waiting for the perfect conditions.

6. Real Talk: Financial Perfection Is but Myths That Need Unlearning

If you're still undecided about whether to act or wait for the perfect star alignment, maybe some myth-busting will help you move along:

Myth 1: Every financial mistake is a major setback.

Truth Bomb: Everyone makes mistakes. The important thing is to learn from them and adjust your approach. Focus on progress, not perfection.

Myth 2: Financial perfection means everything is perfectly optimized.

Truth Bomb: Every financial plan is unique, and there isn't one solid formula for it. Life throws curveballs, and your financial goals will evolve. What you can do is focus on making good, consistent decisions regularly, which is a valuable discipline your wallet will thank you for.

Myth 3: Financial perfectionism means financial success.

Truth Bomb: Having financial goals and being responsible with money are great, but don't worry about being perfect; otherwise, you'll end up stressed and anxious. Financial success is about making consistent, well-informed decisions over time, never about a flawless financial situation.

Myth 4: Falling short of hitting perfect financial goals makes me a failure.

Truth Bomb: Perfectionism often leads to an "all-or-nothing" mindset. Financial progress is about incremental improvements and learning from your mistakes.

Myth 5: A flawless financial plan equals security.

Truth Bomb: A solid plan can give you financial security, but it doesn't need to be perfect! Life can be unpredictable, so flexibility is crucial. Learning to adapt and adjust trumps a spotless financial plan.

Myth 6: Financial mistakes are a no-no.

Truth Bomb: Have we emphasized enough that everyone makes mistakes? Yes, everybody messes up with money at some point in their lives. Think of them as valuable learning experiences instead of failures. Use them to improve and get better at working for your financial future!

Myth 7: My finances must always be under control.

Truth Bomb: Nobody can have anything under perfect control. Life circumstances, economic factors, and unexpected events can all influence financial situations. Accepting this can help you focus on those things you can indeed control.

Myth 8: High income guarantees financial security.

Truth Bomb: Smart budgeting and responsible spending habits can take you far. Many people on modest incomes have achieved financial security.

Myth 9: Financial perfectionism ensures happiness and fulfillment.

Truth Bomb: Financial stability and smart money management contribute to overall well-being, but equating perfectionism with happiness is plain wrong. Pursuing perfection only leads to stress and dissatisfaction. True happiness comes from living a balanced life and nurturing relationships, rather than obsessing over financial perfection.

7. The Dream That Is Financial Perfectionism

Financial perfection sounds lovely. Only it does not exist. We're very sorry to burst your bubble, but here's why you should let the idea go:

Perfectionism is a flawed concept. At its core, financial perfectionism is an illusion – a mere product of norms, cultural influences, and our personal beliefs. It's a fool-proof way of managing money in which every decision leads to the best outcomes, and every goal is achieved without fault. The thing is, life is messy and is not perfect itself, which makes this whole financial perfection idea far from reality.

Perfectionism, like everything else, evolves: "perfect finances" is subjective, it largely depends on what your idea of "perfect" is. Moreover, perfectionism itself is a moving target – it changes with time, with the ever-evolving economy, market trends, and with your milestones, too. Since financial perfectionism is ever-changing, it's better to focus on continuous learning, growth, and adaptation in managing finances. Accept the imperfections that come with money management and learn to be flexible. This way, we can develop healthier and more sustainable financial habits that can move with our ever-changing realities.

8. Embracing Financial Resilience

While pursuing financial perfection may seem like the ultimate goal, it's important to realize that perfectionism in finances is not the key to long-term financial security. We should instead focus on financial resilience that offers a more practical and sustainable path to financial well-being.

Imagine you're out sailing. Financial perfectionism would be like trying to navigate a perfectly calm sea with a course so rigid that there is zero room for error. You panic at the slightest wave, fearing disaster; every gust of wind feels like a threat.

Financial resilience, meanwhile, is like getting your boat ready to brave any weather. You have strong sails, a sturdy hull, and enough supplies in case a storm comes. You can change course if need be, knowing full well you are equipped with the proper skills and resources to weather anything that comes your way.

Unexpected expenses? A financial storm hits? You're good. When you are financially resilient, you have what you need to stay afloat and keep sailing toward your destination.

While financial perfectionism might cause you stress and anxiety as you constantly worry about making the next move, financial resilience empowers you! It creates the discipline in you to be prepared and flexible and ultimately reach your financial goals with a smoother, more satisfying journey.

Moving Forward with Money, One Step at a Time

Overcoming financial perfectionism is a journey that requires a shift in mindset and approach to money management. Instead of striving for flawless financial outcomes, focusing on progress over perfection and embracing the power of small wins along the way are essential. Here are some practical steps to help you move forward with your finances, one step at a time:

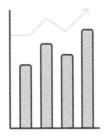

Forget Perfection, Focus on Progress

We know now that striving for perfection leaves us paralyzed, making it difficult to decide and move forward. To overcome this, tell yourself that progress is better than perfection.

What you can try:

1. Grab your phone and download a budgeting app. Start tracking your expenses from the last week.

2. List all your debts. Try to think of a plan to pay them off. Maybe you can dedicate a portion of your pay this month to debt repayment by automatically transferring it to a separate account dedicated to paying off your loans.

Today's your Day 1. Congratulations! Do it again tomorrow and the next day and the day after that and so on. Make it a habit.

Celebrate Small Wins

You don't have to make life-changing decisions today to prove you're seriously handling your finances. You can start by making small changes you can commit to doing regularly. And whatever you do, don't forget to celebrate your victories. Small wins can significantly impact your financial journey, motivating you and giving you the momentum to keep moving forward. Rather than trying to do everything perfectly all at once, focus on taking small, steady steps toward better money habits.

Try doing these:

1. Define a savings target for a week. Say $20. When you've managed to do this, give yourself a pat on the back or a high five. You're on the right track. Keep at it.

2. Instead of buying coffee at work, try brewing your caffeine fix at home. You can also prepare meals you can bring to work, so you won't have to go out and spend for lunch.

Remember, consistency (not perfection) is key to long-term success. By consistently taking action toward your goals, you'll gradually build the strength and move closer to financial security.

Be Realistic

There is no perfect budget. You decide what works for you right now. Letting other people dictate what you need to do with your life can easily mean disaster or stress for you. Work on what's comfortable for you. It need not be perfect. You can even adjust it anytime you want.

1. **Realistic Money Plans.** Create realistic budgets that align with your current financial situation.

2. **Start Small, Dream Big.** Know that small steps toward financial freedom are still progress. If you're struggling to save or invest because you feel like you don't have enough money, start small. Set aside a fixed amount for savings each month, even if it's just a few dollars. You can also consider micro-saving or micro-investing options.

By prioritizing progress over perfection, celebrating small wins, and adopting realistic money plans, you can overcome financial perfectionism and move forward with confidence on your journey toward financial security.

9. Charting the Path to Financial Growth

We've said it before and we'll say it again: perfection is an elusive goal. As we conclude our exploration of financial perfectionism and practical money management, let's reflect on the importance of understanding perfectionism, embracing imperfection, and striving for continuous improvement in our money habits.

Understanding Perfectionism

Perfectionism is a double-edged sword – it can drive us to strive for excellence, but it can also hinder our progress and cause unnecessary stress and anxiety. In personal finance, perfectionism can lead to unrealistic expectations, fear of failure, and delaying or avoidance of making financial decisions. By understanding what drives perfectionism and its impact on our money habits, we can begin to challenge these beliefs and adopt a more balanced approach to money management.

Practical Money Management

It involves proactive financial planning, seeking guidance when needed, and being agile in the face of unexpected challenges.

Learning from Mistakes

We assume you're reading this because somewhere along the way, you may have made a mistake. Or you've tried to do something and ended up feeling disappointed because things did not turn out the way you planned. Whether it's overspending on a want, missing a bill payment, or making a poor investment decision, each mistake gives us the opportunity to improve our money habits. It is important to understand that mistakes happen and that's okay. Sooner or later, we're bound to make them again; what's important is we remember that they're essential tools we can use to refine our financial strategies.

Continuous Improvement

The journey toward financial well-being doesn't happen overnight – it's an ongoing process of growth and evolution. By accepting that we are "works in progress" and committing to continuously improving our money habits, we can create a healthier relationship with money and achieve greater financial security and fulfillment. This means being open to feedback, staying curious and flexible, and embracing change as we strive to improve our finances.

As we study our money habits and look for areas for improvement, let's remember that perfection is not the goal. Instead, let's focus on progress, practicality, and the willingness to learn and grow.

Appendix

Budgeting Essentials

Budgeting is not just about restricting spending, but a strategic approach to managing your finances effectively. It's like a spending plan that tells your income where to go – from bills and groceries to that dream vacation. It tracks your incomings and outgoings, acting as your road map to living comfortably within your means. Just like a house needs a blueprint before it's built, you need a plan for your money. This blueprint will show you exactly where each dollar is allocated, preventing any financial surprises.

Overcoming Common Budgeting Obstacles

There are potential pitfalls and challenges that can arise when implementing and maintaining a budget. Recognizing these pitfalls and having strategies to overcome them can make the difference between success and failure in your budgeting efforts.

Common Pitfalls and How to Tackle Them

Unrealistic Expectations: One of the most common pitfalls in budgeting is setting unrealistic expectations. This can happen when you underestimate your expenses or overestimate your income, leading to a budget that is simply not achievable in the long run.

Strategies for Success 1:

- *Track Constantly:* Keep an accurate log of your spending for at least a month to capture where your money really goes.

- *Estimate Conservatively:* Be realistic about your income, especially if it varies.

- *Plan for Surprises:* Always include a miscellaneous category for unexpected expenses.

- *Stay Flexible:* Regularly revisit your budget to adjust for actual spending and income.

Discipline Dilemmas: Budgeting requires discipline and self-control, especially when spending on your favorite things, experiences, and food.

Strategies for Success 2:

- *Set Clear Limits:* Define spending caps for each category and adhere to them.

- *Use Cash Envelopes:* Withdraw your spending limit in cash for tangible control.

- *Delay Impulses*: Wait before making non-essential purchases to avoid impulse buys.

- *Find Your Squad:* Enlist a friend, spouse, or financial advisor to keep you accountable.

Budgeting Burnout: If you stick too closely to your budget, you may miss out on memorable experiences and moments that cannot return. Over time, this can lead to budgeting burnout, where you become overwhelmed and lose motivation to maintain your budget.

Strategies for Success 3:

- *Simplify Tracking:* Use budgeting tools or apps that automate some of the work.

- *Keep Your Eyes on the Prize:* Focus on your financial goals to stay motivated.

- *Allow for Fun:* Make sure to budget some "fun money" for yourself.

- *Take Breaks:* Periodically step back from budgeting to prevent fatigue.

Inflexibility: While budgeting requires discipline, being too rigid with your budget can also be a downfall.

Strategies for Success 4:

- *Embrace Flexibility:* Incorporate a category for emergencies in your budget.

- *Regular Reviews:* If you are in a different life stage, clearly you should have a different budget plan.

- *Shift Priorities:* Reallocate funds as needed to accommodate unexpected expenses or opportunities.

Ignoring Irregular Expenses: During holiday periods, you will have the tendency to spend more, setting a budget in advance helps.

Strategies for Success 5:

- *Plan Ahead:* Set aside a small amount monthly for these periodic expenses.

- *Use Technology:* Leverage apps that remind you of upcoming irregular expenses.

Neglecting Debt Repayment: It's easy to neglect debt repayment, especially if you've grown accustomed to carrying balances on credit cards or loans.

Strategies for Success 6:

- *Prioritize Debts:* Make debt repayment a prominent part of your budget.

- *Use Snowball or Avalanche Method:* Apply strategic approaches to reduce your debts effectively.

Communicating with Friends and Family: Not being clear about your spending appetite leads to misunderstandings and over-expectation.

Strategies for Success 7:

- *Open Dialogues:* Regularly discuss financial goals and budgeting strategies with your partner or family.

- *Joint Planning:* Engage everyone involved in setting up and maintaining the budget.

Failing to Plan for Emergencies: Life happens and it's important to be ready for whatever life throws your way.

Strategies for Success 8:

- *Emergency Fund:* Allocate a budget category for emergency savings and contribute regularly.

- *Aim for Security:* Build up to three to six months' worth of expenses for comprehensive coverage.

Neglecting Long-Term Goals: While budgeting helps you manage your day-to-day expenses, you should also create a separate savings bucket for future plans.

Strategies for Success 9:

- *Dedicate Funds:* Set up specific savings goals for major future expenses and invest regularly.

- *Regular Goal Review:* Keep your long-term objectives in sync with your current financial strategy.

- *Automate:* From contributions to retirement accounts or dedicated savings funds.

Emotional Spending: Stress, boredom, or seeking temporary gratification can quickly derail your budgeting efforts and lead to overspending.

Strategies for Success 10:

- *Recognize Triggers:* Understand what drives your impulse spending and address it head-on.

- *Mindful Spending:* Incorporate mindfulness practices to manage emotional spending.

- *Budget for Pleasure:* Include a reasonable allowance for discretionary spending to satisfy your cravings without guilt.

Budgeting might not always be smooth sailing, but it's definitely worth the effort. Think of each challenge as a stepping stone toward your financial freedom. It's about more than just numbers; it's about setting a course for your dreams and having the discipline to follow through.

Budgeting Methods: The Right Choice for You

It's also important to review and adjust your budget regularly as your income or expenses change. Budgeting can be your partner to guide you through it and find calm. It can help you take charge of your money, reach your financial goals, and avoid living paycheck to paycheck. Throughout the book we will demonstrate several budgeting methods to help you decide which works best for you, including:

- Cash Stuffing
- Zero-Based Budgeting
- 50/30/20 Budgeting
- Pay Yourself First
- Cash-Only Budgeting

Chapter
Six

Wasting Your Earnings Is Keeping You Broke

WASTING YOUR EARNINGS IS KEEPING YOU BROKE

Imagine it's the end of the month, your bank statement arrives, and you notice your balance is much lower than expected. You don't remember making any big purchases, but when you add it all up you realize it's not one large expense, but a lot of little ones – the small, frequent expenses that we hardly notice day to day. These are what we call "money leaks."

Think about your daily coffee. Spending $4 on it every day doesn't seem like much. But if you add it up, you'll be racking up $120 a month, or $1,440 a year just on coffee!

Now there's nothing wrong with enjoying a coffee once a day, or even more than once, and giving up coffee isn't going to solve all of your financial woes, but it's a good example of how small expenses can easily add up.

In this chapter, we're going to tackle these "money leaks" and uncover why they're so easy to overlook. We'll explore ways you can be more intentional with your spending, identify unnecessary expenses, and develop habits to start building your savings.

By the end of this chapter, you'll have helpful ways to track spending and simple strategies to make smarter choices with your purchases.

1. The Cycle of Living Day to Day

Sadly, many people live paycheck to paycheck where their entire salary goes toward recurring expenses, leaving very little or sometimes nothing at the end of the month for savings or emergencies. It's a scenario that can affect people across all income brackets and causes huge financial stress.

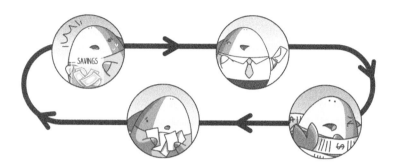

Characteristics of the Paycheck to Paycheck Style

Limited Savings: Being stuck in the cycle of money coming in and money going out, with nothing left to save leaves people with little to no financial cushion. The lack of savings means that an unexpected expense, like a medical emergency, can have a huge knock-on effect of draining what little savings you may have, or preventing those savings from growing over time.

Income Dependency: Relying entirely on each month's paycheck to meet all your financial obligations means there's no room for error. A delay in payment or reduction in hours can put basic needs like rent or groceries at risk. It can also leave you reliant on your current employer, reducing your drive to explore other opportunities to help grow your career.

Vulnerability to Financial Shocks: With no savings or financial safety net, an unexpected job loss or even a minor pay cut can have devastating consequences. Debt can quickly pile up while you try to cover your basic living expenses.

Inhibited Long-Term Financial Planning: If you're stuck with no savings at the end of every month, it can be challenging to try to plan for the future. Any goal you might have, from buying a house to saving for retirement, can seem out of reach.

Breaking the Cycle

Budgeting: If you want to break the cycle, you first need to find out where all your money is going every month. By creating a detailed budget, you can track all your spending. This visibility helps you pinpoint where spending can be reduced.

Emergency Fund: Prioritize building a small emergency fund. No matter the size, it can help in preventing you from falling into debt. Setting aside small amounts like $5, $10, and $15 is a great start! Try to keep the fund separate from your other finances if possible, like in a different account, to remove the temptation of spending it.

Financial Education: Invest time into learning about financial management (which you're doing right now. Well done!). Understanding even basic financial principles can empower you to make better decisions and help you plan more effectively.

Expense Reduction: Every bit counts so reducing your monthly expenses can give you some savings. You could downsize your home or cut back on non-essential services like premium cable packages or subscription services. These changes can reduce your financial stress and get you out of debt. They're not to cause new stresses by forcing you to lose the things you love. You don't have to cut all expenses but prioritize some over others.

2. The Challenges of Saving

Overcoming Psychological and Social Barriers to Financial Security

Saving money consistently may be challenging, but this is a vital step for obtaining financial security. While it may seem straightforward to allocate some of your salary toward your savings every month, there are various psychological and social barriers that often complicate this seemingly simple task. This section talks about these barriers and discusses ways you can develop a strong saving habit.

Instant Gratification Versus Long-Term Rewards

"I'm too tired to go to the gym. I'll go another day!" or "I'll wash the dirty dishes tomorrow." Do these scenarios sound familiar to you?

We are all guilty of choosing the easy path or the quick win, and putting off harder tasks until later. As humans, we're almost hardwired to seek instant gratification, especially now in the era of unlimited choice and immediate access, the temptation to spend now rather than save for later is stronger than ever. There's no shame in it, but it can easily get out of control, leading to impulse purchases again and again, reducing our ability to save.

The best way to combat it is to develop a mindset that values delayed gratification. Set clear, achievable savings goals, like a dream vacation or house deposit, and prioritize these over a fleeting fancy.

The Impact of Social Pressures

We've touched on this previously, but social pressures also play a huge role in our spending habits. The desire to match the lifestyle of friends, colleagues, or influencers, and constantly keep up appearances can lead to unnecessary spending. This phenomenon of keeping up with the Joneses can make saving seem like a far less attractive option compared to the social payoffs received from spending. These pressures are deeply rooted in our need for constant social acceptance and the fear of missing out, and can lead to making financial decisions that provide social gratification, but harm our financial goals.

To navigate this, try to surround yourself with people who share the same financial values, who understand the importance of saving. Talking about financial goals together and the setbacks you have faced can help shift the focus from spending to saving.

Lifestyle Inflation

As people progress in their careers and earn more money, they tend to spend more. This is called lifestyle inflation. An individual might move into a larger house, buy a new car, or eat at fancier restaurants. There's nothing wrong with enjoying the rewards of hard work, but failing to save along the way can seriously impede financial freedom in the future.

It is essential to treat savings as an expense. In other words, when you get your salary, your savings should be paid first – just like rent or a mortgage payment – before you divvy up what's left for everything else.

Saving Strategies

The best budgeting strategies are ones that people will stick with for years because they provide some freedom. The most important part of saving is actually doing it – consistently putting money away over time. Deciding how much money would be enough depends on individual goals as well as obligations. In order to save money, one must become more mindful of their financial situation and take control over it.

Here are a few tips to consider:

1. Track your spending

Sometimes, all it takes is to write down where every dollar is going in order to see patterns and find areas where you could save. Using apps can help you! Some popular examples include Mint.com (owned by Intuit) and You Need A Budget (YNAB). The latter is great for those who need more help staying on track because it's very hands-on.

2. Cut back on non-essentials

There are always ways to cut back on spending; sometimes just reviewing your current subscriptions or monthly services can lead you to realize that you might be paying for things you don't even use anymore.

3. Debunking Myths Around Spending and Budgeting

Challenging Popular Misinterpretations of Finance

Many of us have fixed views about money that prevent us from handling our finances well. These are often myths that negatively shape our spending and saving habits. This section will debunk some of the most popular myths about finances and give you a better perspective on managing your cash.

Myth 1:
"Budgeting is Restrictive and Removes the Fun"

Reality

Budgeting doesn't stop you from having fun but helps you understand your financial limits so you can make rational decisions that are in line with your goals. A good budget provides freedom instead of being restrictive as it makes sure you can enjoy life with fewer worries. This will allow you to allocate funds between necessities and wants, promoting a balanced lifestyle while ensuring financial stability.

Strategy

Start by segregating your expenses and assigning a specific amount for entertainment. This way, you can indulge in recreational activities without having to feel guilty or stressed by unexpected expenses.

Myth 2:
"I Deserve to Spend Because I Work Hard"

Reality:

Although rewarding yourself for hard work is important, consistently overspending can undermine long-term financial security. The trick is to find a balance between self-reward and sound finance management.

Strategy:

Introduce a reward mechanism within your budget; consider smaller, more frequent rewards that are fulfilling yet pocket friendly. Furthermore, diversify rewards; not all treats must be purchases. Sometimes, the best ones are experiences or just personal time.

Myth 3:
"A Higher Income Will Solve All My Financial Problems"

Reality

Just earning more money doesn't automatically address financial problems; instead, it can result in increased expenditure, also known as lifestyle inflation. Without proper management, more money can indeed mean more problems.

Strategy

Concentrate on developing financially sound habits that will not depend on how much you earn. Live within your means irrespective of the salary brackets and invest or save any additional income instead of raising your expenditure.

To shift away from these myths, consider these mindset changes:

- **Embrace Budgeting as a Tool for Empowerment:** Look at budgeting as a dynamic instrument that can help you achieve your dreams and maintain financial peace. Review your plans regularly and adjust them to reflect your evolving goals.

- **Prioritize Long-Term Satisfaction over Instant Gratification:** Learn to evaluate the long-term benefits of saving as opposed to spending for immediate pleasure. This can involve setting specific goals regarding finance and visualizing the positive outcomes associated with reaching them.

- **Never Stop Learning:** Financial literacy is power. Knowledge gaps about money make us fall for common myths. Make good use of books, online courses, and workshops to improve personal finance knowledge.

In order to have a good relationship with money, it is important to bust these popular financial myths. Learning the truth behind these misconceptions can help you manage your money better, make more educated choices, and prepare for a financially safe future.

4. Practical Steps to Stop Wasteful Spending

Implementing Effective Strategies to Enhance Financial Decision-Making

Wasteful spending is one of the biggest setbacks to your finances. It is easy to miss it because it can be spread across small, everyday expenses that can go unnoticed. Unfortunately, these can accumulate over time and drain your resources that could have been better used toward reaching your financial goals. This section provides actionable strategies aimed at transforming wasteful expenditures into wise ones.

Plan Your Purchases

Instead of making impulsive buying decisions, plan your purchases in advance. Before buying something, find out more about the item by doing some research. Compare prices, look for cheaper alternatives, and ask yourself if you really need the item. This will prevent you from making unnecessary purchases.

Set Spending Restrictions

After you've identified all your expenses, set spending restrictions for every category. For example, setting a spending limit for your groceries will prevent overspending and encourage awareness on how you use your money.

Prioritize Quality over Quantity

When making purchases, focus on the quality of an item rather than the quantity. It is better to invest in something that will last longer and serve its purpose well, even if it means paying more for it. While this might seem more expensive, it could actually save you money down the road because you won't have to replace the item as frequently.

Avoid Emotional Spending

Be mindful of your emotional state when making purchasing decisions. Many people engage in "retail therapy" or impulse buying as a way to cope with stress or negative emotions temporarily. Instead of reaching for your wallet, find healthier ways to address these feelings such as talking with a friend or engaging in self-care activities.

Save on Utilities

Check your utility bills for saving opportunities. You can lower costs by making small adjustments like setting a timer for the thermostat, using energy-efficient appliances, and turning off lights when they're not needed.

Refinance Debts

If you have debts with high interest rates, consider looking into refinancing options at lower rates. This could reduce both your monthly payments and total interest paid over time.

Cut Back on Subscription Services

Review all subscription services and memberships. Cancel any that you don't use regularly, and see if there are cheaper alternatives for the ones you do use.

Use Coupons and Discounts

Look for coupons, discount codes, or cashback apps when making purchases. Plan shopping trips around sales whenever possible – especially large-ticket items – to get the best deal.

Buy in Bulk

For products you use frequently, think about buying them in larger quantities (if it's cost-effective). Doing so could save you a significant amount of money over an extended period. But be mindful: only buy non-perishable items or products with an extended shelf life.

Consider Secondhand Options

When purchasing things like clothes, books, or even electronics, consider getting them secondhand. Many times, these items can still be found in great condition and cost a fraction of what they would cost if you were to buy them new.

By following these actionable steps, you can significantly cut down on wasteful spending. Each tactic is designed to make you more money-conscious so that every dollar spent has a purpose. As you transition from mindless to mindful spending, you will begin feeling better about yourself and your finances over time. This newfound comfort will allow for greater focus on personal financial goals rather than unnecessary expenditures.

Doomsday spending is driven by financial hopelessness. In times of extreme financial stress, some may spend impulsively as a way to cope with their emotions. Recognizing this behavior is important; instead of giving in to despair, adopting structured financial planning and practicing mindful spending can help regain control over your money management skills.

5. Building a Sustainable Savings Plan

Building Long-Term Financial Security Through Effective Saving Techniques

Simply deciding to save money is not enough; it must become a habit. You need a consistent approach if you want to make any real progress toward meeting your targets. So, it is crucial to develop a sustainable strategy for saving. Here are some practical steps you can follow:

Set Clear Financial Goals

Step 1: Identify Your Objectives
Start with defining what you are saving for. Are you saving for short-term goals like a holiday or do you have long-term goals like increasing your retirement fund? Writing these goals down will give you direction and motivation to save.

Step 2: Prioritize Your Goals
Not all financial goals carry the same weight. Prioritize them based on their importance and time frame. This helps in effectively allocating your savings so that you do not sacrifice more urgent needs for less critical wants.

Create a Budget That Works

Flexible Budgeting:

As your life continues to change and evolve, so should your budget. Allocate different percentages of your income toward various expenses, including savings, which should always remain fixed regardless of anything.

Use Tools and Resources:

Budgeting apps and financial planning tools can be used to track income, expenses, and savings. These resources can give insights into how you are spending your money and pinpoint where adjustments can be made.

Automate Your Savings

Set Up Automatic Transfers:

Automation can help you build good saving habits. Set up automatic transfers into your savings account each month when payday comes around.

Choosing a Favorable Savings Account:

Look for accounts or other investment options where money can grow faster due to higher interest rates being earned over time. Look for options with the best interest rates and lowest fees to maximize your returns.

Review and Modify Your Plan Periodically

Monthly Reviews:
Have monthly check-ins to track the progress you have made toward existing targets. This helps keep you on course and if there are any issues, you will be able to adjust your plan accordingly.

Be Prepared to Adapt:
Life's circumstances can change unexpectedly. You should be able to adapt your plan to accommodate these changes.

Set Aside Savings for Emergencies

Start Small:
Even a small emergency fund can prevent financial disasters. So, start by setting aside a bit of money every month. Slowly collect enough money to cover one month of living expenses, then gradually increase it to six months.

Keep It Accessible:
This fund should be easy to access whenever needed, so keep it somewhere that is accessible, like in a savings account.

Creating and maintaining a sustainable savings plan requires dedication and discipline, but it is one of the most rewarding endeavors you can undertake.

As we conclude Chapter 6, it's crucial to think about the journey we've taken to uncover the strategies and insights necessary to stop wasteful spending and build a robust savings plan. The goal of this chapter has been not only to educate, but also to empower you with practical tools and knowledge so you can steer your own financial future.

Chapter Takeaways

Finding and Fixing Financial Leaks: We identified how small expenses we don't pay attention to can mess up our finances, then covered various ways to track and cut down on this spending.

Flexible Budgeting: We discussed the importance of having a budget that changes as life does; it acts as a road map for effective money management.

Saving with Intent: We talked about setting clear, prioritized goals for saving money and keeping them in mind throughout one's financial journey, as well as automating savings so that there is no temptation to spend.

Psychological Obstacles: We addressed common misconceptions and psychological blocks toward good personal finance practices and strategies to overcome them.

Empowerment Through Education: We highlighted how education plays a key role in personal finance. By continuously learning and applying what was taught here today, you can enhance your ability to make better choices that can help you reach your goals. After all, financial independence isn't achieved overnight – it's a cumulative result of daily decisions and disciplined practices.

Appendix

Budgeting Method – Envelope System

The envelope system is a straightforward, old-school budgeting method that uses physical envelopes to allocate cash for different expenses. For example, you might have envelopes for groceries, utilities, entertainment, etc. Once you have used up all the cash in an envelope, you cannot allocate more money into that category.

Here's how it works:

1. **Organize Your Finances:** List down how much you make every month and your monthly expenses.

2. **Categorize:** Break down your spending into categories like rent, groceries, fun money, etc.

3. **Label Your Envelopes:** Write each category on an envelope.

4. **Allocate Your Cash:** Withdraw your budgeted cash and pop the right amount into each envelope.

5. **Spend Wisely:** Use the cash from each envelope only for its specific category.

6. **Stick to the Budget:** When an envelope is empty, that's it until next month!

The envelope system is an excellent way to visualize your spending and make it tangible. It helps you stay within your budget by physically separating your money into different categories. However, it can be inconvenient to carry around multiple envelopes filled with cash, and it may not be suitable for larger expenses like rent or mortgage payments, so choose the categories most suitable for this method carefully.

Dos and Don'ts of the Envelope System:

Dos:

Stay on Track: The envelope system requires strict discipline and self-control. Once you have used up all the cash in an envelope, you must resist the temptation to overspend or dip into the other envelopes.

Use Cash: The envelope system works best when you use physical cash. Using debit or credit cards can undermine the purpose of the system, making it easier to overspend.

Tweak (a little): If the cash you have in a particular envelope keeps running out, consider adjusting your budget to allocate more funds to that category.

Plan for the Unexpected: Remember to set aside money for irregular expenses such as car and home repairs. Create separate envelopes for these expenses and allocate some money to it every month.

Don'ts:

Don't Borrow from other Envelopes: If you've used up all the cash in one envelope, resist the temptation to borrow from other envelopes. This can quickly lead to overspending and defeat the purpose of the system.

Don't Use Plastic: Avoid using your credit card as paying with cash is a fundamental aspect of the envelope system. Swiping a card undermines the tangible nature of the system and can make it easier to overspend.

Don't Neglect Fixed Expenses: While the envelope system is primarily designed for variable expenses, remember to include fixed expenses like rent, mortgage, and loan payments. These should be paid directly from your bank account or through automatic transfers.

Don't Forget Savings: Allocating a set amount of money into your savings every month is crucial for your long-term financial health.

Don't Get Discouraged: Implementing the envelope system may take some time and effort to get used to, especially if you're transitioning from a different budgeting method. Be patient and persistent, and don't get discouraged if you experience setbacks or slip-ups along the way.

By embracing these tips and staying committed, the envelope system can be a powerful ally on your journey to financial well-being. Dive in, adjust as needed, and watch your money grow!

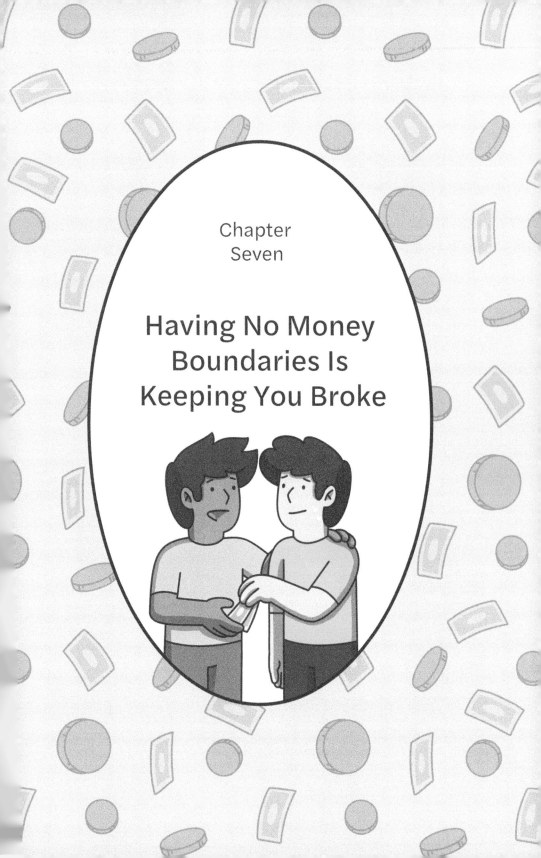

Chapter
Seven

Having No Money Boundaries Is Keeping You Broke

HAVING NO MONEY BOUNDARIES IS KEEPING YOU BROKE

Have you ever looked at your bank account mid-month, puzzled at where your money has gone? Imagine Alex, who, like many of us, decides to unwind on a Friday night after a grueling week. A few clicks on his favourite shopping app, dinner out with friends, and grabbing the latest gadget he's been eyeing – suddenly, his weekend budget has disappeared before it's even Saturday morning.

This isn't just about one weekend of overspending; it's a glimpse into a recurring pattern, a lifestyle without clear financial boundaries. Alex's story isn't unique; it mirrors a modern financial life where the lines between "need" and "want" blur, creating a common cycle of uncontrolled spending, chronic stress, and financial instability.

Why is this pattern so common? Without financial boundaries, our lives can feel like a constant tug-of-war with our bank accounts, where impulse purchases become the norm and saving goals like preparing for retirement seem just out of reach. In this chapter, we discuss why it's important to have money boundaries – not as a restrictive measure, but as a step toward financial stability and freedom.

Financial boundaries can help us regulate our spending, manage our expenses, and secure our financial future. They enable you to navigate through your finances confidently, avoiding unnecessary spending, reducing financial stress, and promoting a healthier lifestyle.

1. Financial Fences: Drawing Lines to Keep Your Money Safe

Understanding Financial Boundaries

Financial boundaries are the principles and limits we establish to manage our personal finances. They act as protective fences around our financial garden, defining what's ours and safeguarding it from unwanted intrusions. Just as a physical fence around a property establishes boundaries that protect and define it, financial boundaries help us manage our spending habits and interactions involving money.

Establishing Your Financial Fences

Creating effective financial boundaries starts with recognizing the need to safeguard your financial health. This is crucial not just for maintaining stability but also for achieving goals you have set for yourself. Start by setting these boundaries:

Recognize Your Financial Space: Begin by understanding where you currently stand, financially. How much do you earn and what are your expenses and debt? This overview provides the foundation on which you can start building your boundaries.

Define Your Financial Limits: Set clear and specific limits on your spending, saving, and borrowing. For example, you might not want to spend more than

20% of your income on rent, or that your credit card debt should not exceed a certain amount.

Implement Rules for Financial Interactions: Determine how you will handle money transactions with others. This could include rules for lending money to friends or how you manage shared expenses with a partner or housemates.

Types of Financial Boundaries

Financial boundaries can be grouped under several categories, each serving a distinct purpose in your financial life:

Personal Spending Limits: These are self-imposed rules that dictate how much you are willing to spend in various categories of your budget. For instance, setting a monthly limit for dining out, entertainment, or shopping helps ensure that you don't overspend and that funds are allocated for savings and essential expenses.

Savings Goals: Establishing clear targets for savings – such as your retirement funds, emergency accounts, or specific purchase goals (like saving for a home or a vacation) – is another form of financial boundary. These goals motivate you to save regularly and promote good money habits.

Credit Usage: Limiting how and when you use credit is a crucial boundary that prevents debt from piling up. Deciding what types of purchases or situations justify the use of credit, and setting caps on credit spending, can protect you from high-interest debt traps.

Financial Interactions with Others: These boundaries relate to how you manage financial relationships, including lending money to friends or family, managing shared expenses, or negotiating financial responsibilities in a partnership. Clear guidelines and open communication about these topics can prevent financial misunderstandings and conflicts.

How Do Financial Boundaries Work?

Setting and maintaining these boundaries require ongoing attention and adjustment. Firstly, you'll need to understand your finances and goals. From there, you develop guidelines that align with your financial priorities and values. These guidelines should be revisited and adjusted as your financial circumstances evolve, ensuring they continue to serve your needs effectively.

Characteristics of Effective Financial Boundaries

Clarity: Financial boundaries should be clearly defined and understood. Ambiguity leads to oversights and breaches that can quickly cause problems.

Consistency: They must be consistently applied. It reinforces good financial habits and reduces the temptation to make exceptions "just this once."

Flexibility: While consistency is crucial, good financial boundaries also need an element of flexibility to accommodate unexpected changes in your financial landscape, such as emergencies or shifts in income.

Communication: Especially in relationships, communicating your financial boundaries clearly and regularly is vital. This ensures that everyone involved understands and respects these boundaries, which is crucial for maintaining healthy financial interactions.

By defining what is and isn't allowed in your financial life, boundaries can help you determine what your limits are, avoid unnecessary spending, and promote better money management. They provide a framework within which you can make confident decisions, knowing that each choice supports your broader financial objectives.

2. The Perilous Path: Consequences of Not Having Financial Boundaries

Navigating life without financial boundaries is like driving a car with no idea of how to get to your destination, without a map and not asking for directions. Without clear guidelines for your spending and communication with others about money, you're at risk of getting lost, frustrated, and potentially running out of gas (money) before reaching your destination (financial goals). Here are the consequences of not having financial boundaries:

The Creep of Debt

Uncontrolled spending, fueled by impulse purchases and a lack of budgeting, can lead to a mountain of debt. Without boundaries, credit cards become tempting solutions that quickly spiral out of control. Interest charges accumulate, and soon, you find yourself trapped in a cycle of minimum payments that hinder your ability to save or reach your financial objectives.

Imagine you see a trendy new gadget. Seized by impulse, you buy it using your credit card, even though it's not in your budget. This, piled on top of other unplanned spending, leads to maxed-out cards and high monthly interest payments, leaving less savings for that dream vacation.

Saying 'Yes' to Debt: The Cost of Generosity

Without clear communication about lending money or shared expenses, you become the go-to person for financial aid because you often say "yes." This can lead to resentment toward friends or family who may inadvertently take advantage of your generosity. You end up lending money you can't afford to lose or covering the bill for group outings, leaving your wallet – and spirit – drained.

Consider a friend who often asks for loans, promising to repay but seldom does. Obligated to help, you lend money, straining your budget and nurturing a seed of resentment toward your friend.

The Stress Spiral

Financial anxieties are the bedfellows of those without clear boundaries. The constant worry about money – running out of it, managing unexpected expenses, or meeting loan repayments – can manifest in various ways, impacting your relationships, work performance, and health.

Without a budget or spending limits, you're in a constant state of worry about overspending and not having enough for bills. This stress permeates your life, keeps you awake at night, and fosters tension with loved ones.

Strained Relationships

Money matters, when not openly discussed, can damage relationships. Imagine a partner's resentment as you splurge, or a family member's hurt by your inability to assist financially because you never set clear lending boundaries. Without open communication and respect for financial limits, money can become a major source of discord.

If you and your partner differ in spending habits, without communication and boundaries, your overspending on discretionary items could lead to bitter arguments and a resentful atmosphere.

Dreams Delayed, Goals Derailed

Without boundaries, saving for the future becomes a struggle. Each unplanned expense or indulgence chips away at your ability to accumulate enough money for a down payment, a comfortable retirement, or that dream getaway. Without boundaries, your long-term goals remain elusive.

You envision owning a home in five years, but without a budget and spending limits, impulsive purchases and frequent dining out erode your down payment fund, postponing your dream of home ownership.

185

Missed Opportunities

Lacking a financial plan and boundaries, you may miss out on beneficial investments. Juggling unexpected expenses and debt leaves little room for opportunities that could grow your wealth.

A friend shares a promising investment opportunity, but because of your consistent overspending, you have no spare cash to invest, missing out on a chance to boost your financial portfolio.

Poor Credit Score

Unrestrained spending and an over-reliance on your credit cards could cause you to go into debt. This will lead to a poor credit score and affect your eligibility for getting a loan in the future.

Frequent credit card max-outs and missed payments cause your credit score to plummet. When you want to buy a car, you're met with high-interest rates on loans, ratcheting up the cost.

Lack of Control

Financial boundaries empower you with control over your money. Without them, you're adrift in your own financial journey, reacting to unexpected expenses, feeling powerless to make any change, leading to frustration and hopelessness.

The incessant calls from creditors due to unpaid bills underscore a sinking feeling of being overwhelmed and the stark reality of a financial life adrift.

Unhealthy Financial Habits

Without boundaries, impulse buys and neglecting to budget can become the norm, making it even more difficult to attain financial stability.

Stressful days see you turn to retail therapy, an emotional spending habit that, while temporarily soothing, drains your savings and derails your financial objectives.

Vulnerability to Scams

Scammers prey on those who seem financially vulnerable or lack control. Without financial literacy and strong boundaries, you're an easy target for scams that could rob you of hard-earned money.

You fall for a scam under the guise of a call from your bank, pressuring you to transfer money to fix an alleged account issue, only to find your accounts pilfered.

By understanding and implementing financial boundaries, you create a safeguard for your finances, empowering informed decision-making, wealth-building, and the realization of your goals. Consider it as seizing the steering wheel on your financial journey – you're the driver, and your boundaries are the road map guiding you to your desired destination.

3. Types of Money Boundaries and How They Work

Think of setting money boundaries like defining the rules for how you manage your finances. These rules are vital as they guide you through your financial decisions, helping you avoid missteps and steering you back on course toward reaching your targets. In this segment, we'll look at the various types of financial boundaries you can establish, and how each contributes to steering you toward your goals.

Boundaries for Yourself: The Traffic Laws of Your Financial Journey

Just as traffic laws ensure safety and order on the roads, financial boundaries with yourself create a structured and secure financial environment. These personal rules help you manage spending, saving, and investing, promoting a healthy financial lifestyle.

Setting Spending Limits: Sticking to the Speed Limit

Setting spending limits is like sticking to speed limits – they prevent reckless financial behavior and ensure you stay within safe spending zones.

Implementing Spending Limits: Begin by reviewing how much you make every month and how much you spend. Look for categories where spending can be capped, such as dining out, shopping, or entertainment. For instance, if your monthly entertainment budget is $200, resist the temptation to exceed this limit, just as you would avoid speeding on the highway.

Benefits of Spending Limits: These limits help you prioritize essential expenses and savings, reducing the risk of financial instability. They act as guardrails that keep you from falling over.

Budgeting: Your Road Map

A detailed budget serves as a financial map that outlines your income, expenditures, and objectives. It provides a clear path forward and helps prevent financial missteps.

Creating a Budget: List down how much you make every month and all your expenses such as rent and grocery bills. Allocate funds accordingly, ensuring that essential needs are met before spending on wants.

Staying on Course: Examine your budget periodically and adjust it to reflect any changes that have emerged in your life. This ongoing adjustment ensures your financial plan remains relevant and effective, much like updating a GPS for the best route based on current traffic conditions.

The 'Needs Versus Wants' Tollbooth

Being able to tell the difference between an essential expense that is necessary for survival and a want which is something that is desired but not essential is crucial for financial stability. This helps in making informed spending decisions, ensuring that essential needs are prioritized over optional wants.

Prioritizing Needs: Set aside the required funds for necessities like housing, food, healthcare, and transportation. These are akin to paying a toll – essential for your journey to continue smoothly.

Managing Wants: Limit expenditures on non-essential items. Treat these like luxury stops on your journey – they are enjoyable but should only be pursued after fulfilling all essential needs.

The 'Unsubscribe' Detour

Regular subscriptions can quickly drain finances. Actively managing these can free up significant funds.

Reviewing Subscriptions: Every few months, evaluate all subscription services (streaming media, gym memberships, magazines). Cancel any that are not essential or not providing value for their cost.

Financial Benefits: Reducing these fixed expenses increases your financial flexibility, allowing more funds to be redirected toward savings or debt reduction.

The 'Retail Therapy' Roadblock

Impulse buying, often triggered by emotional needs, can derail financial plans. Establishing boundaries to manage emotional spending is crucial.

Recognizing Triggers: Identify situations that lead to impulse spending, like stress or social influences. Understanding these triggers allows you to develop strategies to cope without spending.

Alternative Coping Strategies: Instead of shopping, consider other ways you can relieve stress, such as going for a walk. These alternatives provide satisfaction without financial consequences.

Boundaries with Others: Building Bridges of Clear Communication

Crafting financial boundaries with others is about laying down clear and respectful communication lines, not just erecting barriers. These boundaries are like bridges that connect you to your friends, family, and partners in a way that maintains both your financial integrity and your relationships.

The 'Splitting the Bill Express Lane' (Open Communication About Shared Expenses)

Transparent and upfront communication about shared expenses prevents awkwardness and ensures fairness with finances. Whether you are dining out with friends or planning a holiday with family, setting expectations early keeps everyone on the same financial page.

Implementing Shared Expense Rules: Before any money is spent, discuss and agree on how costs will be shared. Apps that track group expenses can be helpful in keeping everyone informed and accountable.

Benefits of Clear Guidelines: This approach not only avoids misunderstandings but also strengthens trust among participants, ensuring that no one feels burdened or taken advantage of.

The 'Loaning Lane' (Navigating Lending Money)

Lending money to friends or family can be fraught with risk. Establishing clear guidelines and terms for loans safeguards relationships and finances.

Setting Terms for Loans: If you decide to lend money, specify the amount, repayment schedule, and any interest charges in writing. Treat it as a formal agreement, even with loved ones, to ensure clarity and seriousness on both sides.

Alternative Support: If you are not comfortable or do not have the means to lend money to a loved one but would still like to help, look for non-monetary ways you can assist them.

The 'Gift-Giving Gate' (Managing Expectations Around Gifts)

Gift-giving, especially during holidays or special occasions, can strain budgets. Setting up boundaries around gift expenses helps manage personal finances without compromising relationships.

Establishing Gift Budgets: Discuss and set spending limits for gifts with family and friends. This can prevent competitive spending so everyone enjoys gifting without the pressure.

Creative Alternatives: Suggest non-material gifts, like experiences or homemade presents, which can be more meaningful and less financially demanding.

The 'Stop Sign' Strategy (Dealing with Persistent Financial Pressure)

Sometimes, despite clear boundaries, people may persistently pressure you for financial help or engage in financially toxic behaviors. Knowing how to handle these situations is crucial for your financial peace.

Saying No Respectfully: Learn to say no firmly and respectfully when faced with unreasonable financial demands. Provide your reasons clearly and suggest alternatives where appropriate.

Limiting Exposure: If certain relationships consistently lead to financial strain, consider limiting your financial interactions with those individuals. This might mean declining to participate in financially burdensome activities or politely withdrawing from joint financial commitments.

In essence, establishing and maintaining both types of financial boundaries – those with yourself and with others – creates a strong framework for your financial well-being. By setting clear guidelines for spending and saving, you not only protect your finances but also create relationships built on transparency and mutual respect. These boundaries empower you to navigate through financial landscapes with confidence, ensuring that every financial decision is in line with your goals and values. As you continue to reinforce these boundaries, they become not just financial safeguards, but stepping stones to greater financial freedom and security.

4. Crafting Your Financial Blueprint: The Essence of Money Boundaries

Creating a financial blueprint with well-defined money boundaries is like drawing a detailed map for your financial journey. It doesn't just guide you; it ensures that every step you take aligns with your broader financial goals. Let's explore how to effectively draw this map and navigate your path to financial stability and success.

Clear and Defined Boundaries

Start by clearly defining your financial boundaries. These should be specific, unambiguous, and tailored to your personal financial situation, helping you differentiate between acceptable and unacceptable financial behaviors.

> "I commit to saving at least 15% of my monthly income. This will directly go into a high-interest savings account before I allocate funds to other expenses."

Personalized Money Boundaries

Your financial boundaries should reflect your personal circumstances, goals, and values. They must be adaptable to changes in your financial status and life priorities.

> "As a freelance graphic designer, my income varies every month. I've set a flexible spending limit that can be modified based on my earnings, ensuring I always live within my means while saving consistently."

Flexible Yet Firm

Flexibility within your financial boundaries lets you modify your plans to accommodate the changes in your life.

> "When I receive unexpected medical bills, I adjust my entertainment and dining out budgets to maintain my financial balance without dipping into savings meant for emergencies."

Consistent Application

Apply your boundaries consistently across all areas of your finances to develop strong, sustainable financial habits.

Track your spending and find out if you managed to stick to your boundaries. If you didn't, reflect on the reasons and fine-tune your strategies to fit your spending habits better.

Realistic and Achievable

Set realistic boundaries that reflect your financial situation. Unrealistic boundaries are discouraging and unsustainable.

Try using a visual aid like a flowchart to set and adjust your financial boundaries.

Empowering and Enforcing

Money boundaries should empower you and help you manage your finances confidently and effectively. Think of your boundaries as tools for empowerment, not restrictions. They are designed to help you build the financial life you aspire to.

Boundary Enforcement

Regular reviews and adjustments to your boundaries ensure they remain effective and relevant.

Develop a quarterly financial review checklist that includes evaluating your budget effectiveness, investment returns, and progress toward savings goals. This ensures you stay aligned with your financial objectives.

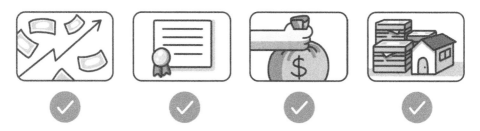

Think of your financial blueprint as a living document that grows and evolves with you. By establishing and maintaining clear, personalized, and flexible money boundaries, you not only safeguard your current assets but pave the way for future financial successes. Each boundary you set should feel like a stepping stone toward achieving your dreams. Challenge yourself to not just set boundaries but to live by them, making smart, informed financial decisions that bring you closer to your goals every day.

5. Setting Money Boundaries

Navigating your finances effectively goes beyond having good intentions; it requires a structured approach to managing your money. Setting money boundaries for yourself is crucial in creating a financial framework that not only guides your spending, saving, and investing but also aligns with your long-term life goals.

Budgeting: Crafting Your Financial Compass

Why it's Important: A budget is your financial compass, guiding every dollar to ensure it's working for you. Here's how to turn your budget from a monthly chore into a powerful tool for financial freedom:

Practical Steps: Start by finding out where your money is going every month. Categorize your expenses and set limits based on your financial priorities, such as essential living costs, savings, and debts.

Incorporate a pie chart in your budgeting app or spreadsheet to visually break down your spending categories. This will help you see, at a glance, if adjustments are needed.

Setting Saving Goals: Plotting Your Financial Milestones

Connect to Life Goals: Saving goals should be direct reflections of your personal aspirations – be it a dream vacation, homeownership, or a comfortable retirement.

Actionable Advice: You can set automatic transfers to facilitate saving. This makes it easier to stay committed.

Implementing Spending Limits: Keeping Your Spending in Check

Behavioral Impact: Establishing spending limits is essential for ensuring you live within your means.

Review your last three months of bank statements. Identify one area where you tend to overspend and set a specific, reduced spending limit for the next month. Track your progress and adjust as needed.

Developing an Investment Strategy: Building Your Financial Future

Long-Term Growth: A well-crafted investment strategy is your blueprint for building wealth. It should include your goals, risk tolerance, and timeline.

Reflect on your current investments. Are they aligned with the level of risk you are comfortable with and your financial goals? If unsure, speak to someone who can help you review your investment strategy.

Maintaining Financial Independence: Preserving Your Financial Identity

Empowering Independence: In relationships, maintaining some level of financial independence is vital. It ensures you have financial security and freedom.

With your partner, discuss the importance of individual financial boundaries. Agree on what expenses to share and which ones to manage independently, fostering both unity and respect for personal autonomy.

Enforcing Financial Boundaries: Embracing Change

Continuous Improvement: Regularly updating your financial boundaries is key to adapting to life's changes and unexpected financial shifts.

Create a quarterly financial review checklist. Include items like assessing budget efficacy, reviewing investment performance, and updating saving goals. This will help you stay proactive about your financial health.

Your financial boundaries are not just rules but the principles that define your approach to money management. They help forge a path toward a financially stable and fulfilling life. As you refine these boundaries, remember they are tools to empower you – not restrictions that confine you. Take this knowledge and use it to build a financial plan based on your values.

Chapter Takeaways

Harnessing the Power of Financial Boundaries

In this chapter, we've explored the critical role of financial boundaries in establishing a secure and prosperous financial life. By understanding and implementing these boundaries, you can prevent the common pitfalls that lead to financial instability and stress. Here are the key actions and insights from this chapter:

Establish Clear Boundaries: Start by clearly defining what you can and cannot do with your finances. Whether it's setting spending limits, saving goals, or investment rules, these boundaries help you navigate your financial landscape confidently.

Personalize Your Financial Plan: Tailor your financial boundaries to reflect your unique circumstances, goals, and values. This customization ensures that your financial plan works effectively for you, not just in theory but in everyday life.

Maintain Flexibility: While consistency is crucial, your financial boundaries should also accommodate changes in your financial situation and personal life. This adaptability prevents your financial plan from becoming obsolete or impractical.

Apply Boundaries Consistently: To reinforce good financial habits, apply your boundaries consistently across all areas of your finances. Regular practice solidifies these habits, making them second nature.

Review and Make Necessary Adjustments: Reviewing your finances periodically allows you to stay aware of your financial health and make any adjustments, if needed.

Use Tools to Help You: Use tools such as budget trackers, investment calculators, and savings apps to help you keep to your financial boundaries. These tools offer practical support in managing your finances effectively.

Empowerment Through Education: Continue to educate yourself about financial management and personal finance. Knowledge is power, so being well-read will enable you to make better, more informed decisions.

Build and Sustain Healthy Financial Relationships: Communicate and enforce your financial boundaries with others. This clarity prevents misunderstandings and ensures that your financial interactions are healthy and productive.

Remember, financial boundaries aren't restrictions but empowering tools that guide you toward financial freedom and stability. They provide the framework within which you can make confident and informed financial decisions, ultimately leading to a more secure and fulfilling financial future. Embrace these boundaries, adjust them as needed, and watch how they transform your financial life.

Appendix

Budgeting Method – Zero-Based Budgeting

In the quest for financial control, zero-based budgeting stands out as a rigorous method that makes every dollar work for you. Here, you are supposed to assign your entire income into various categories such as expenses, savings, debt repayment, and investments until you have nothing left. This approach helps you account for every penny you earn and forces you to be intentional about how you spend your money.

Here's what you can do:

1. **Sum Up Your Earnings:** Tabulate how much you make every month from all your revenue streams – from your job, side hustles, or investments.

2. **List Your Expenses:** Write down all expenses, from fixed spending such as rent to irregular costs like groceries and entertainment.

3. **Assign Every Dollar:** Allocate every dollar of your income to identified categories until you hit zero.

4. **Adjust as Needed:** Review your budget from time to time, especially if your earnings or expenses change.

Dos and Don'ts of Zero-Based Budgeting:

Dos:

Be Vigilant: Monitor your cash flow and stay on top of every dollar to ensure you don't overspend.

Involve Everyone: Make budgeting a family affair. This approach helps ensure that everyone's priorities are considered, and teaches valuable financial habits to all family members.

Stay Flexible: Life is unpredictable. Be ready to tweak your plans in response to the changes in your life.

Embrace Technology: Use modern tools to keep your budgeting precise and manageable. Apps can alert you to overspending or help you shift funds on the go.

Don'ts:

Don't Ignore Annual Costs: Always set aside a bit each month for irregular expenses like insurance premiums or holiday shopping.

Don't Be Too Rigid: Allow some wiggle room. Strict budgets can lead to burnout and discourage you from sticking to your financial plan.

Don't Lose Sight of the Future: With so many things to do every day, many of us get distracted by what's happening right now. But don't let that affect your future goals.

Don't Overextend Yourself: Resist the temptation to stretch your budget to cover non-essentials. Prioritize needs over wants, especially when funds are tight.

Implementing zero-based budgeting might seem daunting, but its benefits are profound. With commitment and discipline, this budgeting method can illuminate your financial pathway.

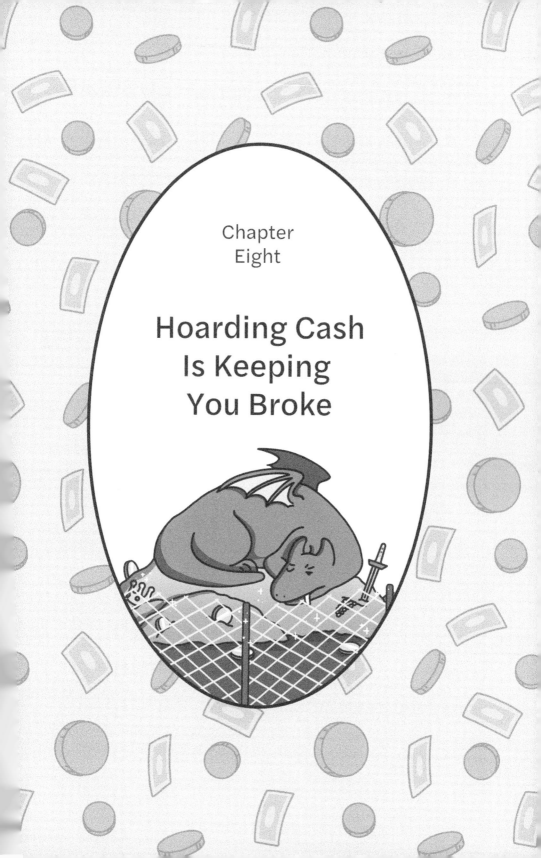

Chapter
Eight

Hoarding Cash
Is Keeping
You Broke

HOARDING CASH IS KEEPING YOU BROKE

Let's say you're the type who diligently saves money. You've meticulously organized your life savings, housing them in several bank accounts according to purpose: regular bills, vacation and fun, retirement, and even emergencies. Pretty neat. However, when you review your accounts, you think, "I have a decent amount of money. So, why does it feel like it's never enough?"

It's common knowledge that we should have funds that are easily accessible with us at all times – just in case, right? You don't know when life will surprise you with a blown tire, an injury, or a bill you didn't expect.

But while it's comforting to know that you're prepared to deal with emergencies, did you know that hoarding cash could be stopping you from growing your wealth?

Think of it this way: If you have $10,000 tucked away in a savings account that gives you 1.5% interest per annum, your savings would have grown to $11,605 in 10 years. That's pretty decent, right?

Now imagine if you had placed the same $10,000 into a mix of investments with a guaranteed 7% annual return. In 10 years, you will have bagged $19,672 worth of earnings! See the difference?

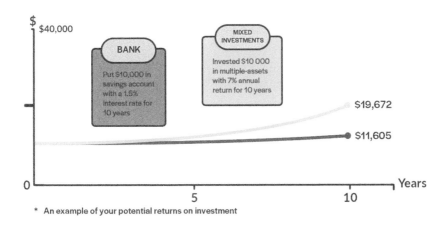

* An example of your potential returns on investment

Money can grow over time, but you have to know how to maximize its potential. It's great that you have cash to spare anytime you need it, but that same stash could multiply over time if you let it.

By not investing, your money slowly loses its value over time. We have inflation to thank for that.

Economists define inflation as the increase in prices of goods and services over time. Basically, all the stuff we buy! This decreases our purchasing power. Think of the same $10,000 you have. We're pretty sure you won't be able to buy the same things with it 10 years from now.

Yes, it's great to keep cash but having too much money just sitting idly by will make you lose out on the potential growth it could achieve through strategic investments.

It's all about finding the balance between having enough cash available for short-term needs and unexpected events and investing your money to outpace inflation.

The key is understanding your finances. Have you thought about your goals and targets? Would you like to take a trip around the world or retire in the south of France? Having a vision of your future can help you find that balance between cash savings and investments.

Finding that balance sets you up to achieve financial freedom. In this chapter, we'll be your guide, helping you master your money.

1. What Is a Liquidity Trap and Are You in One?

Ever feel like your money is stuck in quicksand, sinking so fast and you have no idea how to stop it? You work hard and you save even harder. Your bank balance keeps on growing, giving you that satisfying feeling. And somehow, your dream retirement seems to be within reach.

That is until you realize that what you have in your bank does not seem to account for much, even if the figures stay the same or increase. Over time, inflation has been eating away at your money's purchasing power, slowly but steadily shrinking the value of your savings. When things become more expensive, you suddenly need more dollars to buy the same item – making that comfortable retirement you dream of seem so far away.

Welcome to the liquidity trap.

What Is a Liquidity Trap?

Thinking of putting your money in a safety box at home? While it lies safe and secure, and access is 100% not a problem, the chances of it growing are close to, if not zero. This is the liquidity trap – you have money that is safe and accessible, but it doesn't grow in value over time.

Keeping your money in low-interest bank accounts offers extra protection for your cash in exchange for less-than-impressive returns.

We've all been there, really. Hoarding cash because we're scared we'll lose it to some shady investments or simply because we want to feel secure knowing that there's cash available whenever we need it. The thing is, when you play it a little too safely, it puts your money at the risk of losing its value over time.

But hey, that's why we're here. In the following sections, we will show you how to make your money work for you in your quest for financial independence!

Post-It.

Liquidity. A business term that measures one's ability to convert their assets into cash.

Mutual Fund. An investment that pools funds from different investors to buy different types of assets like stocks and bonds.

Money Market Funds. A type of mutual fund that is generally less risky compared to other options. Much like a safe that's easy to access and grows your money slowly through time. Typically secure, it invests in reliable sources like short-term loans to businesses or governments, reflecting the current interest rates in the returns you earn.

2. Why Do We Hoard Cash?

We explained that parking your life savings in liquid and not-so-hardworking assets only makes them miss out on growth opportunities because they can't put up a fight with inflation. Keeping this up only sucks you even deeper into the black hole that is the liquidity trap.

You need to get out of it fast, but to do so, you must first understand why hoarding cash is detrimental to you.

Two Factors Why Keeping Cash Holds You Back

Inflation Rocket Ship

How often have you heard old folks say, "Things were not this expensive when we were young!" Time and inflation have decided to team up in what seems to be an ill twist of fate. Prices have skyrocketed over the years (and they will do so without stopping), leaving your money somewhat powerless to buy the things it could once pay for.

Remember how your grandparents told you that a movie ticket cost just $0.25 back in the day? Try going to a cinema today, and chances are you'll pay at least $9. The same amount of money won't get you as much as it did 50 or 60 years ago because inflation would have pulled the prices up.

This is why savings that aren't invested or earning returns effectively lose value in the long run. Prices creep up over time and your cash buys less and less.

Stuck in the No-Investment Launchpad

Inflation sucks in the value of your money as days go by because you won't take your chances at investing. This hesitation not only helps inflation defeat your purchasing power, but it also limits your chances of growing your wealth.

Try looking at investing in a new light: it can be your rocket booster! Instead of letting your money slowly lose its buying power, investing can help launch your cash on growth exploration missions. You harness the power of compounding returns by putting your money into productive assets like stocks, bonds, real estate, or businesses.

If you place $10,000 in an investment that gives you 7% annual returns every year, your investment would be more than $76,000 in 30 years!

The sooner you launch your money on its financial adventure, the better, because your money will have more time to grow.

Post-It.

Compounding Effect. Compounding earns you money on your principal and on the interest you accumulated, which helps your money grow faster. Think of it like a snowball rolling downhill: it only gets bigger the longer it goes. The longer you leave your money in an investment that has compounding interest, the more time it has to grow!

Why Do People Keep Cash Rather than Invest?

It's sound advice to always keep a portion of your cash readily available. Nobody wants to be caught cashless in emergencies, after all. This sense of security extends to investing as well. When you have cash, fluctuations in the financial market become the least of your worries, and you face no risk of losing all your hard-earned money. Cash is a straightforward, tangible asset that's always accessible. This makes it a bit challenging to convince cash-preferring people to spare some of their money for investment. To help us understand better, let us explore a few reasons why they prefer to keep their money in cash rather than invest it:

Focusing on the Immediate Future Versus the Distant Future

Some of us concentrate so much on meeting daily needs that achieving long-term growth often takes a back seat. And because cash is easily accessible, the thought of putting money up for investment easily spells inconvenience especially when you suddenly need the money.

We say: Think of investment like planting a seed for a brighter financial future!

Ghosts of Losses Past

Suffering traumatic losses in previous years either from a failed business venture, fraudulent activities, or even bad investments can scar anyone for life. If things turned out badly in the past, choosing to play it safe and sticking with cash is understandable. By keeping cash, they can be sure it's safe with them and that they need not worry about the risks of losing money again. Investments always come with the risk of losses, which is why people with low-risk appetites opt for the stability of cash.

We say: There are a lot of investment options to explore, even ones that come with lower risks!

Investments and Financial Market Horror Stories

News about financial scandals can make investing seem scary. We see headlines about "get-rich-quick schemes" and bad actors in the industry – enough to make anyone want to keep their cash under the mattress!

We say: With the right knowledge, you can become more financially literate which can make you a savvy investor, not an easy target.

Lost in (Financial) Translation

Investing can feel like a whole new language, full of confusing terms and complicated charts. No wonder some people just stick with what they know and can fully understand.

We say: Like learning a new skill, we can start with the basics and walk you through things step-by-step.

Retiree State of Mind

Security is the top priority for retirees living on a fixed income. Having a readily available cash cushion makes perfect sense. Holding onto their only source of income or what's left of their life savings is imperative.

We say: Don't worry, because there are also ways to invest that can make your money available for you when needed while helping your money grow!

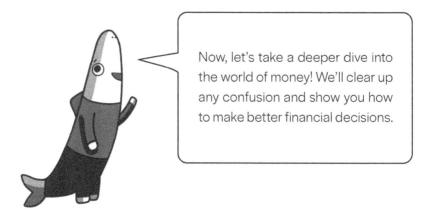

Now, let's take a deeper dive into the world of money! We'll clear up any confusion and show you how to make better financial decisions.

3. Understanding Money

Most of what we own may have been purchased using money. Money plays a big role in this world. We can get what we want – be it food, gadgets, or sometimes experiences – in exchange for money.

More than this, money has various functions. You can use it to buy things today, like a cup of coffee or your groceries. You can also save it and use it for bigger purchases in the future, like a dream car or an art program in France. What's more, you can even grow it over time as long as you use it wisely, like investing. By doing so, you are boosting your money's "purchasing power."

While there are things that matter more than money, we can all agree that it is essential. It's a tool we need in our everyday lives, and we can make the most of it. Let us show you how!

How 'Money Makes the World Go Round'

The functions of money: How does money work in our daily lives?

All right, it may be exaggerated to say that money makes the world go round. Maybe not in the literal sense of the word, but it does play a crucial role in keeping things moving along. As mentioned, we use it in our everyday lives, something we'll have a hard time living without. It will make no sense to talk about our finances without money since it's somewhat synonymous with earning, spending, and growing wealth.

In case you missed it, here are some of the ways money proves its usefulness:

- *Keeping Your Fridge (and Tummies) Full:* From grocery stores to restaurants, money lets you buy the food that satisfies your hunger. Relying on this exchange are the farmers, producers, bakers, and everyone responsible for bringing your food from the sources to your table.

- *Juicing Up:* Needless to say, the world runs on money. We use it to pay for electricity, water, internet, and phone services – basically everything that keeps your home and devices functional and connected.

- *Staying Healthy:* Doctor visits, medicines, medical procedures, even aesthetic ones, all require money. Thanks to money, your basic healthcare needs to stay happy and free from illnesses are accessible.

- *Never-Ending Learning:* From daycare to college to post-graduate degrees, including training programs to enhance one's skill set, to learning conventions, down to that online digital marketing course – everything that you need to invest in your education needs money.

- *Getting Practically Anything:* That mouth-watering food, the latest gadget, or a fun karaoke with friends, you pay for them with money whether in hard cash, card, or online transfer.

- *Treating Yourself to a Shopping Spree:* When you put your money down, you get to bring home the trendiest outfit or those fancy shoes and call them your own.

- *Having Fun:* From movie nights to world tour concerts to that grand prix you've been dying to witness firsthand, money is your ticket to enjoying them.

- *Asking for Help:* When we want to buy things we can't afford now, we borrow money, spend, and pay back later.

4. Money Up Close

The Time Value of Money

Earlier, we discussed how your money is more valuable today than it will be in the future. This concept is also known as the "time value of money." It's very much like a seed that you plant, nurture, and grow over time.

Here, "planting" refers to investing. If you keep a seed in your shed for years without planting it, the less likely it is to grow. This is basically because letting money sit around lessens its earning capacity. But investing your money wisely lets you grow your money through the interest it can earn, boosting its value.

Understanding this idea of time value is crucial for all types of financial decisions like why saving for your retirement as early as you can is good for you or why getting loans for big purchases might be more beneficial for you. Stay tuned as we dig deeper into the time value of money.

Understanding the Concept

Imagine you wake up with $100,000 in your account. What would you do with it? Would you spend it on a dream vacation? Would you lend it to a friend in need? Would you invest it? Or, maybe, take up another $100,000 loan to finally get your hands on that $200,000 sports car of your dreams?

Remember that whatever decision you make today can and will impact your future finances.

Here's what could happen to your $100,000 for every choice you make:

- *Spend it all:* You only live once, and it's not every day that you get to wake up richer by $100,000! Once you spend it, though, you wake up with the money gone forever and a feeling as if it never really happened.

- *Lend it to a friend at a 5% interest rate:* Not only will you get your $100,000 back after 10 years, but you will also earn an extra $62,889 in interest using the future value calculation. Sweet!

- *Make a wise investment with a 7% annual return:* Fast-forward 10 years. Using the future value calculation, your $100,000 could easily grow to $196,715 – almost double your capital! Congratulations on making your money work for you!

- *Buy your dream sports car with a loan:* You decided to take a $100,000 loan that has a 6% interest and 5-year repayment tenure to get that shiny new car. After accounting for amortisation, you would have coughed up

$115,997 in five years! Not only does the car cost more than its original $200,000 price, but your $100,000 is also gone.

Can you see the difference the time value of money makes? Every decision you make affects your finances in an entirely different way. By using present value and future value calculations, you can assess potential financial outcomes before making decisions about money.

The $100,000 Question: Who Benefited the Most?

Leigh the Investor

Both the lender and the investor win! They made good use of their cash and made the time value of money work to their advantage. The early investment grew their money through interest, dividends, or capital appreciation. Investing early is key: the longer you stay invested, the more time your money has to grow.

Spencer the Spender

No benefits here except maybe for the fleeting thrill of spending money on whatever he wanted. By spending at once, he denied his money the potential future growth from compounding returns.

Barry the Borrow-Then-Spender

At the bottom of the list is the borrower-then-spender who not only used his money but got himself into debt just to get a fancy car.

Post-It.

1. *Dividends.* Tiny shares of profits from companies.

2. *Capital.* A general term for resources and assets that provide the owner an edge or an advantage. In business, it is the money (and resources) needed to build, run, and grow a company.

3. *Capital Appreciation.* An increase in the value of investment made.

Using Present and Future Value in Planning Your Finances

Present Value is like asking, "How much money do I need to save to buy a three-bedroom lakefront property?" It helps you calculate the amount of money you need to save up to achieve your future goals.

Suppose you want to buy a new car that costs $20,000 in five years. Present Value helps you identify the amount of money you will have to save every month in order to make that purchase.

Future Value, on the other hand, is like asking, "If I set aside a few dollars today, how much will they be worth in the future?" Like a time machine, it tells you how much your cash can grow over time based on interest or returns when you invest or keep it in savings accounts.

> If you place $5,000 into a bank account, the Future Value calculation calculates the interest and lets you know how much that money will be worth in, say, 10 years.

These two calculations are like handy tools you can use as you make your financial freedom journey. Helping you plan your savings goals is **Present Value** while **Future Value** helps you approximate the rewards of saving wisely (and early). Isn't that cool?

Remember these two terms as we'll be using them throughout this chapter.

Present Value and Future Value Applications in Personal Finances

Concept	Definition	Where It Applies
Present Value	How much you need to save right now to achieve a future goal.	• Saving for major purchases/goals (e.g., house, car, etc.) • Retirement planning • Evaluating job offers/raises • Understanding loan repayments
Future Value	The approximated value of an investment, cash, or asset in the future based on an estimated growth rate.	• Saving goals (e.g., retirement, education) • Investment growth projections • Understanding loan repayment amount in total • Evaluating job offers/raises

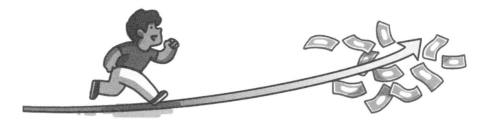

Practical Examples:

Scenario	Present Value	Future Value
Saving for a $30,000 car in 5 years	How much do you need to save monthly to have $30,000 in 5 years?	If you save $X monthly, it will grow to $30,000 in 5 years.
Retirement planning	How much do you need to invest today to have $1 million when you retire?	If you invest $X now, it will grow to $1 million by retirement.
Taking a $200,000 loan	What you borrowed today is worth $200,000.	Total repayment is valued at $X over 30 years, including interest

Make Present Value and Future Value work for your financial future by considering the time value of money.

Compound Interest: The Money-Making Machine

The Basics of Compounding Returns

Ever heard of a money tree? Compound interest works on a similar concept. With a money tree, you hope to grow money as fruits. With compounding interest, you literally make your money multiply. Your interest can be reinvested, multiplying your money further.

Never mind that you started investing a small sum. Even a tiny seedling can grow into something big. Imagine investing $5,000 in an asset that gives you 7% annual returns.

Every year, your investment grows; in the first year, your money grows to $5,350, then goes up to $5,724 in the second year after compounding the previous year's earnings.

Fast forward 30 years, at 7% interest rate, your initial $5,000 investment could be worth almost $40,000! Thanks to the wonders of compounding interest, what little savings you had has grown significantly!

Comparing Different Investment Scenarios

For better appreciation, we've drawn up some situations to describe the amazing money-making power of compounding interest over time:

All Saving, Zero Investing Alice

- Initial savings: $10,000 at age 25

- No additional contributions

- Annual growth rate: 0% as cash is not invested

- Total wealth at age 65: (still) $10,000

Early Investing Emma

- Initial investment: $10,000 at age 25

- Annual growth rate: 7% compounded annually

- No additional contributions

- Total wealth at age 65: $149,745

Can you see the striking difference between Alice and Emma's total wealth at the end? The only thing the two did differently was to invest. Emma's decision to put her $10,000 to work versus Alice's choice to just keep her cash sitting idly meant over $126,000 difference in their accounts. Here, we've proven that investing your money wisely as early as possible can mean exponential growth for your savings, thanks to compounded returns. If you can, try to add (consistently) to your contributions for an even better bottom line.

Compounding Made Successful

Based on the scenarios described previously, you might observe some key factors that make compounding work hard for you, no matter the type of investment you choose:

- **Start Early, Think Long-Term**

  We can't stress it enough: The sooner you begin, the better! Compounding thrives when you give it time – the longer, the better.

- **Make Consistent Contributions**

  While upfront sums give you a great head start, know that the most impactful wealth compounding happens when you consistently add new funds.

- **Reinvest Your Earnings**

  Since you've taken the risk by investing anyway, why not push the envelope more and reinvest your investment earnings instead of going on a spending spree? Reinvesting returns is probably the greatest favor you will ever give your savings because it brings compounded earnings that turbo-charge your wealth growth over time.

Ultimately, strategic investing is arguably one of the best things you can do to boost your money. By taking advantage of compounding interest and returns over decades and nurturing it with discipline and patience, even the smallest amount of money can grow immensely. While it's true that no investment comes without risks, there's no harm in using this exponential growth potential to achieve a secure financial future.

5. Factors Affecting the Value of Money

The value of money is always changing, thanks to various economic factors that can either make it lose its purchasing power or make it more valuable. You probably know how inflation affects money. Here, we introduce two major forces that drive these money fluctuations: interest rates and currency fluctuations. Let's see how they contribute to the rising or falling of money's worth.

Interest Rates

Interest rates pretty much tell you how much your savings and investments can generate. When interest rates rise, savers earn more from interest-bearing accounts. It also works the opposite way: falling rates negatively affect this growth potential, decreasing it.

If you invest $10,000 into an asset that earns 5% compounded interest annually, you would make an additional $2,762 after 5 years. However, if interest rates were only at 1%, your $10,000 investment would only be gaining about $500 at the 5-year mark.

Higher interest rates let your money compound and appreciate quickly before considering inflation's effects. But when interest rates are low, cash savings get stuck, losing their purchasing power to even the slightest inflation over time.

This interest rate affects everything from savings accounts and loans to business lending and bond investing. High interest rates mean borrowing money from financial institutions, such as banks, will be more expensive.

Inflation

To expand on inflation, which is the gradual rise in the prices of goods and services over time, it's important to note that as prices increase, each unit of currency loses some purchasing power, meaning it can't buy as much as it once could.

Assume that a basket of groceries costs $100 today. If inflation averages 3% every year, that same basket would cost around $103 one year from now, $106 two years out, and so on with continued compounding. In essence, your $100 becomes worth less and less every year due to inflation.

While we cannot stop inflation's destructive impact on money's purchasing power over time, we can counter it by investing in assets that can outpace it and provide protection against its detrimental effects. Remember, cash savings, wages, bonds, and other fixed-income streams become particularly vulnerable to devaluation.

Deflation

Deflation happens when there is a general decline in the prices of everyday goods and services. On the surface, this works to your benefit as the falling prices let your money buy more than it could before. However, deflation often signals deeper economic problems like slowing demand which could lead to even bigger problems like unemployment, among others.

Currency Movements

Inflation and deflation aside, the value of money is silently affected by how a national currency strengthens or weakens compared to other currencies on the global foreign exchange markets. These fluctuating exchange rates impact a currency's purchasing power.

Let's say the US dollar (USD) is 10% stronger versus the currency of your earnings. This means the things you buy that are priced in USD become 10% more expensive for you. This is because the strength of USD diminishes the purchasing power of your local currency.

6. Debunking Cash Hoarding Myths

We're always advised to keep cash with us and we find ourselves heeding this advice. Supporting this advice are these cash-keeping myths that deserve a good shattering.

Myth 1: Cash Never Loses Value

False. One wave of inflation will result in cash steadily losing its purchasing power over time. This is why your $100 today won't buy you the same stuff around 20 or 30 years from now. Investing will help your money keep up with, if not outpace, inflation.

Myth 2: Investing Opens You Up to Losses

You can choose not to invest and let inflation eat away at your money's purchasing power and deny it the chance to reach its full potential for growth. Yes, investing always comes with risks, but investing wisely helps you grow your money and keep up with inflation. Holding onto your cash has 0% risk, but likewise, you risk missing out on growth opportunities for your savings.

Myth 3: I Don't Have Enough to Invest

Even small amounts of money can grow significantly when invested consistently over a period of time, thanks to compound interest and return rates. When you keep too much cash, you rob your money of its growth potential.

7. Putting Money to Work

The Difference Between Saving and Investing

While both are good for your finances, saving and investing work differently. Saving protects your money in the short term while investing makes your money work hard for long-term growth. While saving prioritizes liquidity and security, investing puts your money to productive use as it becomes your tool for outpacing inflation and growing your money. Other differences include:

Saving

- Setting money aside for future use

- Preserves your money's value in the short term but doesn't grow your money significantly

- Keeping cash in a savings account, money market fund, or fixed deposit account

- Having available cash for emergencies or short-term goals is the purpose

- Interest rates on savings are typically low and often don't keep up with inflation

- Your money is safely stored in the bank (hopefully not under your mattress) but isn't really growing

Investing

- Putting your money into assets to generate more income

- Comes with a money loss risk but has the potential for growth

- Can be stocks, bonds, mutual funds, real estate, or a business venture

- The purpose is to increase your money through compounding

- Has a higher probability for returns from investments to significantly out-pace inflation over time

- Significant price appreciation when invested in productive assets

Ways to Put Money to Work

What good would it bring you if your money were sitting on a couch, streaming videos online the entire day? Why not give it a nudge and make it work for you? Here are some ways you can get your cash moving:

- **Settle High-Interest Debts**

  High-interest debts will make you poor with the impossible charges they give you. Paying off debts like credit cards or personal loans is a productive use of your money. Saying goodbye to the high-interest rates is like earning money minus the risk.

- **Invest in Productive Assets**

  An effective method to grow your wealth is by investing in assets that can yield an income or increase in value over time. These include rental properties, dividend-paying stocks or bonds, and starting a business.

- **Educate/Upskill Yourself**

  You can never go wrong by investing in yourself. Whether through further studies or skills development, they have the potential to boost your income.

- **Do the (Side) Hustles**

  Use your cash to start a side business like selling food or crafts online or offering your freelancing skills – anything that can bring in extra cash on top of your day job. If you have what it takes to earn more, what's stopping you, right?

The key is to find ways to grow your money, save you money, or help you earn more in the future. Watch yourself achieve your financial goals when you put your money to (hard) work!

Unproductive use of money is spending your money in ways that don't give you any returns or growth over time. Here are some common examples for you to avoid:

- Impulsively buying stuff without considering your budget or limits. You may enjoy it at the moment, but it just really strips you of money you can put to better use.

- Buying depreciating assets like cars and the latest gadgets that quickly lose their value over time.

- Giving in to social pressure by keeping up with the Joneses and racking up high-interest debt (hello, credit cards!)

Is Your Money Working Hard or Hardly Working?

It can sometimes be tricky to tell if you're using money wisely. Here are some examples:

- **Risky Investments.** Putting all your funds into a high-risk asset might not be the best idea because you run the risk of losing a portion – if not all – of your investment. Think twice before making any high-risk investments.

- **Home Improvements.** Renovating your home can increase its value and provide a return on investment, if you eventually sell. Try not to overdo it and splurge on unnecessary upgrades. It's unlikely you'll get your money back when you put it up for sale.

- **Buying Cars.** The convenience of having a car can never be overstated. Aside from their convenience, cars can also be used to make money. But if you're buying one just to show off, and getting a fancy one at that, you'd do well to cancel your purchase. Remember, cars lose value over time, and getting a fancy one can leave you drowning in debt.

Money working hard means it's growing, saving, and earning you more money. If it's not doing that or just the opposite, then your money is hardly working. Take a look at the table below:

Money Working Hard	Money Hardly Working
Generates additional income streams (rent, interest, dividends, profits)	No income or returns generated
Has asset appreciation potential (stocks, real estate)	Assets depreciate over time
Enhances future income-earning potential (education, skills)	No enhancement to income-earning abilities
Builds long-term wealth through compounding	Diminishes wealth over time
Maximizes the power of compounding returns	Erodes purchasing power due to inflation
Assets/investments retain or increase in value	Money spent with no lasting value
Aligns with long-term financial goals	Potential for instant gratification, but no long-term benefits

Is Your Money Working for You or Against You?

Depending on how you manage it, money can work for or against you. Below is a table that illustrate these points:

Money Working for You	Money Working Against You
Savings & Investments: Building wealth through compounding interest and asset appreciation. This can provide financial security.	**Debts:** High-interest debts drain your resources and hinders wealth-building.
Earning Potential: Investing in education and skills to increase income.	**Lifestyle Inflation:** Increasing expenses with higher income, preventing effective saving and investing, and wealth-building.
Leverage: Using money to acquire assets or make investments that generate more money. Taking out a loan to buy a property that appreciates in value or using capital to start a successful business are some examples.	**Opportunity Costs:** Spending money on one thing means missing out on other opportunities. Poor financial decisions or impulsive purchases can lead to missed opportunities for investing or achieving important goals.
Opportunities: Having money opens doors to travel, networking, and exclusive access to events, groups, or companies.	**Psychological Effects:** Money can sometimes lead to greed, anxiety, and a sense of entitlement. These can later strain relationships and lead to poor decision-making.

Money Working for You	Money Working Against You
Financial Security: A solid foundation gives you security and reassurance.	**Financial Stress:** Lack of money can make you anxious, strain relationships, and impact your overall well-being.
Freedom & Flexibility: Money allows you to live the life you choose.	**Impulsive Spending:** Mindless spending and lack of financial discipline can deplete your resources.
Wealth Building: Compound interest and wise investments can grow wealth exponentially.	**Instant Gratification:** The inability to resist instant gratification can prevent you from achieving your long-term goals.
Legacy: Accumulated wealth can be passed on to future generations.	**Keeping Up Appearances:** The pressure to maintain a certain lifestyle can lead to overspending.

By maintaining a balanced perspective, you can get money to work toward your financial freedom and not against it.

The Time Value of Money in Your Financial Plan

Life always confronts us with financial choices – from small daily expenses to major decisions like financing a home. Let's look at how the time value of money plays a role in planning our personal finances. Understanding how time impacts your financial plans can guide you to plan your money better.

The True Price Behind the Tags

Time Value of Money helps you see how much something truly costs, particularly for big-ticket expenses spread out over years. If you are planning to buy a property, you might look at the purchase price listed and think you can afford it. But after factoring in the 30-year home loan, you'll understand how much more you will be paying for that property. This can help you make a better-informed decision on whether to purchase the house or not.

Retirement Planning

The sooner you start saving for retirement, the longer your money gets to grow. Imagine setting aside only $5,000 at age 25. Thanks to compounding interest effect your initial $5,000 could balloon to more than $70,000 by the time you hit 65, even without additional contributions!

If you start when you are 45, you'll need to make a much bigger effort to get the same earnings. Understanding the time value of money helps you set realistic savings targets based on how much time you have left. Think of it like having a road map to a comfortable retirement!

Timing Major Purchases

Whether buying a home, car, business, or other major long-term asset, the timing of that purchase can affect the overall value of your money. Take vehicles as an example. Given the consistent depreciation in value for most vehicles, buying a new car usually represents a terrible time value, with some models losing 20% of their value within the first year alone. By buying a low-mileage, issues-free used car that's ideally two to three years old, your money retains much more value than buying a new unit.

Investment Growth Projections

If you're interested in growing your wealth by investing, the number of years your money is invested dramatically impacts its ability to multiply over time due to compounding.

For instance, if you invest $10,000 today, your money could grow to more than $76,000 in 30 years if your annual returns are maintained at 7%. If you leave it to grow for another 10 years, the ending balance could be about $150,000!

By exploring various investment amounts, time frames, and expected returns, you can set realistic goals for your money. Imagining that pot of cash in the future can be one great motivator to keep saving and investing wisely. So, start growing your wealth today!

No two financial road maps are the same, so tailor yours according to your needs and circumstances.

- **Career Choices:** How might your income change throughout your working years?

- **Saving & Investing:** Start small and develop a healthy savings habit as your income grows.

- **Life Stages:** Plan for big-ticket expenses like a house or a car without losing sight of your long-term goals.

- **Rainy Day Fund:** Build an emergency fund for unexpected expenses while keeping your plans unharmed.

- **Balance Is Key:** You can still make the most of today while preparing for your future.

- **Growing Your Wealth:** The time value of money can help in your wealth-building that can, in turn, benefit future generations.

More than just a financial concept, the time value of money serves as a powerful lens that, when understood and actively applied, can create discipline, help you make smarter choices, and keep your focus on your priorities.

Finding the Balance: To Keep Cash or Not

There is still wisdom in keeping cash, but knowing how much cash to keep and how much to invest is the balance you need to aim for.

Why Keep Some Cash on Hand?

- *Daily Expenses:* You should set some cash aside for your daily needs like groceries and bills. Define a budget for your payables and stick to it. This way, you can avoid getting into credit card debt.

- *Emergency Fund:* It's wise to keep a stash of cash for when life throws you a curveball. Having an emergency fund protects you from unexpected costs like car repairs or hospital bills. Remember to set aside savings that can cover your living expenses for at least three to six months.

- *Short-Term Goals:* For short-term goals such as buying a gadget, keep the funds somewhere that is easily accessible so you can grab it when you chance on the perfect deal.

- *Peace of Mind:* Nothing spells peace and quiet like feeling financially secure. If having a certain amount of cash in your bank account relieves your stress, then keep your money there by all means! Just don't forget to create a separate "buffer account" to avoid accidentally splurging on your daily needs. Don't forget that inflation is always there, so keep your cash moving!

Why You Shouldn't Keep Your Cash on Hand

- *Long-term savings and investments:* Money intended for medium and long-term financial goals, like retirement funds or wealth-building savings kept in low-interest bank accounts, will only stifle their growth. Liquid cash accounts typically offer very low, close-to-zero interest rates. Investing them in various channels can generate higher returns.

239

8. Start Making Money Work for You

Take it one step at a time:

Educate Yourself: Investing can seem daunting, but countless resources are available to help you learn the basics. Read books, take online courses, or seek guidance from a financial advisor, if you feel overwhelmed.

Set Clear Financial Goals: Think about what you would like to achieve with your money. These objectives will help you identify what investment plan and strategy you can use.

Build an Emergency Fund: Before you dive into investing, make sure you have a cash cushion for emergencies. This prevents you from dipping into your investments whenever an unexpected expense arises.

Think Long-Term and Stay the Course: Investing is for the long haul. There will be periods of volatility and temporary losses but don't let short-term fluctuations derail you. Instead, stay committed to your goals and let compounding interest grow your money.

Start Small: Contrary to popular belief, you don't need a lot to start investing. Many platforms allow you to invest less than $100. So start small and increase your contributions progressively.

Diversify: Diversification is the best way to spread your risk. When you invest in different assets, you reduce the likelihood of losing all your assets at one go.

9. Can Money Really Buy Happiness?

Whether money can truly buy happiness is a question unique to each person. While a Tesla might not necessarily guarantee joy, knowing that you are financially secure can take the weight off one's shoulders. That's one big worry resolved! The truth is, when you are not constantly stressed about how to make ends meet or how to settle bills or healthcare, it's easier to shift your focus on the things that truly matter – like quiet time with loved ones or pursuing what your heart desires.

Money may not buy you happiness, but it definitely can contribute to a happier, healthier you. Here's how:

The Power of a Mind at Peace: For most people, security and stability mean having a roof over our heads, food on the table, and access to healthcare.

Experience Is Key: It can be satisfying to know you can go on that dream family vacation or take that art class at any time you wish. Money can help open doors to experiences that bring joy, spark creativity, and create lasting memories.

Freedom to Choose: Financial security can give you the freedom of choice. Maybe it's starting your own business or touring the world. The choice is yours to make.

Rainy Day Relief: Life can be hard to predict, and that's why having a fund that can help you during these times is essential. Having one makes dealing with it bearable and bouncing back quicker.

Helping Others Feels Good: For many people, nothing can quite compare to the happiness brought by giving back and paying good things forward. Money can be an instrument in making the world a better place when it is used for volunteering or donating to various causes.

Remember, money is a tool. It has the power to create a more comfortable and secure life. It can also lift off burdens weighing you down and open doors to new experiences.

10. Conclusion: Master the Money Flow

Are you all set to unlock your money's true potential? This chapter discussed why keeping cash isn't the best option to lead you to financial freedom. Here's a quick recap of what we covered:

Cash Isn't Always King. Keeping cash with you or in your bank account does not work to your benefit as it robs your money of the chance to grow to its fullest potential. Letting it chill in a low-term back account only invites inflation to diminish its purchasing power.

There is Power in Investing. Investing can leverage the time value of money and compounding interest to build your wealth. The earlier you invest, the better returns await.

Take Action Today: Look up investment options, consult a financial expert, and start crafting a plan to make your money work hard for you.

Appendix

Budgeting Method – 50/30/20

This method ensures that you cover essentials, save diligently, and still enjoy life's pleasures. It splits your after-tax income into three categories of differing percentages, making it easy to know what to spend, and not to spend.

Here's how it works:

Calculate and Allocate: Sum up all of your income and split it based on the following:

- *Essentials (50%):* This chunk covers necessary expenses like housing, food, and utilities. It's about keeping the lights on and the wheels turning.

- *Wants (30%):* This portion is for the nice-to-haves, such as dining out, hobbies, and subscriptions. It's your financial breathing space to enjoy life.

- *Savings and Debt Repayment (20%):* This final segment is your future-focused funds – savings, investments, and extra debt payments. It's about building a buffer and securing your financial future.

The 50/30/20 budget is easy to use, but it may not work for everyone, especially if your essential expenses exceed 50% of your after tax income or if you have significant debt to pay off. If this is you, try adjusting your expenses or percentages so your money makes sense to you. You can also reduce your wants or find additional sources of income.

The beauty of this budget lies in its simplicity and flexibility. It provides a clear framework for allocating your money without getting bogged down in too many categories or intricate calculations. It also allows for some discretionary spending, which can make it more sustainable and enjoyable than a strict, bare-bones budget.

Dos and Don'ts of the 50/30/20 Budget:

Dos:

- *Track Spending Closely:* Keeping a detailed record helps ensure adherence to your 50/30/20 budget plan.

- *Be Realistic:* Honestly assess your spending habits and lifestyle needs. Accurately allocating for your essentials and discretionary spending ensures the budget is both realistic and effective.

- *Prioritize Financial Goals:* Though only 20% of your budget goes toward savings and debt repayment, prioritize these funds as they help you achieve goals such as owning your own property. Small, consistent contributions grow over time.

- *Adjust as Necessary:* The 50/30/20 budget isn't set in stone. If life throws you a curveball – an unexpected expense, or a change in priorities – tweak your budget to keep it relevant and effective.

- *Enjoy 'Guilt-Free' Spending:* Embrace the freedom within the 30% allocated for wants. If you stay within this limit, you can indulge without impacting your essential expenses or financial goals.

Don'ts:

- *Don't Ignore Irregular Expenses:* Always factor in occasional costs like insurance premiums or holiday gifts. Planning for these in your budget prevents unwelcome financial surprises.

- *Don't Neglect Saving for Emergencies:* While 20% might also cover debt repayment, ensuring some of this goes into an emergency fund is crucial for financial security.

- *Don't Overspend in Any Category:* Stick to the allocated percentages for needs, wants, and savings. This discipline helps avoid the need to borrow from one category to cover overspending in another.

- *Don't Treat the 30% as a 'Free-for-All':* While discretionary spending offers flexibility, it's important to remain mindful and avoid frivolous splurges.

- *Don't Get Discouraged:* Transitioning to a new budgeting method can be challenging. Remain patient and persistent, and don't be disheartened by initial setbacks.

The 50/30/20 budgeting method helps you cover your essentials, have a little fun, and stack up savings for a rainy day. So, as you adopt this budgeting framework, remember: it's designed to grow with you and help you carve out a path to real financial freedom. Stick with it, tweak it as you go, and soon you'll see not just your savings, but your whole financial perspective transform.

Chapter
Nine

Ignoring Debt Is Keeping You Broke

IGNORING DEBT IS KEEPING YOU BROKE

The Harsh Reality: Debt Is a Silent Dream Killer

When you first step into adulthood and independence, it's a thrilling time filled with potential. You're on your own, making decisions, building a life, dreaming of a successful career, a home like the bungalow down the road, and adventures around the world. Initially, your financial slate is clean; there are no overdue credit card and mortgage payments to worry about. Yet, the temptations to take on debt are everywhere; they are potential financial landmines that rob you of your income, freedom, and ability to build wealth.

Meet Emily, a recent college graduate whose entry into adulthood was marked by these very dreams and challenges. Like many, she was quickly drawn to the allure of easy credit, seeing it as a means to fulfill immediate desires without fully grasping the long-term consequences.

Most people find themselves saddled with one form of debt or another, from modest credit card balances to significant 30-year mortgages. Debt is remarkably easy to acquire yet proves extremely difficult to escape. It starts small, appearing harmless at first, but it can rapidly trap you in a vicious cycle if you're not careful.

While you can use debt to grow your wealth, using it for depreciating assets like cars, vacations, clothes, and more is financially imprudent. These purchases lose value instantly, whereas the debt endures, accruing interest month after month.

Now let's delve into the deceptive nature of debt. We'll explore the common pitfalls that lead to the debt trap and how it can spiral out of control. We will challenge some of the most persistent myths and most importantly, we'll arm you with practical strategies to manage your payments. From understanding the warning signs to learning effective ways to manage and ultimately eliminate it, this chapter will guide you step-by-step toward reclaiming your financial freedom.

1. The Debt Trap

The Debt Spiral: How It Usually Happens

Jane left college three years ago and she immediately found a secure executive job, and all these years she has been managing her expenses well. But somehow, she just can't get rid of this debt, her credit card balance.

Her debt story began with a seemingly harmless decision: signing up for a no-annual-fee credit card. Jane's first major purchase was a $1,000 phone, bought under the assumption that a low minimum payment of 2% or $20 was manageable. However, two years later, despite regular payments, she still owed $893 on that phone.

Because the minimum monthly payment amount makes everything so affordable, soon, she racked up thousands of dollars in purchases. Before long it becomes harder and harder to pay off each month. No matter how carefully she plans her monthly payments, the balances never seem to go down much. Does this sound familiar?

The minimum payment structure, designed to appear affordable, often leads to a ballooning debt load due to accumulating interest, trapping consumers like Jane in a cycle of debt repayment that can extend nearly a decade longer than expected. In Jane's case, it would take her eight years to pay off the original $1,000 debt.

At the end of the eighth year, she would have paid the credit card company a total of $1,458 for her phone purchase. Because credit card companies charge between 15% and 22% (depending on the current interest rates) on her unpaid balances, the extra $458 goes to paying interest charges.

What It Looks Like Living in Indebtedness

The initial convenience of credit cards quickly transitions to a burden. Before long, your credit cards have accumulated a $7,000 debt. On top of that, you still have $32,000 in student loans and a $30,000 car loan.

Each month a huge chunk of your paycheck goes toward paying off your loans. You begin to miss out on one or two payments because you have to juggle with other essential needs such as rent and meals, causing your credit score to tank from missed payments and maxed-out credit limits.

Now your dream of buying your own home is close to impossible. With all the debt weighing you down, you don't have room to save for the house deposit and banks may not offer you a mortgage because of your scratched credit score. You're trapped in a vicious cycle – unable to pay down your debts and you can't plan and save for your future.

Stages of Indebtedness: Moving from Small Debt into Bankruptcy

The path from manageable debt to a serious, overwhelming debt trap often follows a pattern with several stages:

- *Initial debt:* Most people start with small amounts of debt such as a credit card balance of a few hundred dollars. This debt may be manageable initially.

- *Income disruption:* A job loss, pay cut, medical emergency, or other financial shock reduces income while expenses remain the same or increase.

- *Using credit to cover shortfalls:* With less income, people start relying more heavily on credit cards, payment deferments, and other forms of borrowing to pay bills and maintain their lifestyle.

- *Snowballing interest and fees:* As balances grow, interest charges and late fees compound the debt burden rapidly, making it harder to catch up.

- *Credit maxed out:* Eventually, credit limits are reached, and no new borrowing is possible, exacerbating cash flow problems.

- *Depleting savings and assets:* People drain emergency funds, cash out investments, or raid retirement accounts trying to stay afloat financially.

- *Missed payments and defaults:* With no way to cover minimum payments, defaults occur on loans, mortgages, credit cards, leading to penalties, higher interest rates, and collections calls.

- *Asset seizure:* Creditors may eventually take legal action, garnishing wages or seizing assets like homes and cars, if payments aren't made.

- *Bankruptcy consideration:* With no way to dig out, bankruptcy may seem like the only option to get relief from overwhelming debt.

The key factor is the downward spiral where temporary cash shortfalls lead to more borrowing, fees compound the balance owed, and income can't keep up – trapping people in an inescapable cycle of debt.

Debt Trap Common Reasons: How Debt Creeps into Your Life

- *Living beyond your means:* When you spend more than you earn, you will be funding your spending using borrowed money.

- *Unexpected expenses:* If you don't have an emergency fund, you might be compelled to use your credit card or take a loan to pay for unexpected expenses like medical bills or home repair.

- *Job loss or reduced income:* You can't pay for your living expenses because you lost your job or received a pay cut.

- *Lack of financial literacy:* Poor money management skills, such as not budgeting properly or not understanding the true costs of credit, can lead to overspending and debt accumulation.

- *Using credit as a lifestyle:* You buy everything, from essentials and discretionary spending, using your credit card. Some people become accustomed to living on credit, continuously carrying balances on credit cards or taking out new loans to maintain their lifestyle.

- *Student loans:* The rising costs of higher education can saddle individuals with significant student loan debt. It can be difficult to pay off if you have to take care of high living expenses and other debts such as car loan and mortgage.

- *Business failures:* Entrepreneurs who take on debt to start or expand a business can end up in debt, if the business fails.

- *Addictions or compulsive behaviors:* Addictions to gambling, shopping, or other compulsive behaviors can lead to overspending and debt problems.

Addressing the root causes, such as improving financial literacy, and learning how to manage your finances can help prevent or manage debt accumulation.

This vicious cycle of debt, high interest costs, depleted savings, and credit damage can lead to living paycheck to paycheck in perpetuity. Breaking out of the debt cycle is not impossible, but it takes financial discipline, curbed spending, and methodically paying down debt balances over time.

2. The Impact of Debt on Personal Finances

The domino effect of debt: Ignoring debt can lead to a domino effect, impacting other financial areas of your life and hindering progress toward financial goals. Debt influences not just your finances but cascades into your emotional and professional life.

Finances

Debt can have a profound effect on your finances. High debt levels drain a substantial portion of your income, leaving little room for saving or investing for the future. As interest charges on debt accumulate, it becomes increasingly challenging to pay down the principal amount. Additionally, a poor credit score resulting from excessive debt can make it difficult to obtain a loan with favorable rates, further compounding the financial burden.

Emotional Toll: Stress, Anxiety, and the Weight of Debt on Mental Health

Having massive debt can have a profound effect on individuals emotionally. The constant worry and anxiety about making payments and managing creditors can lead to significant stress and mental health challenges. Debt can also strain personal relationships, as financial pressures and disagreements over spending and debt management arise. The emotional burden of debt can manifest in various ways, such as difficulty sleeping, decreased productivity, and a general sense of hopelessness or despair.

Opportunity Cost: How Debt Holds You Back from Achieving Financial Goals

Debt can be a stumbling block to success. If you spend a large portion of your income repaying debt, you won't have much left for other goals such as savings and investing. Additionally, the interest paid on debt represents an opportunity cost, as those funds could have been invested and grown over time. Debt can also limit career choices or risk-taking opportunities, as individuals may feel trapped in their current financial situation, unable to take calculated risks or pursue their desired paths due to the constraints of debt.

The Broader Impact of Debt

Furthermore, the impact of debt can be far-reaching, affecting not only an individual's financial situation but also their overall quality of life. The stress and emotional toll of debt can strain personal relationships, impact job performance, and limit opportunities for personal growth and development. Breaking free from the cycle of debt is important for financial independence.

Moving Forward with Confidence

Understanding the full impact of debt is the first step toward financial change. By recognizing how debt affects not just our bank accounts but our overall quality of life, we can start to make better choices. If you are committed to change and employ effective strategies, you can break free from the debt cycle, restore financial health, and open the door to new opportunities for personal and professional growth. Embrace the journey with resilience and optimism, knowing that each effort to diminish debt enhances your financial stability and overall well-being.

3. Dispelling Common Debt Myths

Debt and credit often spark stress and confusion, leading to pervasive myths that can result in poor financial decisions and perpetuate unnecessary cycles of debt. Let's address and debunk some of these common myths, providing clear explanations and actionable advice to help you navigate your financial landscape more effectively.

Myth: All Debt Is Bad Debt

Reality: Not all debt is bad, if it's managed properly. Strategic debts, such as student loans or mortgages, can be investments in your future, potentially increasing your earning power or building your assets.

Action Step: Evaluate the potential return of a debt before taking it on. If it contributes to your financial growth or adds significant value to your life, it might be worthwhile.

Myth: There's No Way Out of Debt

Reality: There is always a way to manage and eventually overcome debt. It requires a structured approach and sometimes the help of financial professionals.

Action Step: Compile all your debts and arrange them from most expensive (the highest interest rate) to identify which debt is costing you the most. Seek advice from credit counselors if you feel overwhelmed.

Myth: Not Having Credit Cards Helps Your Credit

Reality: Responsible usage of your credit card helps you build your credit score. Regular use and timely payments can improve your credit score significantly.

Action Step: Use your credit card to pay for small purchases, but remember to pay your bill in full and on time every month to build your credit history without accruing unnecessary interest.

Myth: No Credit Is Better Than Bad Credit

Reality: Having no credit history can be just as limiting as having bad credit, especially when you need to make significant financial decisions like buying a home.

Action Step: Before applying for a bank loan, build your credit score through the responsible use of a credit card. Make sure to keep your utilization low and always pay on time.

Myth: Why Having Lots of Credit Cards Might Not Be as Bad as You Think

Reality: Owning multiple credit cards can actually improve your credit score by reducing your credit utilization ratio, as long as you manage them responsibly and don't accumulate debt.

Action Step: If you choose to have multiple cards, keep track of different billing cycles and due dates. Use a spreadsheet or a financial app to manage your accounts effectively and avoid missed payments.

Understanding the truth behind these common myths is crucial. By dispelling misconceptions, you will be better equipped to navigate the complexities of credit and debt. Remember, each step taken toward debunking these myths not only clarifies your financial path but also strengthens your ability to achieve and maintain financial health. As you continue to educate yourself and apply this knowledge, you'll find that managing debt becomes less intimidating and more empowering.

4. Taking Control: Ways to Manage Debt

Recognizing the Red Flags

If any of these warning signs sound familiar, you should take immediate action before your debt spirals out of control:

- *Robbing Peter to Pay Paul:* Constantly juggling payments, paying one creditor with money intended for another bill, indicates that you are finding it hard to manage your debt obligations.

- *Making Minimum Payments:* Paying the minimum that is required means you're barely treading water, and the interest charges are piling up, making it harder to get ahead.

- *Hiding Bills:* If you find yourself stashing away unopened bills or feeling anxious when the mail arrives, it could mean you're avoiding facing the reality of your debt situation.

- *Maxed Out:* If you've reached the credit limit on most or all of your credit cards, it's obvious that you are depending too much on borrowed money to fund your lifestyle.

- *Debt Collectors Calling:* When debt collectors start calling you regularly, it means you've fallen behind on payments, and your creditors are getting serious about collecting what you owe.

- *No Savings:* If you're unable to save any money because all your income goes toward paying off debt, it's a sign that your debt levels are unsustainable and leaving you financially vulnerable.

- *Sleepless Nights:* If you find yourself lying awake at night, stressed and anxious about your mounting debt, it's a strong emotional indicator that your debt situation has become a significant problem in your life.

Ways to Manage Indebtedness

If any of these situations sound familiar, it's time to take your debts seriously and develop a plan to get them under control before they spiral out of control. If more than 50% of your paycheck goes toward paying off debts, you have to do something about your debts as soon as possible. If not, they will slowly but surely take bigger bites into your paycheck.

Stop digging a bigger hole: Even before you put a repayment plan together, the first step is to stop taking on more debt. Put away the credit cards and don't borrow any more money until you've got a handle on your existing debt.

Coming Up with A Plan

The best way to manage your debt is to come up with a detailed debt repayment plan.

1. List All Your Debts

- *Action:* Compile all your debt and list all the details.
- *Worksheet:* Use a spreadsheet to track each debt detail, which will help you see the big picture and prioritize repayments.

2. Assess Your Financial Situation:

- *Action:* Calculate your income and expenses to determine the amount you can realistically allocate toward repaying debt every month.
- *Worksheet:* Create a budget worksheet to balance your monthly income against your expenses and debt repayments.

3. Choose a Method to Repay

Now that you know your exact debt position and how much monthly repayment you can afford, chose your repayment strategy:

- *Snowball Method:* You prioritize paying off your smallest debt first.

- *Avalanche Method:* Prioritize your most expensive debts; those with the highest interest rates.

4. Consider Debt Counseling

If based on your current financial circumstances, the debt load is simply too much for you to handle, even with a structured repayment plan, explore options to negotiate with creditors. Some of them are willing to restructure your payment plans. However, be warned that this could affect your credit score.

- *Action:* If you're overwhelmed, seek help from a non-profit credit counseling agency for guidance on budgeting and debt management.

- *Benefit:* They can help negotiate with creditors or enroll you in a debt management plan with potentially lower interest rates.

Stay Motivated and On-Track

Paying off debt is a journey that requires consistency, persistence, and unwavering commitment. Here are some tips to help you stay on track:

- *Temporary sacrifice for long-term gain:* The sacrifices you make today can give you a more comfortable and enjoyable future later on. As the saying goes, "Suffer now, enjoy later."

- *Celebrate your victories:* Clearing off debt can be a lengthy and challenging journey. To help you stay motivated, celebrate every time you achieve a milestone (even small ones).

- *Stay accountable:* Get support from friends and family who can keep you accountable by providing guidance and encouragement. Share your goals and progress with them, and let them provide encouragement and accountability when you start to veer off course.

- *Visualize your debt-free future:* When the going gets tough, take a moment to visualize what your life will be like once you're debt-free. Imagine the freedom that comes with being able to manage your finances, and use that as motivation to keep pushing forward.

- *Avoid temptation:* It may be tempting to revert to previous spending patterns, especially when you start to see progress in your debt repayment efforts. Stay vigilant and avoid temptations that could derail your progress, such as impulse purchases or taking on new debt.

Action Tools:

- *Downloadable Worksheets:* Available on our website, thesimplesum.com, these tools help you track and plan your debt repayment effectively.

- *Interactive Budget Planner:* Use our online planner to manage your finances and adjust your plans as needed.

Staying motivated throughout your debt repayment journey is essential for success. Celebrating small wins can give you the encouragement you need to keep going. Keep your eyes on the prize – a debt-free life – and remember that every payment you make is an investment in your future financial well-being.

5. Conclusion

As we wrap up this chapter, think about the crucial lessons we've discussed about managing debt effectively. Debt doesn't have to be a life sentence – it can be managed, and with the right strategies, completely overcome. Here are the key takeaways to carry with you:

Chapter Takeaways

Recognize the Warning Signs: Early recognition of debt issues is essential. Whether it's juggling payments or using credit for essentials, identifying these red flags early can prevent a minor debt problem from becoming a crisis.

Develop a Strategic Repayment Plan: Organizing your debts and understanding your financial landscape is foundational. Use the tools and worksheets provided to create a personalized plan that prioritizes high-interest debts and sets achievable milestones.

Stay Committed and Motivated: Paying off debt can be a long process. Celebrate your progress, no matter how small, and stay connected with supportive friends or family who can encourage you along the way.

Educate Yourself Continuously: Understanding debt and the various tools and strategies for managing it is crucial. Continuous learning helps you adapt to financial challenges and make informed decisions.

Speak to a Professional: Don't be ashamed to reach out to a professional for advice if you find yourself overwhelmed. Credit counseling services can provide valuable guidance and help negotiate terms that might otherwise be out of reach.

By embracing these principles, you can transform your approach to debt from one of fear and stress to one of control and confidence. Every step taken brings you closer toward being debt-free! Empower yourself with knowledge, and let that knowledge guide you to financial freedom.

Appendix

Budgeting Method – Pay Yourself First

Unlike traditional methods that focus on bills and expenses first, the "Pay Yourself First" strategy flips the script – you allocate some money for savings before covering other expenses. By doing so, you are prioritizing your savings (and your financial security).

Here's how it works:

- *First Action – Save:* As soon as your paycheck arrives, a predetermined percentage goes straight into savings or investment. Think of it as the first "bill" you pay each month – but this one's paying your future self!

- *Don't Sweat It:* Automate this process by transferring money to your savings account on payday. It's effortless, and you won't even miss the money.

- *Budget the Remainder:* This method simplifies spending decisions and curbs the temptation to overspend.

Prioritizing your savings allows you to grow your funds over time and develop a habit of saving regularly. However, it may be challenging if you have a tight budget or significant debt to pay off.

Dos and Don'ts of the 'Pay Yourself First' Method:

Dos:

- *Set Automatic Transfers:* Arrange automatic transfers so your savings are in a separate account, which minimizes the risk of you spending it.

- *Do Start Small:* If your income is limited, start by saving a small amount of money every month then increase it when you have the means to.

- *Do Consider Savings Essential:* Just like you wouldn't skip paying your rent or utilities, don't skip paying yourself. Make your savings a priority.

- *Review Your Progress:* Analyze your progress from time to time to ensure that it matches your financial goals. If you find that they are misaligned, make adjustments to your plan.

- *Do Celebrate Small Wins:* Saving money can be challenging, so remember to celebrate the small milestones that you achieve. This can motivate you to stay on course.

Don'ts:

- *Don't Forget Emergencies:* While the "Pay Yourself First" method emphasizes saving for long-term goals, don't neglect the importance of building savings for a rainy day.

- *Don't Deprive Yourself:* While saving is important, don't deprive yourself of all discretionary spending. Allow for some fun and enjoyment within your budget to make the process more sustainable.

- *Don't Ignore Debt:* Prioritize paying off your debts as soon as possible, especially those that charge high-interest such as a credit cards.

- *Don't Be Too Rigid:* While your success in saving depends on how well you stick to your plan, don't be so rigid that you can't adjust when life circumstances change. Be flexible and adapt as needed.

- *Don't Neglect Other Financial Priorities:* While saving is crucial, don't neglect other important financial priorities, such as maintaining adequate insurance coverage or contributing to your retirement accounts.

Adopting the "Pay Yourself First" method is a commitment to your financial well-being. By prioritizing your savings, you ensure that every paycheck contributes toward your long-term dreams and stability.

NOT UNDERSTANDING CREDIT IS KEEPING YOU BROKE

Do you really know what credit is and how it affects you every day? Understanding credit goes far beyond just knowing you can buy now and pay later. It's about the impact it has on your future financial options and overall economic stability.

Think about the last time you used your credit card for everyday shopping or a big-ticket item. It might seem simple to swipe and forget until the bill comes, but each purchase has a ripple effect. If you're not paying off your balance each month, those ripples can turn into waves of debt that build up faster than you expect.

In this chapter, we will demystify credit, breaking down how it works, the true cost of borrowing, and how to use it to your advantage rather than letting it become a financial burden. We'll clear up common misconceptions and arm you with the knowledge so that you can understand the pros and cons of borrowing money, and how your financial goals can benefit from it. Ready to take control of your credit? Let's get started on a path to a more secure financial future.

1. Understanding Credit and Debt

Defining Credit, Debt, and Its Costs

Credit allows you to borrow money with the promise of future payment. Debt, on the other hand, is the amount of money owed to a lender, creditor, or friends and family. When you take on credit, you incur debt, which must be repaid with interest and/or fees.

The cost of debt includes:

- *Interest:* This is the amount charged by the lender for the privilege of borrowing money, usually expressed at an annual percentage rate (APR).

- *Fees:* Lenders may charge additional fees for services such as loan origination, late payments, or account maintenance.

The Different Types of Credit:

Revolving Credit (Credit Cards):

Credit cards are a type of revolving credit, you only pay the interest on the balance that you owe. When you are issued a credit card, you are given a credit limit amount that you can spend. You can keep using the card within that credit limit. Therefore, as long as you make payments for the portion spent and you spend within the limit, you can swipe that card without worries. The cost is the interest charged on your outstanding balance each month.

Key Points:

- Pay interest only on the balance carried over
- Essential to pay off monthly to avoid interest

Non-Revolving/Installment Credit (Student Loans, Car Loans, Personal Loans, and Mortgage):

Also known as installment credit, you borrow a fixed amount of money for a specific purpose (general purposes in the case of personal loans), like paying for college or buying a car. You get the full loan amount upfront, and then you pay it back through scheduled payments over a set period, plus interest charges.

Key Points:

- Fixed amount borrowed and repaid in installments

- Predictable, fixed monthly payments

Secured Debt (Mortgages, Auto Loans):

When you take out a secured debt, you're putting up an asset as collateral, like your house for a mortgage or your car for an auto loan. If you completely miss your payments, the lender is allowed to take your house or car or whatever asset you have put up as collateral. Secured debts often have lower interest rates because the collateral reduces risk for the lender.

Key Points:

- Requires an asset as collateral that guarantees you will pay

- Lower interest rates due to reduced lender risk

Unsecured Debt (Credit Cards, Personal Loans):

With unsecured debt, you're not putting up any collateral. There is nothing of value that the lender can take from you in case you fail to repay the loan, which puts them at risk of losing the money they let you borrow. As a result, unsecured debts like credit cards and some personal loans tend to have higher interest rates.

Key Points:

- No collateral required
- Higher interest rates due to increased risk

The Real Cost of Debt

Let's say, you borrow $100 from your friend today and promise to pay it back in a year. Do you think that it's fair to pay him a fee in return for lending you the money? If he didn't lend the money to you, he could have invested the $100 which has the potential to earn returns or interest over time

This is the concept of "the time value of money," which means that whatever money you have now has more value compared to the same amount of money in, let's say, three years or so. It's because money can earn interest or returns over time.

When you borrow money, you always have to pay back more than you borrowed due to interest charges. When you take a loan, essentially, you're borrowing someone else's savings or investment, typically from lenders or banks. In exchange for letting you use their money upfront, you pay interest – a fee for borrowing. The amount of interest that you will have to pay is based on the chances or risk you pose of not repaying the loan, which is often based on factors such as credit score, among others. If you are identified as a high risk, you will likely be charged a higher interest rate, and you will end up paying more.

How much interest rate you pay depends on the type of loan, duration of the loan, and if you give the lender any collateral.

Interest rate is the "price" of borrowing money.

> For example, if you borrowed $10,000 with 1 year payment term and 5% interest, the cost of your loan would be $500 (5% of $10,000).

If the interest rate is high, you will have to pay more for the same amount of money you borrowed. And if you take a longer payment term (3 years instead of 1 year to pay, for example), you will have to pay more accumulated interest fees, which in total adds to your overall debt burden.

So, when you're borrowing money, for whatever purpose, you must know the interest rate and how it affects the amount you have to pay back in total. Comparing interest rates and minimizing the cost of borrowing can help you save a lot of money.

Cost of Borrowing Comparison:

The cost of borrowing generally follows this order from lowest to highest in interest charges:

- Secured debts like mortgages and auto loans (lower risk for lenders)

- Non-revolving credits like student loans (fixed payments)

- Installment credits like personal loans

- Revolving credits like credit cards (higher risk for lenders)

'The True Cost' When You Buy on Credit

When you buy something on credit, you're borrowing money from a lender to make that purchase now and make repayments over time. It may seem like a good deal at the time, but there is a hidden cost that comes with using credit, and that is the cost to borrow. If you consider the interest cost and other charges, sometimes it doesn't look like such a good deal.

Let's take the example of buying a $2,000 computer using your credit card. You might think, I don't have the full $2,000 right now, but I can just put it on my credit card and pay it off over time. Sounds reasonable, right? But here's the math:

- The credit card company isn't lending you that money for free. They'll charge you a fee on the amount you haven't paid yet – the outstanding balance. Let's say the interest rate on your credit card is 18% per year. That means for every month you don't pay off the full $2,000, you're compounding interest charges. If you only pay the minimum amount due monthly (let's say $40), it could take you more than six years to pay off that $2,000 computer, and the amount of interest charges you have to pay would be $1,722 plus the original $2,000 cost.

- Now, let's look at a bigger purchase, like a $500,000 home. Most people can't afford to pay that kind of money upfront, so they take out a mortgage from a bank. Let's say the mortgage has a 4% interest rate over a 30-year term. By the time you've paid off the mortgage, you'll have paid around $360,000 in interest charges on top of the $500,000 principal amount. That's a lot of extra money just for the privilege of borrowing!

The bottom line is, when you buy something on credit, you're not just paying for the item itself – you're also paying interest charges to the lender, which can add up significantly over time. The true cost of that purchase ends up being much higher than the sticker price. It's important to factor in those interest charges and understand how many years or months until you can settle the payments, so that you can decide if taking the loan is even worth it.

The Debt Trap of 'Affordability'

The illusion of affordability is when something seems affordable or within your means, and it's not too expensive to fit your budget. It's an illusion because it tricks you into thinking you can afford it when it might put you into debt because based on the state of your finances at the moment, it's not really something you can afford to buy. If you could, you would have paid the full amount in cash.

Let's take credit card use as an example. When you're at a store and want to buy something, swiping your credit card and paying later seems so easy and affordable in the moment. The item might cost $100, but you think, "I can just put it on my card and pay it off later." However, the interest fees will start accumulating if you only pay the minimum amount due instead of the full amount, and suddenly that $100 item becomes more expensive than you thought it was, because you paid more in the long run.

The key is to look beyond the initial affordability illusion, have a repayment plan, and think of your long-term finances. Can you truly afford the true costs of this purchase, plus interest, plus potential changes in your financial situation? Don't let the illusion of a manageable monthly payment trap you into debt you can't sustain. Being realistic about what you can afford long-term is crucial.

For a $1,000 purchase:

At 18% Annual Percentage Rate, making a minimum 2% payment ($20/month), it's going to take 87 months (more than 7 years) to pay off, and you'll pay $797 in interest.

To pay it off in 12 months, you need to pay $92/month, with a total interest of $100.

The key things to note:

- Minimum payments can lead to being trapped in debt for decades with crazy interest costs

- Aggressive payoff of 12-18 months saves thousands in interest

- The higher the balance, the more critical it is to pay it off quickly before the interest accrues

So, when making a credit card purchase, calculate what monthly payment you'd need to pay it off in 12-18 months. If that fits your budget, it's affordable. If not, you're likely getting trapped in an illusion of affordability that will lead to years of compounding debt.

Use the 50/30/20 rule in budgeting. Only spend 50% of the money you earn on necessities such as housing, food, etc. Then 30% on non-essentials, and 20% on savings/investing and debt payments. This ensures new debts fit your budget long-term.

The key is taking a hard, honest look at the full, long-term costs of any debt or recurring payment. If it puts you over budget, causes you to dip into emergency savings, or requires an unrealistic set of life changes, then it's unaffordable even if the upfront costs seem manageable. Slow and steady financial prudence avoids the affordability illusion's traps.

2. Demystifying Credit

Use of Credit in Your Wealth-Building

Credit has good and bad consequences – it can make you rich or make you poor. It all depends on if you know how to use it wisely. Credit gives you access to opportunities that might otherwise be out of your reach. It can help you start a business or invest in your education for a better future. However, if you misuse credit, your finances can quickly spiral into a web of debt, hampering your financial progress and leaving you struggling.

Consider the scenario of investing in real estate: property prices generally appreciate over time, making early investment appealing. However, saving enough to buy property outright can take years. By using a mortgage, you can begin your investment sooner, allowing rental income and property appreciation to work in your favor, increasing your equity in a valuable asset over time.

(Remember, buying an investment property is similar to other investments – there are pros and cons to consider. You need to take the same considerations and calculate if you can afford the debt. If interest rates go up, your monthly mortgage payments could go up too, and suddenly, you might find it tough to keep up. And while you might think about raising the rent to cover these extra costs, that isn't always possible – or the right thing to do. So, take your time, weigh your options, and make sure this strategy fits into your overall financial plan.)

Good Versus Bad Use of Credit

Debt can be different for everybody. There are types of credit, used responsibly, that can be affordable and get you ahead in life. But other forms are just financial quicksand that will drag you down.

Good Use of Credit

- Mortgage for a home purchase: Invests in an appreciating asset.

- Student loans: Enhance earning potential by investing in education.

- Business loans: Provide capital to start or expand a profitable venture.

- Home improvement loans: Increase property value.

- Consolidating high-interest debt: Lowers interest costs and simplifies finances.

- Investing in income-generating assets like rental properties: Provides regular income.

Bad Use of Credit

- *Using credit card for discretionary purchases:* The fees you pay in interest are high, which does not increase wealth.

- *Payday loans or cash advances:* The interest rates are extremely high. You can fall into a trap of taking loans repeatedly.

- *Financing depreciating assets like cars or electronics:* These assets lose value rapidly.

- *Using credit cards for cash advances or balance transfers:* Comes with fees and often higher interest rates.

- *Borrowing to fund an unsustainable lifestyle:* Leads to debt without returns.

- *Financing luxury items or vacations:* Creates debt for non-essential expenditures.

The key factors that differentiate good and bad uses of credit are:

1. *Purpose:* Good credit is used for investments or purchases that generate returns or appreciate in value. Bad credit is used for consumption or depreciating assets.

2. *Ability to Repay:* Good credit is taken on when there is a clear plan and ability to repay the debt comfortably. Bad credit is often taken on without a realistic repayment strategy.

3. *Interest Rates and Fees:* Good credit typically involves lower interest rates and fewer fees, while bad credit often comes with high costs and hidden charges.

4. *Long-Term Impact:* Good credit use builds wealth, improves credit scores, and creates opportunities. Bad credit use leads to debt cycles, damaged credit, and financial stress.

By understanding and applying these principles, you can use credit strategically as a way for you to build wealth and achieve your long-term money goals, rather than as a means to fund an unsustainable lifestyle or make impulsive purchases.

3. Mindful and Responsible Use of Credit

Using credit wisely is key to maintaining financial health. It's not just about whether you can use credit, but whether you should. Every time you consider using credit, you're facing a decision that could either enhance your financial stability or undermine it.

Borrowing money is not inherently good or bad – it depends on your circumstances and the purpose of the loan. As a general rule, you should borrow when it's an investment in your future, like purchasing a house, funding a start-up, or getting a Master's degree.

When You Should Consider Borrowing:

- **For Appreciating Investments***:* Borrow when the asset is likely to increase in value over time. For instance, purchasing a rental property that you can later sell for a profit not only provides ongoing rental income but also capital gains. Using a mortgage to facilitate this investment can be a strategic move.

- **For Personal Development:** It's wise to invest in yourself. Taking a course or earning a degree that boosts your qualifications and enhances your earning potential is a sound reason to take on student loans. These are investments that pay dividends in the form of higher future earnings.

- **For Necessary Purchases with Manageable Interest Rates:** Sometimes, special financing offers like "zero interest for 12 months" make sense for essential purchases that are payable within a specific amount of time without interest. This is ideal for items you need immediately but can budget to pay off quickly without extra cost.

When You Should Avoid Borrowing:

- **For Depreciating Assets:** Avoid borrowing for items that lose value quickly, like cars, trendy gadgets, or clothes. These purchases might feel good in the short term but aren't financially wise as they generate no returns and depreciate rapidly.

- **When Interest Rates Are Prohibitively High:** Steer clear of loans with high interest rates that dramatically inflate the cost over time. This is akin to paying multiple times the item's worth under burdensome terms – definitely not a savvy financial move.

- **To Support an Unsustainable Lifestyle:** Living beyond your means by using credit to simulate a wealthier lifestyle is unsustainable. This often involves maxing out credit cards for luxury items that you can't afford, leading to a dangerous cycle of high-interest debt.

Key Factors to Consider Before Borrowing:

- **Purpose of the Loan:** Evaluate if the loan is for an asset that appreciates or provides a return, or if it's for immediate consumption.

- **Ability to Repay:** Assess whether you can comfortably manage the loan repayments within your budget without compromising other financial obligations.

- **Interest Rate and Cost of Borrowing:** Consider the overall amount you have to pay, including interest and other charges, to determine if it's reasonable.

- **Potential Return or Benefit:** Consider the financial or personal growth benefits that the loan will facilitate.

By thoughtfully taking these factors into consideration, there is a good chance that you can use credit responsibly, ensuring that every loan supports your financial health and long-term goals.

When to Use Credit: A Decision-Making Guide

To help you make smart choices about using credit, here's a simple decision-making process you can follow. Imagine this as a flowchart where each answer leads you to the next step:

Identify the Purchase:

- Is this purchase necessary or is it a want? (Necessity might justify using credit, especially if it's an emergency or an investment.)

Consider Financial State at the Present:

- Is there an existing loan that you have yet to pay off?

- Can you afford the additional monthly payments without stress?

- Are your job and income stable?

Evaluate the Real Cost of Credit:

- What interest rates are you looking at?

- How much will this purchase cost in total with interest?

- Could you save up and buy it later instead?

Long-Term Impact:

- Will this purchase appreciate in value or is it for immediate consumption?

- How will this affect your credit score? (Remember, utilization and on-time payments impact your score.)

Decision:

- If all signs point to a manageable and strategic use of credit, go ahead.

- If doubts remain, it might be better to wait, save, or explore other options.

Practical Tips for Using Credit Responsibly

- *Emergency Fund First*: Always try to have money ready for emergencies that covers your expenses of up to six months before using credit for non-essential purchases.

- *Budget for Repayments:* Include your credit payments when you make your budget every month. It should not be more than 20% of your net earnings.

- *Understand the Terms:* Read the fine print on interest rates, admin or processing fees, and penalties. If you are aware of all these, you can choose the best option and avoid surprises.

Using Credit as a Tool

Credit should be a tool that helps build your financial future, not something that leads to a debt trap. For example, you can use a credit card for necessities and then pay it in full monthly – your credit score will improve without having to pay interest. On the contrary, using your card to buy the latest gadget without a plan to pay off the balance quickly can lead to unnecessary debt.

Remember, every credit decision should be within your overall strategy that supports your plans for finances in the long-term. By following these guidelines and using the decision-making flowchart, you can ensure that every time you reach for your credit card, you're making a choice that is in tune with your money health.

Watch Out for the Pitfalls

The Dangers of Minimum Payments:

The attraction of paying only the minimum amount due on your credit card bill is deceptive. At first, it seems like a manageable way to handle debt, but this approach mainly covers interest without reducing the principal. This cycle can extend indefinitely, essentially causing you to pay interest on top of interest, which can trap you in a persistent state of debt.

Preventive Steps Before Using Credit

Making informed decisions about taking on debt is crucial. Consider these critical questions to ensure that you are committing to credit responsibly:

Credit Cards:

- Do I have a clear budget to manage full payment of the balance each month?

- If I am unable to pay the full balance immediately, can I manage the resulting interest charges?

- Are my credit card expenses necessary or are they driven by impulse buying?

Car Loans:

- Have I compared interest rates from various lenders?

- Are the monthly payments manageable within my budget, even if my financial situation changes?

- Have I accounted for all costs associated with owning a car, including insurance, maintenance, and fuel?

Mortgages:

- Am I ready for the long-term financial commitment that comes with a mortgage?

- Have I accumulated enough for a significant down payment to reduce the borrowing amount?

- Will I be able to handle the monthly payments if there's an increase in interest rates?

Student Loans:

- Have I looked into all options available to me such as scholarships, financial grants, and programs for work and study?

- Am I strictly getting a loan that equates the amount necessary to cover my educational costs?

- Is my repayment plan feasible based on my career prospects and expected future income?

These questions are designed to prompt careful consideration of the financial implications of debt. By thoroughly assessing your needs, capabilities, and potential risks, you can use credit to your advantage without falling into common financial traps.

The Credit Card Lesson

Getting approved for a credit card for the first time is a considerable leap into the world of personal finance, especially for young people. What often trips many up is not realizing how missed payments and maxing out limits can hurt your credit score. A low score makes it tough to get out of debt and blocks access to financial tools that could help you grow your wealth.

Here is how sticking to paying only the minimum amount due can trap you in debt:

Imagine you buy a $1,000 smartphone with your credit card, which has an 18% annual interest rate. On a monthly repayment schedule, this means you'll be charged a 1.5% monthly periodic rate (18% annual rate divided by 12 months). The card requires a minimum monthly payment of 2% of the balance or $20, whichever is greater.

Month 1:

- Starting Balance: $1,000
- Interest Added: $15 (1.5% of $1,000)
- Payment Made: $20
- Remaining Balance: $995

Month 2:

- Interest Added: $14.90 (1.5% of $995)
- Payment Made: $20
- Remaining Balance: $989.90

Month 3:

- Interest Added: $14.85 (1.5% of $989.90)
- Payment Made: $20
- Remaining Balance: $984.75

After just three months, you've paid $60 toward your debt, but your balance has barely decreased. If you only make minimum payments:

- After one year: You still owe about $935.
- After two years: You owe $893.
- After five years: You owe $778.

In the end, it would take more than eight years just to pay back the original $1,000, and you would have paid an extra $458 for interest charges alone!

This cycle of only paying the minimum drags you deeper into debt because most of the money you paid is spent for the interest charges instead of reducing what you owe. High interest keeps piling up, making it hard to get out from under the debt.

Breaking the Cycle

The best way to tackle this is to settle more than just the minimum amount due. This approach reduces the principal amount much more quickly, and cuts down the total interest fees you pay. Avoid the credit trap by planning to pay off purchases quickly rather than letting them linger and grow.

By understanding how credit works and committing to better payment habits, you can use your credit card as a tool for convenience and building your credit score, without falling into debt.

4. Measuring Creditworthiness

Cracking the Credit Score Code: What It Really Means for You

Do you know what a credit score is? Surprisingly, many overlook how important a credit score is leading to potential financial difficulties. Understanding your credit score is crucial in managing your financial health effectively.

What Is a Credit Score?

A credit score is the benchmark of how worthy you are to get credit. It determines how capable and responsible you are to pay your debt. It's your credit history, which lenders or financial institutions consider before approving applications for loans and credit lines. Sometimes, even potential employers look at your credit score to check how risky it is for them to hire you. Your credit scores are calculated and maintained by credit bureaus and credit reporting companies (differ from country to country).

Cracking the Credit Score Code

Understanding how credit scores work gives you control of your financial future. Most credit scoring models are between 300 to 850. If you score high, it generally shows that you have a lower risk of defaulting on loans or credit obligations. If you have a low score, it's considered that there is a strong chance that you will not be capable to pay back the loan.

The Credit Score Breakdown

There are several factors used to calculate your credit score, each carrying a different weight. Here's a breakdown of the major components:

- *Payment History (35%):* This influences your credit score most signifi-cantly. It reflects your habit of paying bills on time, whether it's for a loan, a credit card, or any other financial obligations.

- *Credit Utilization Ratio (30%):* This measures how much of your credit limit you are actually using. Ideally, you should try to utilize only 30% or below of your limit.

- *Length of Credit History (15%):* A higher score is possible if you have a longer credit history that you built over the years, as it is a good demon-stration of your capability to manage your finances and payments over a long period of time.

- *Credit Mix (10%):* When you have a variation of credit accounts, it can positively affect your credit score. Examples are credit cards, car or home mortgages, and even installment loans.

- *New Credit Inquiries (10%):* Whenever you submit an application for a new loan, it can temporarily affect your credit score negatively.

The Impact of Credit Scores

Understanding the numbers behind your credit score is more than an academic exercise; it directly affects your financial opportunities and challenges. Here's why they matter:

- *Loan Approval and Interest Rates:* Financial institutions check credit scores to determine how worthy you are for credit and the interest rates they'll offer you. If you have a high score, it's likely you will get loan terms and interest rates that are easier to manage, saving you a lot of money over the course of a loan.

- *Opportunity for Large Sum Borrowing:* Buying a property is a big commitment, probably the biggest sum of money that you'd borrow. Lenders heavily take your credit score into account when you apply for a mortgage. A poor score can disqualify you from securing your dream home. Because of your low credit score, the banks may not want to lend too much money to you, hence you will need to pay a higher deposit amount which you may not have.

- *Employment Prospects:* Employers often look at a credit report before hiring someone, particularly for roles that involve financial responsibilities or access to highly sensitive information. A poor credit score can negatively affect your job prospects.

Keeping your credit score to a good number is vital for your long-term stability. It enables you to access better loan conditions, secure housing, and even affects your career opportunities. By keeping informed and managing your credit smartly, you can make sure that a financially stable future is possible.

5. Managing Your Creditworthiness: The Power of Credit Scores

Playing Smart with Credit

Debt Management for Credit Improvement:

Imagine your credit score is like your reputation or credibility with banks and lenders. The higher it is, the more they trust you to pay back what you borrow responsibly. Managing your existing debt well is key to building and maintaining a good credit reputation.

It's kind of like if you borrowed money from a friend. If you make your payments on time and don't overextend yourself by borrowing too much, your friend will be more likely to lend to you again in the future because you've shown you're responsible. But if you miss payments or max out what you've borrowed, your friend may hesitate to lend more since you've damaged that trust.

With credit, paying at least the minimum amounts due on time for things like credit cards, loans, etc. shows you're reliable. Paying more than the minimums when possible gets you out of debt faster. It's important to keep your credit utilization – how much you owe compared to your credit limit – below 30% to show you're not over-leveraged.

It's also crucial to keep the number of your credit accounts to a minimum, as it may look risky. Using credit responsibly over time by only borrowing an amount you can comfortably pay, will build a very good credit history.

Essentially, paying your bills on time, keeping debt levels manageable, and avoiding credit overuse convinces lenders you're low-risk. This responsible behavior elevates your credit score, proving you've got a good credit reputation and you're lending to again.

Success Story: Maria's Journey from Poor to Excellent Credit

Meet Maria, who once struggled with a credit score of 580 (which is considered low) because she missed payments and maintained a high balance on her credit card. Determined to turn her finances around, Maria took several decisive steps:

- Created scheduled or automatic payments for her bills to make sure the payments were timely.

- Reduced the balance on her credit card to below 30% of her available limit.

- Refused to open new credit accounts unnecessarily.

- Regularly checked her credit report for errors and corrected them promptly.

Over two years, these actions helped Maria increase her credit score to 740. With her improved score, she secured a more affordable interest rate for a mortgage, which means she gets to pay less interest over the course of the loan, and qualify for better credit card offers. Maria's story shows that with consistent good money habits, you can dramatically improve your credit score and financial opportunities.

Best Practices for Using Credit Responsibly

Some credit safety tips to avoid painful debt burdens:

- Live below your means and save for bigger purchases if possible, so you don't have to borrow as much.

- When you do need to borrow, make a plan and a budget so you know you can afford the payments.

- Try to pay with cash for smaller daily stuff. Credit cards are for bigger planned expenses.

- Pay all bills on time, no exceptions. Autopay can help with this.

- Don't constantly open new credit accounts you don't need. It can look risky.

- Check your credit reports regularly for errors or fraud.

- Use credit deliberately as a tool to build assets, not rack up expenses you can't repay. That's the path to winning with your money long-term.

6. Conclusion

Throughout this chapter, we've explored the intricacies of credit scores and how they can profoundly affect your finances. From securing loans with favorable rates to affecting your job prospects, having a positive credit score is an invaluable asset in today's economy.

Chapter Takeaways

- Manage debt wisely: Ensure that you don't miss your payment due dates, keep your credit utilizations low, and avoid applying for new loans that you don't really need.

- Stay informed: Review your credit report periodically to check for accuracy and to understand where you stand.

- Plan for the future: Use credit strategically to build assets and enhance your stability when it comes to finances.

Keep in mind that you can use credit to your advantage. When used wisely, it can open many doors. It's not only about borrowing money, it's also about broadening your opportunities and securing your financial future.

Appendix

Budgeting Method – Cash-Only Budgeting

In a world where digital transactions are quickly becoming the norm, the cash-only budgeting method serves as a tangible and effective approach to managing personal finances. This method involves using cash for all your purchases and expenses, rather than relying on credit. You allocate funds for different expenses, withdraw that amount in cash and only use cash for those purchases. This helps prevent overspending, especially with credit cards.

Here's how it works:

- *Plan Your Spending:* Start by figuring out the amount you usually allocate for categories like eating out, groceries, bills, and transportation.

- *Withdraw Cash:* Withdraw the total amount you've allocated for the month and divide it into categories.

- *Spend Wisely:* Use only the cash allocated for each category for your purchases. When it's gone, it's gone.

You can also have a digital version by having a separate "expense account." Link the account to a debit card. All cash withdrawals, links to e-wallets, and expenses are paid from this account. Knowing how much "cash" you have in hand helps with being aware of how much you are spending, thus, preventing you from spending too much.

Here's how It works (digital version):

This mirrors the cash-only method but uses digital tracking:

- *Start with an Account:* Open a bank account that you can use separately for expenses alone.

- *Transfer Funds:* At the start of each month, transfer the budgeted amounts into this account.

- *Track Your Spending:* Use your debit card for purchases, ensuring you only spend what's available.

Cash-only budgeting can be an effective way to curb impulse purchases and overspending, as you have a tangible representation of your remaining funds.

Dos and Don'ts of Cash-Only Budgeting:

Dos:

- *Be Disciplined:* Stick strictly to the cash available. It's tempting to dip into other categories, but discipline is key.

- *Use Envelopes or Containers:* Physically separating your cash into labeled envelopes or containers makes it much easier to visualize your remaining funds and not lose track of your spend.

- *Plan for Irregular Expenses:* Set aside cash for annual or irregular expenses like insurance premiums or vehicle maintenance.

- *Allow a Little Fun Money:* Allocate a small amount for spontaneous treats or outings to keep the budget flexible and fun.

- *Involve Your Family:* Share the budgeting process with your family members to ensure everyone understands and supports the financial plan.

Don'ts:

- *Don't Borrow Between Categories:* Once the cash in one enve-lope is spent, resist the urge to borrow from another.

- *Don't Use Credit or Debit Cards:* Stick to cash to feel the impact of money leaving your wallet, which psychologically helps reduce spending.

- *Don't Forget Regular Bills:* Make sure regular bills like rent or mort-gage are automatically taken care of through your bank.

- *Don't Carry Too Much Cash:* For safety reasons, it's best to avoid carrying large amounts of cash with you. Only withdraw the cash you need for your variable expenses at the beginning of each budg-eting cycle.

- *Don't Get Discouraged:* Implementing cash-only budgeting is not as easy as it looks, especially if you are transitioning from a differ-ent budgeting method. Be patient and persistent, and don't get discouraged if you experience setbacks or slip-ups along the way.

Cash-only budgeting doesn't only involve putting a limit on spending; it's also about financial awareness and discipline. It teaches valuable lessons in resource management and helps build a foundation for strong financial habits. Whether you choose the tangible feel of cash or the convenience of a digital version, the principles of cash-only budgeting can lead to profound insights into your spending habits and pave the way to a more secure financial future.

Envelope System (Cash Stuffing) and Cash-Only Budgeting are closely related and often overlap in practice, but they have some distinct characteristics:

Cash-Only Budgeting

- *Fundamental Concept:* This method involves using only cash to handle all daily transactions. The idea is to avoid using credit cards and digital payments to prevent overspending and to gain a better awareness of physical money flow.

- *Methodology:* You withdraw a set amount of cash for your needs and use only this cash for all spending. Once the cash is out, spending in that category or overall must stop until the next budget period.

- *Flexibility:* Generally less flexible as it restricts spending to the cash on hand, with no explicit allocations for different categories unless combined with another system like envelopes.

Envelope System

- *Fundamental Concept:* This is a way of earmarking cash for specific spending categories, typically using physical envelopes. Each envelope is labeled for a different expense category, such as groceries, dining out, entertainment, etc.

- *Methodology:* At the start of each budget period, you fill each envelope with the budgeted amount of cash for that category. You spend from the assigned envelope for specific expenses. Once you empty an envelope, you should not spend in that category anymore.

- *Flexibility:* Provides structured flexibility within the confines of each category. If there's money left in one envelope, it can be reallocated to another or saved for future expenses in the same category.

Key Differences

- *Purpose:* Cash-only budgeting primarily focuses on preventing the use of credit and controlling overall spending by limiting transactions to cash. The Envelope System is more about allocating and managing finances across various categories, ensuring that spending stays within predefined limits for each area of expense.

- *Usage:* The Envelope System requires more initial setup and management, categorizing expenses and adjusting allocations as needed. Cash-only budgeting is simpler in setup but requires discipline to avoid the temptation of drawing more cash or using non-cash payment methods.

- *Adaptability:* The Envelope System can be more adaptable within the budget period. You can shift funds between envelopes if necessary (though this can dilute the method's effectiveness if done frequently). Cash-only budgeting is stricter, as it doesn't inherently involve dividing cash by categories unless combined with an envelope-like system.

Combining Both Methods

Many people find a combination of both methods effective. They use the envelope system to manage and allocate their budget into categories and commit to using only cash from those envelopes for their spending. This hybrid approach maximizes the benefits of both systems, providing both overall spending control and category-specific financial management.

FEARING INVESTING IS KEEPING YOU BROKE

You've wanted to grow your money for as long as you can remember, imagining a future that is worry-free and financially secure. You have a well-paying job and have savings in the bank. When you have the time, you make money from your hobbies because you know side hustles can help you achieve your goal. There is one thing, though that you've been hearing a lot about and been meaning to explore for a while now: investing. People around you, even the stuff you read on the news and on your socials mention its wealth-building potential and how one should try it. And you want to! But you're scared, aren't you?

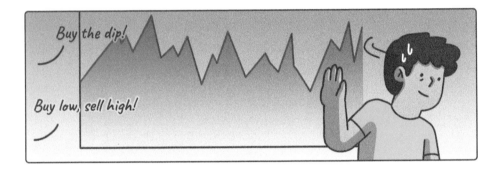

Want to know a secret? You're not alone. Many people fear investing, and it's perfectly understandable. You don't master investing overnight. It takes time and a whole lot of effort. You need not worry, though, because we're here to help you overcome that fear. In fact, it's what this entire chapter is for. Let's help you get acquainted with investing, and who knows, you might just end up becoming an investing master yourself!

So why don't we get down to business and look at this fear of yours straight in the eye, shall we?

1. Understanding the Fear of Investing

Investing can be scary, even for those who understand the importance of growing their money. Earning money is one thing. Investing that hard-earned money is another. The thought of losing it because of bad investment decisions is a bitter pill to swallow. If you feel the same, you can breathe – it's fine, it's normal.

At the root of this fear is the worry of making mistakes. Well, guess what? Everybody makes mistakes! Yes, even seasoned investors. What's important is that we learn from our mistakes and apply our lessons to improve our investing strategy.

There's also the fear of the unknown: we have no idea how the markets will perform, we are clueless about financial jargon that sounds so complex, and we cannot predict the future. While there are things that are beyond our control, it doesn't mean we're so helpless that we don't even want to try investing. Remember, there's always something we can do.

First things first: we need to identify what sets off our fear of investing.

Investment Fear Triggers

- *Losing Money:* Everyone worries about losing their hard-earned cash. It's a risk you can take, though, as long as you know how to diversify or spread your money around different investments.

- *Market Unpredictability:* Financial markets are full of uncertainties that are hard to stomach. They may be hard to predict, but historically, even though bumpy, markets have this tendency to climb up over time.

- *Biases:* You might have failed once at investing, gotten hurt, and resolved never to do it again. You can't let this thinking rule over you. Remember, your past does not define you or your future. Try to move past it for the sake of your financial future.

- *Intimidating Jargon and Topic Disconnection:* The world of finance looks complex, and people find it intimidating. Try not to worry, jargon can be broken down easily: "diversification" only means spreading your cash around several investment options; "asset allocation" is just choosing where to put your money based on the amount of risk you can tolerate which is simply the "ups" and "downs" you are comfortable with. Easy, right? We also have a section in this chapter dedicated to key investing terms you must familiarize yourself with. You're welcome!

It's natural to feel apprehensive about investing, because it sounds complicated. Start with simple jargon and work on overcoming these mental barriers one step at a time.

2. The Risks of Investing

Maybe you're scared to invest because you've seen a family member or a close friend fail at theirs. You're worried you'll lose all your money because you might mess up.

We're not going to sugarcoat it: yes, investing always comes with risks, but the bright side is that it also involves returns. One thing is for sure: you won't know unless you try. For your peace of mind, know there are ways to avoid messing up. Before we get to that, let's look at a few common reasons behind bad investment decisions:

- *Going in Blind:* When you dive in heart first without any research, you risk failing. A good understanding of the investment, its potential risks, and market movements is important in your investment decision.

- *Letting Your Emotions Decide:* When you let your heart instead of your head decide for you, you're likely in trouble. Fear, greed, excitement, and overconfidence, can all affect your ability to make a sound decision. Remember to listen to your head and think things through before deciding.

- *Chasing Trends:* What works for others might not necessarily work for you. Not every hot investment suits your investing appetite. It helps to back things up with research and consider your goals more than the virality of an option.

- *Ignoring Risks:* The better the potential to make money, the more risk you'll have to take. When you focus only on the return without considering the risks, the odds may not rule in your favor. Carefully examine an investment and try diversification.

- *Sticking with a Single Option:* Putting all investment funds into a single asset or a limited number of assets can be a riskier move than a helpful one. Spreading your money out also spreads the risks compared to concentrating on one asset.

- *Getting in Debt to Invest:* Leveraging or borrowing just so you can invest can be very risky. It's wise to invest only what you're comfortable with.

- *Not Knowing When to Say Goodbye:* Investing without a clear plan for when to sell or exit the investment means missing out on opportunities to make money. Avoid holding onto investments for too long and know when to sell to maximize returns!

- *Falling for Scams or Fraud:* If an investment gives exceptionally high returns, it may be a scam. Always keep an eye out for get-rich-quick or Ponzi schemes that take advantage of unaware, trusting investors.

Post-It.

Ponzi Scheme. A scam posed as an investment that promises unrealistic returns with minimal risks. By using money coming in from new investors to pay off earlier ones, this swindling tactic creates an illusion of success. Once the flow of new money stops, the entire scheme collapses.

---

3. The Risks of Not Investing

While investing seems risky, there are also significant risks to not investing at all. Here's why:

Stunted Financial Growth Due to Inflation: Imagine having a garden. You want it to flourish, right? To achieve that, you wouldn't keep your seeds in a jar; you'd plant them so they can grow. The same goes for your money. Leaving it in a savings account won't let it grow much. What's more, inflation will surely eat away at your money's purchasing power while it sits in your bank account over time. When you invest, you help your money grow faster than inflation, and maintain and even increase its purchasing power.

The Opportunity Cost of Not Growing Your Money: If you have $1,000, keeping it in the bank at a 1% annual interest, it will give you only around $1,350 after 30 years. As opposed to investing the same $10,000, which could earn an average of 7% interest every year, fast-forward 30 years, and you would have made more than $76,000! The striking difference is your opportunity cost – or the potential gains you miss out on – by not investing.

Falling Behind on Long-Term Financial Goals: Whether buying your own house, saving up for your kids' education, or a comfortable retirement, achieving these long-term goals can be a bit challenging if you rely on your income alone. It's like trying to finish a marathon by walking – you'll eventually get there, but it'll take much longer. Investing gives your money that boost to help you reach your financial finish line faster.

Market trends may not always be favorable, but as long as you invest wisely, diversify your options, and stay the course for the long haul, you are giving your money the chance to grow substantially. Often, the biggest risk is not taking any risk at all by leaving all your money sitting idle.

4. Investing Myths That Need Forgetting

If it's not fear of losing your money or making mistakes that are holding you back, these myths might have done their parts tricking you into believing investing isn't for you.

Myth 1: Investing is a 'rich people thing.'

This couldn't have been more wrong! Investing is actually for anyone who wants to see their money grow over time. You don't have to be a millionaire to invest. With the likes of retirement accounts and affordable investment apps, anyone can easily become an investor and watch whatever small amount they have grow into something big.

Myth 2: Investing is like gambling.

Investing and gambling are worlds apart! While gambling is about luck, investing is about making smart money choices, like putting your money into different asset types, such as stocks, bonds, real estate, etc. Remember, it's about taking calculated risks, not blind bets.

Myth 3: Only those with a lot of money can invest.

You don't need a lot of money to invest! These days, to invest, you can start with a small amount, $5 or $10 a month, thanks to apps and services you can manage via your mobile phone. No matter how small your starting investment is, the key is to consistently add to it, much like a plant needs steady watering and attention to grow. With time, the help of compound interest, your small amount can blossom into something impressive!

Here's the reality: investing is for everyone. Don't let these myths hold you back from growing your wealth. With a little learning and some serious planning, you can take on investing and use it to reach your financial goals.

5. Learning to Invest

The Different Stages in Learning to Invest and Your Circle of Competence

Your investing journey is made up of different stages that basically describe your knowledge of investing. Before we dive into them, let's introduce you to a mental model popular in the industry, developed by renowned businessmen, philanthropists, and investors themselves, Warren Buffet and Charlie Munger.

Simply put, the circle of competence (CoC) describes your level of expertise, representing what you know and understand very well: it could be a hobby, a skill, or an investment strategy. Following this logic, the concept says that you should only invest in businesses or industries that you have a very clear understanding of, or strictly within that innermost circle. You use your circle of competence as a guide in picking investment products out of thousands of options. The point is to stay within your area of competence, where you have an edge. Anything outside your circle of competence should be avoided. According to the model, you run the risk of making bad decisions and losing money by jumping into something totally alien to you so it's recommended to stick with what you know best.

As with everything that can be learned, your circle of competence grows over time as you gain more experience and knowledge.

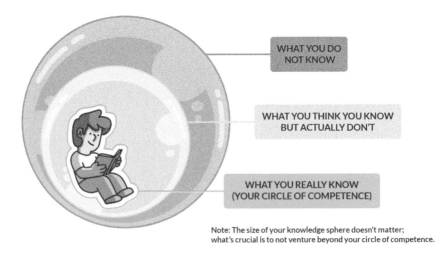

WHAT YOU DO NOT KNOW

WHAT YOU THINK YOU KNOW BUT ACTUALLY DON'T

WHAT YOU REALLY KNOW (YOUR CIRCLE OF COMPETENCE)

Note: The size of your knowledge sphere doesn't matter; what's crucial is to not venture beyond your circle of competence.

Now, let's look at the stages in learning to invest and how your circle of competence expands in every phase:

Beginner Stage

Taking baby steps, you start learning the basics of investing, familiarizing yourself with different investment types or asset classes like stocks, bonds, mutual funds, etc. Think of it as building your investing foundation. You explore risk and return, diversification, and asset allocation and try to get a grasp of financial markets and how they work, picking up helpful terminologies.

Circle of competence: relatively small, as you're just starting out

Investment types to explore: simple and low-risk, like bank accounts, fixed deposits, or money market funds. It's like putting your money in a piggy bank or a safe deposit box – it's easily accessible, gives you a small return, and it doesn't grow much

Education Stage

Now that you've mastered the basics, you're ready to learn how to choose the type of investments. You can then move on to checking out investment strategies like value investing, growth investing, and diversification. You will also have a better understanding of how factors like inflation, interest rates, and exchange rates affect your investments.

Circle of competence: begins to expand with every bit of knowledge gained

Investment types to explore: slightly more complex investments like index funds or index-linked exchange-traded funds (ETFs)

Practical Stage

You're ready to test things out. Start investing with a small "experimental" amount from your savings and try opening investment accounts like brokerage or retirement. You can even start working out an investment plan with your financial goals, plans, risk profile, and time frame you want to keep the investment.

> *Circle of competence:* widens with every practical application of your learnings
>
> *Investment types to explore:* paper trading or a simulated account can help you practice making investment decisions without risking real money

Implementation Stage

This is when you start to invest with real money. Remember to keep the amount small. It's time to put all those practice and learnings to work and build yourself a diversified portfolio to spread out the risks.

> *Circle of competence:* keeps on growing with firsthand investing experience
>
> *Investment types to explore:* you can now invest using real money, but it's best to stick to simple investments like individual stocks, bonds, or mutual funds. You may be in a live setting now, putting your skills and knowledge to the test, but don't forget that you're still learning and growing.

Continuous Learning Stage

Think of it as a lifelong learning experience. To keep up, you need to stay informed on market movements, economic conditions, and even changes in investing regulations. Reading and taking courses will expand your investing knowledge. Refine and refocus your strategy based on experience and changing goals.

> *Circle of competence:* what once was a small circle has now become a bigger one that only keeps on growing
>
> *Investment types to explore:* you move on from traditional investment products to more diverse ones, always backed by continuous research, practice, and experience.

Advanced Stage

My, my, look how far you've come. You are not only a professional investor but an expert at that (we hope!). You're now looking at more complex investments and strategies with the skills you've developed in portfolio management, risk management, and tax optimization. You may now even be considering professional certifications or designations like a certified financial planner or a chartered financial analyst.

> *Circle of competence:* it has grown so much that you've managed to master the things you only thought you knew before
>
> *Investment types to explore:* complex investment products and strategies not suitable for beginners like options, futures, or alternative investments

One thing to remember is that investing is a continuous pursuit that takes time and dedication. Your progress from one stage to another is entirely up to the level you are comfortable committing to. Note that seeking help from financial professionals or experienced investors can do wonders for you, especially when you're starting out. As for your circle of competence, you'd do well to observe your boundaries and limitations to avoid poor decision-making.

Learning Stages of Investing Gamified

Imagine you're a gaming newbie who dreams of competing in e-sports tournaments. Your journey to becoming a professional gamer can be likened to investing.

Gaming Noob (Beginner Stage): You choose a game and check out its mechanics and basic controls. CoC is small, and you find yourself restarting the game again and again. Forget competing with pros for now so you won't get discouraged.

Boot Camp Trainee (Education Stage): You start studying game strategies, watching tutorials, and learning advanced techniques from more experienced players. CoC expands as you gain theoretical knowledge about the game.

Beta Tester (Practical Stage): You take practicing seriously, applying the strategies and techniques you've learned so you're prepared for the real deal. CoC grows with your every practice, testing out different game scenarios.

Live Gamer (Implementation Stage): You're confident enough to take your chances in mini-tournaments, testing your skills against other players in a competitive setting. CoC grows to include not just gameplay but also tournament prep and mindset.

Quest Finder (Continuous Learning Stage): The more competitions you enter, the more experience you gain. You keep up with game updates and evolving strategies. CoC expands with every win and loss, teaching you to adapt accordingly.

Pro Gamer (Advanced Stage): CoC grows to include mastery of multiple games, professional-level gameplay, team management, and even game analysis, coaching, or e-sports business operations.

Knowing your comfort level is a key investing aspect. Just like no beginner tackles the big boss, you are not expected to take on complex investment products until you're confident you have the knowledge and skills to do so.

By observing boundaries and staying within one's level of expertise, gamers and investors alike can minimize risks, learn more, and practice more. This way, their circle of competence continues to expand, building their confidence to fight bigger battles or explore new investment types.

6. What Investor Type Are You?

You can be a passive investor, an active one, or someone caught in between. Let's walk you through each of them to know more:

Passive Investor

They are looking into putting their investing knowledge to the test but are not quite ready to spend most of their time monitoring stocks. It's like investing on autopilot! They are mostly stage 3 investors (practical stage) who prefer simple, low-cost, and low-maintenance investments that let their money grow over time. Some examples are index funds or index-linked exchange-traded funds (ETFs) that track a broad set of companies or assets, following market trends.

Core-Satellite Approach Investor

In between the no pressure passive type and the right amount of control active investing offers are the core-satellite approach investors. Knowledge-wise, they are equipped to invest but they also need to expand their skill set before they can go full active investing.

Their portfolio is divided into two main components:

Core Portfolio (Passive Investing): A large chunk of investments are made up of low-cost index funds (ETFs) that move with the market. This provides broad exposure to different types of investments while maximizing returns.

Satellite Portfolio (Active Investing): This is the smaller yet more custom-built portion of the portfolio that is actively managed. One can explore specific securities based on interest and research, matched with analysis, and stock-picking abilities.

These are typically stage 5 to 6 investors (continuous to advanced learning stages) with a higher level of investing knowledge and confidence to complement the active portion of this approach. They prefer that perfect balance between having a solid foundation and some room for more personalized investments.

Active Investors

Their stock-picking characteristics set them apart from passive investors. They choose individual stocks, bonds, or other investments to outperform the market. To become an active investor, one must have an understanding of the investing ropes, and keen eyes for market and stock analysis, complemented by a high risk tolerance. They have usually reached the advanced stage of learning how to invest (stage 6). In addition, they should be able to keep their cool and manage their emotions no matter the market direction.

Many investors move from passive to active investing as they gain more knowledge and experience. Some are fine being passive or core-satellite investors the whole time. It is entirely up to you, as long as you are comfortable with your chosen strategy.

7. Starting Your Investing Journey

The Must-Know Investing Core Concepts When Starting Your Investing Journey

To help you understand investing better and decide whether you want to explore this wealth-building tactic, here are a few core concepts you will likely come across and must understand:

Financial Planning: We can't stress it enough: you need a financial road map. Investing is only one part of it. Having a plan helps you avoid aimless investing, which can cause you to veer off course. More importantly, it serves as your guide, making sure your investment choices align with your financial goals.

Risk and Return: Risk and return always go together – you can't have one without the other. Generally, the higher the potential return of an investment (or how much your money grows), the higher the risks involved. Knowing the risk-reward relationship is important for better decision-making.

Investment Products: There are many types of investment products you can pick from to invest in, from stocks, bonds, mutual funds, and exchange-traded funds (ETFs) to real estate investment trusts (REITs). Take the time to learn about them – their risks and potential returns – and use them to build a well-rounded portfolio.

Diversification: Whether you are a rookie or a seasoned investor, investing in a variety of investment types is key to spread risk. Diversification helps mitigate risks by ensuring you're not putting your money on a single asset class or security. In case one investment fails, you won't lose everything.

Asset Allocation: How you divide and assign the money you want to invest by the type of investment, like stocks, bonds, cash equivalents, or alternative investments. Let's say your portfolio is a cake – asset allocation is how you slice that cake – you may want a bigger slice for stocks and a smaller slice for more complex investments. Where you invest should be based on your positions and according to your objectives, the upside and downside that you can tolerate, and how long you want to stay invested.

Compound Interest: Earn interest on interest. This helps your money grow faster. The key is to invest early and reinvest your earnings for greater returns.

Investment Costs and Fees: Investments also come with costs and fees. Familiarizing yourself with management fees, trading commissions, expense ratios, and other similar fees can help you minimize costs and maximize your returns.

Time Horizon: The time frame you intend to stay invested. If you are looking at holding the investment for a long time, you can take more risk because, technically, if the market fluctuates in the short-term, you have time to wait for the market to recover.

Exchange Rates: Not only do they tell you how much a specific currency is worth in another one, but they can also significantly affect your investments. You will need to understand and monitor foreign currencies and their exchange rates, compared to your home currency, if you're looking to invest in international markets.

The Key Steps to Jumpstart Your Investing Journey

Have a Plan

Goal Setting: What are your investment goals? Is it a cozy retirement home by the beach? A rainy day fund? Or education expenses for the kids? Identifying them clearly helps you make appropriate investment decisions.

Risk Profile Assessment: Ever thought about what your risk appetite is like? How much risk you're willing to take or your risk profile helps determine the investment strategies that suit you best.

Build a Strong Foundation

Set Up a Fund for Unexpected Events: It's crucial to save enough money for unexpected expenses like emergencies, accidents, and the like before you invest. This fund should typically cover three to six months' worth of living expenses and must be readily accessible.

Pay Off High-Interest Debt: Before investing, you might want to clear any credit card balances or debts that you may have. Similar debts often exceed potential investment returns.

Prepare Investing Capital: Try to avoid investing using loans. Other options, like micro-savings and micro-investing, are available in case you haven't saved up for investing yet. They come with investing platforms that are convenient to use. Micro-savings is especially useful/relevant for those with limited capital. What's cool is that you can invest as you save.

Choose Your Investments

When picking an investment product, consider the unique risk-reward relationships. It's important that it aligns with your risk profile, your set timeline, and your overall financial plan.

Diversification: Be careful not to place all your eggs in one basket to help spread out any risks you may face and give your returns a boost.

Monitor and Adjust

Investing is a lifelong learning process. Regularly reviewing your investments and monitoring their performance makes it easier to adjust your portfolio as needed. If you change your goals or prefer a different level of risk, regular check ins keep you on track.

8. Invest as You Save: Micro-Savings and Micro-Investing

As lightly discussed previously, micro-saving and micro-investing platforms are popular investing starting points for beginners, especially the young generation. These apps make investing more accessible for those who want to start investing but don't have a lot of money.

Micro-savings

Put your spare change to good use through micro-saving. This approach makes small amounts work for you as they accumulate over time. Micro-saving apps round up your everyday spending. Your $4.50 coffee fix becomes $5.00, with the extra 50 cents sent to your savings!

Micro-investing

With micro-investing, you can start with as little as a few bucks and buy various investment products. Like micro-savings platforms, they have easily downloadable apps that make it easy to start investing without the need for a hefty capital.

Just threw in my first few bucks!
I can't wait to have my own place.

Upside:

Starting Small: You can start investing without a lot of money, making it accessible to those with limited cash to spare.

Automation: Many micro-saving and micro-investing platforms offer automation features, making the process a breeze. With minimal effort, you can see your money grow.

Habit Forming: You're training yourself to develop healthy financial habits by consistently putting small amounts aside.

Diversification: Micro-investing platforms often offer diversified portfolios, giving you much-needed exposure to various asset classes while minimizing risks.

Downside:

Fees: Be on the lookout for platforms that charge fees or require account minimums before signing up. These fees can affect your returns, especially those with smaller balances.

Limited options: As portfolios are automated, they may not always be to your liking or incompatible with the risks you're comfortable taking.

Dependency: Instead of letting these platforms invest for you, why not sharpen your investing skills? This way, you can take control of your finances. After all, there's no better person to put your portfolio together than you!

Micro-savings and micro-investing can be useful tools to build financial discipline and gradually grow your wealth, especially after traumatic investment experiences. Just make sure to check on possible charges, investment options available, and ultimately, how they fit into your overall financial road map.

Investment Booboos to Avoid

Sure, investing can grow your money, but it doesn't mean there are no humps and bumps that can derail your investing journey if you're not careful. We came up with a list of investing mishaps you must avoid at all costs:

> **Investing with Your Heart:** Letting your emotions get the best of you when making investing decisions can result in poor choices and undesirable outcomes. That's why it's a must to approach things calmly. When investing, it's better to put your mind over your heart.

> **Diversify:** What happens if you put all your money in one investment and it falls apart? Yes, your hard-earned money goes down with it. Diversification is key to mitigating risks and losses.

> **Chasing Hot Investments:** Not all that glitters is gold, so they say. It's the same with investing. Try not to be tempted by an investment that seems to perform so well at the moment. Investing considers more than just historical performance so try to get over the hype if you can.

Overconfidence and Overtrading: A winning investment streak can easily inflate your confidence, pushing you to trade more often and speculate even more. While it's great that you're winning, sticking to your plan might be more beneficial for you than trying to outdo a notoriously unpredictable market.

Impatience: When you invest, make sure you invest for the long-term. It's a tough industry to crack, requiring patience and discipline to adhere to a plan, especially when the market fluctuates. It helps to remind yourself why you're investing in the first place and to keep hanging tight.

Watch out for these potential pitfalls and avoid them completely when you can for a smooth investing journey!

9. Conclusion

Investing can be a lot to take in, especially if you have had bad experiences that left you scared of making the same mistakes. The fear of losing your hard-earned money is reason enough to stop you from dipping your feet into investing, not to mention the uncertainty surrounding the market.

We got to the bottom of those fears, remember? And if there's one takeaway you've got, it's that with enough research and a whole lot of patience and dedication, investing is another thing you can master.

Never let the complex financial jargon overwhelm you. It can always be broken down into simpler, everyday terms. As for your circle of competence, we hope reading this chapter has somehow expanded it a bit, giving you the confidence to see investing in a different light.

We won't hide it, mastering the art of investing will take time. What's important is that you take the first step. Now, you just have to press on and stay the course. A bright financial future is within reach!

P.S. Don't forget to check out our investment calculator!

www.thesimplesum.com/investment-calculator/

Appendix

Asset Classes

They are types of investments grouped together according to characteristics, risk profiles, and potential returns. The different types' performances are affected differently by market forces. Some common asset classes include stocks, bonds, cash equivalents, real estate, commodities, and alternative investments like private equity and hedge funds.

Cash Equivalents

When needed, you can quickly sell these investments and change them to cash, like a savings account. They are usually safe and offer small returns. They are also your best bet for rainy-day savings or monies that you will need very soon.

Fixed Deposits (FDs)

Also known as time deposits, an FD is a bank account offered by banks that earns interest over a fixed period. FDs are considered low-risk investments.

Commodities

Covering a broad range of products, commodities are any and all things you can buy and sell. They include gold, silver, oil, agricultural produce (wheat, corn, soybeans), and industrial metals (copper, aluminum). Be warned, though: investing in commodities can be pretty risky, we say do your research first!

Exchange-Traded Funds (ETFs)

ETFs are either index funds or mutual funds traded on exchanges like stocks. Let's say an ETF holds shares of companies in the energy sector. The performance of the ETF depends on the performance of the sector.

Fixed-Income Securities

Also known as debt instruments, pays you a fixed amount. A common example is bonds, where you agree to loan the government or companies your money, and they promise to pay you back with a fixed interest.

Generally considered safer investments than stocks, debt instruments offer a sequence of returns and the promise of repayment. However, the price doesn't increase over time, so the value of your investment doesn't go up as well.

Forex (Foreign Exchange)

This refers to buying and selling one currency for another, banking on the possibility of making a profit from the difference in the forex rates.

Index Funds

They are investment funds that benchmark market indices, like the S&P 500. It's like buying into great companies, following their market behavior instead of picking out individual stocks. It's a passive way of investing in several companies all at once.

Money Market Funds

They are investment funds that put their money in government bills and fixed deposit. They are a safe investment if you don't want to stay invested for a long time.

Mutual Funds

Mutual funds represent a pool of money from many investors managed by professionals who decide which assets to invest in based on a variety of strategies.

Real Estate Investment Trusts (REITs)

REITs invest in properties. Instead of buying the physical properties yourself, say a building or a lot, you can invest in a REIT, effectively sharing in the company's property rental income or potential increase in value.

Stocks or Equities

When you buy shares of a listed company, also known as equities, you become a partial owner. A stock is a slice of that company that you buy. You own that slice so when business is good for the company, the stock (like your slice) price goes up, which can mean earnings for you. Then there are dividends the stocks pay you, much like a token you get as an owner.

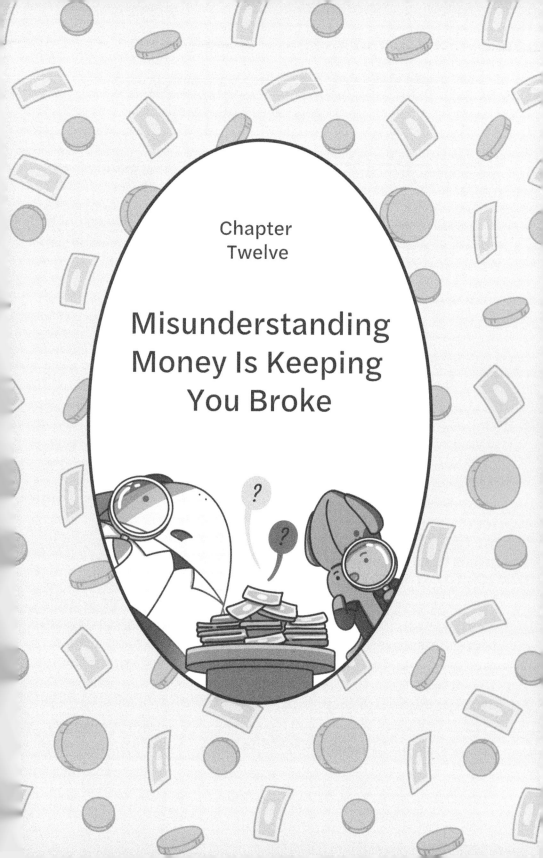

Chapter
Twelve

Misunderstanding Money Is Keeping You Broke

MISUNDERSTANDING MONEY IS KEEPING YOU BROKE

Have you ever reached the end of the month, coffee in hand, puzzling over your bank statements, wondering where all your money disappeared to? This scene is all too familiar in many households. Despite earning a decent income, you find yourself barely scraping by, trapped in a cycle of financial frustration. This isn't just your story – it's a narrative shared across countless living rooms and kitchen tables.

In this chapter, we will confront the myths and misconceptions that often warp our financial understanding and explore clear, actionable strategies to mend your monetary mindset. Think of it not just as learning, but as embarking on a path to financial healing and empowerment.

Money and emotions are deeply intertwined, much like our relationships with people. Our connection to money is wrought with emotions, beliefs, habits, and personal histories that define our financial behaviors. For some, money symbolizes security and freedom; for others, it represents a constant source of anxiety or shame. These emotional undercurrents influence how we earn, spend, save, and manage money – often without us even realizing it.

Consider the emotional weight of money: the sinking feeling of an unexpected bill, the elation of a pay raise. These reactions show that money isn't just numbers on a page; it's a concept steeped in psychological significance, capable of triggering a spectrum of emotional responses from joy to fear.

A dysfunctional money relationship is characterized by harmful patterns: chronic overspending, poor savings habits, avoidance of financial planning, or recurring conflicts over money. This broken dynamic usually stems from unhealthy attitudes, excessive emotional baggage, and a misalignment between our stated life goals and our actual financial behaviors.

When caught in such a cycle, the size of your paycheck becomes irrelevant. True wealth and financial freedom remain just out of reach, like driving a car with the parking brake engaged – no matter how hard you press the accelerator, you're stuck. But there's hope. Healing your relationship with money is not only possible; it's empowering. Throughout this chapter, we will dive into understanding your unique financial perspective, uncover the roots of your money mindset, and most importantly, learn how to shift it from a source of stress to a foundation of prosperity and peace. Let's break the chains of misunderstanding and rebuild a relationship with money that is healthy, mindful, and prosperous.

1. Understanding Your Relationship with Money

Decoding Your Monetary Mindset

What does your relationship with money really look like? Let's explore the depths of your financial persona.

At the heart of it, your relationship with money is a complex tapestry woven from your thoughts, emotions, habits, and behaviors. These elements dictate how you earn, spend, save, and manage your finances, both daily and in the long run. This relationship influences everything from your mindset on wealth-building to your gut reactions during financial surprises.

Key Components of Your Monetary Relationship

Spending Habits

1.

Example: Think of Emma, who pauses to consider the long-term value of every purchase. She contrasts sharply with Tom, who lives for the thrill of luxury buys, giving little thought to tomorrow. Where do you see yourself on this spectrum?

Saving Patterns

2.

Example: Reflect on your last significant purchase – did planning for it feel like a chore or a challenge? Or was it a satisfying milestone in your financial journey? Your approach to saving, whether you view it as a safeguard or a sacrifice, highlights your financial priorities and resilience.

Emotional Associations

3.

Scenario: Imagine receiving a large, unexpected bill. Does it trigger panic, or do you view it as a manageable inconvenience? The emotions you associate with money – be it anxiety, empowerment, or indifference – play a pivotal role in your financial decisions.

Money Management Skills

4.

Self-Assessment: Consider how confident you feel about creating and sticking to a budget. Does the thought of tracking your expenses energize you, or does it bring a sense of dread? You money management can either be a source of empowerment or a barrier to financial confidence.

Each of these facets – spending, saving, emotional responses, and skills – contributes to the overall health of your financial life. By examining these aspects, you can begin to identify patterns that may be holding you back or propelling you forward. Understanding your monetary mindset is the first step toward reshaping it to better support your goals and dreams.

In the next sections, we will introduce strategies to transform your relationship with money from a potential source of stress to one of strength and confidence. Prepare to turn insights into actions, as we chart a course toward a more empowered financial future.

What Is Your Relationship with Money and Why Is It Important?

The Ties That Bind: Unraveling the Importance of Your Money Mentality

Why do some individuals enjoy a healthy and positive relationship with money, while others wrestle with financial stress, impulsive spending, or a persistent scarcity mindset? The fabric of each person's relationship with money is woven from a complex interplay of internal and external factors. These influences shape how one perceives, values, and interacts with money throughout their lifetime.

Internal Factors Shaping Your Money Relationship

Internal factors originate from within the individual – their thoughts, beliefs, experiences, and core psychology. These factors shape a person's inner world and deeply influence their attitudes, emotions, and behaviors when it comes to money matters.

Money Mindset

Core Influence: Your mindset encapsulates your general attitude toward money, including earning, spending, saving, and investing. Consider the abundance mindset, which embraces the potential to grow and multiply wealth, versus the scarcity mindset, which views money as a finite resource that must be conserved. These perspectives are not formed in isolation; they evolve from deeper internal influences such as beliefs, past experiences, and even personality traits.

Personality Traits

Impact on Finances: Personality greatly dictates financial behavior. For instance, a person with high impulsivity may frequently indulge in unplanned spending, whereas someone who is risk-averse might shy away from potentially lucrative investments. Traits like conscientiousness and self-discipline are typically linked to positive financial habits such as diligent saving and prudent budgeting.

Personal Values and Goals

Guiding Financial Decisions: The values you cherish and the goals you pursue directly influence how you manage money. Someone who prioritizes financial security is likely to focus on saving and conservative investments, while another who values experiences may allocate funds toward travel and adventure, shaping their spending patterns accordingly.

Family Upbringing and Culture

Foundational Influences: Early experiences within the family and the broader cultural context set the groundwork for your financial behaviors. A person raised in a financially constrained environment might constantly feel the need to save or may experience anxiety about spending, whereas someone from a wealthier background might not appreciate the value of money or lack budgeting skills.

Financial Knowledge and Self-Awareness

Educational Impact: Understanding financial principles plays a critical role in shaping one's financial practices. Lack of knowledge can lead to poor decision-making, while a well-informed individual is more likely to engage in effective money management.

External Factors Influencing Money Relationships

While internal factors originate within the individual's psychology, external circumstances represent outside forces and realities that have a profound impact on shaping money mindsets and behaviors – for better or worse.

Life Experiences and Events

Defining Moments: Important life milestones, such as a career breakthrough or a financial setback, can profoundly alter one's financial outlook and behavior. Experiences like bankruptcy or sudden wealth can dramatically change one's approach to saving, spending, and investing.

Financial Education and Literacy Programs

Role of Learning: Access to financial education significantly affects financial competence and confidence. Educational programs, whether in schools or through community initiatives, equip individuals with essential skills and knowledge to navigate their financial landscapes effectively.

Income Level and Economic Status

Economic Influence: Your economic environment plays a substantial role in shaping your financial mindset. Individuals at different income levels face unique challenges and opportunities, from managing scarcity to allocating abundance.

Societal and Cultural Influences

Cultural Context: The societal norms and cultural backdrop to which one is exposed influence financial attitudes and actions. Consumerism encourages spending, while other cultural norms might emphasize frugality and saving, highlighting how societal values mold personal finance strategies.

Understanding these complex and intertwined factors provides a clearer picture of why people interact with money in vastly different ways. By exploring these dimensions, you can begin to unravel your own money mentality and take steps toward cultivating a healthier, more empowered financial life.

2. Decoding Your Monetary Mindset: Understanding the Connection Between Internal and External Factors

While it's helpful to distinguish internal and external factors, these forces are not isolated; instead they interact in a continuous feedback loop that dynamically impacts one's money relationship over time.

Signs of a Broken Money Relationship

To better understand the nature of a "broken money relationship," let's look at Sarah's example, a talented professional who hopes to own a business. Despite having a solid business plan and market potential, Sarah is paralyzed by a fear of failure and doubts about her financial acumen, keeping her from taking the plunge.

A broken money relationship refers to dysfunctional and self-destructive patterns of attitudes, emotions, beliefs, and behaviors surrounding finances. It's an energetic dynamic where subconscious programming keeps you struggling, stuck, or blocked from achieving true financial abundance – no matter how positive your conscious efforts might be.

Identifying these signs is your first powerful step toward financial liberation and a thriving relationship with wealth.

The Cost of a Broken Money Relationship

A fractured financial relationship can have consequences far beyond your wallet, affecting your emotional well-being, relationships, and overall quality of life. Let's explore the steep price of a fractured fiscal relationship.

Financial Consequences

Debt Accumulation: For example, Sarah, despite her steady income, finds herself repeatedly falling into the debt trap. Her impulse purchases, driven by emotional triggers and a lack of awareness, force her to live beyond her means, leaning on credit cards and loans. This behavior could lead her into a deep debt spiral, compounded by high interest rates and making financial recovery increasingly challenging.

Inability to Save or Invest: Sarah struggles to save for future needs. Her short-term gratification needs and a scarcity mindset may prevent her from saving for essential business capital or investing in growth opportunities. This lack of foresight can leave her vulnerable to unforeseen expenses and stall her business before it starts.

Missed Opportunities for Financial Growth: Sarah wants to be an entrepreneur and have her own business but is paralyzed by fear and insecurity about her financial acumen. This hesitation prevents her from pursuing opportunities that could potentially increase her wealth and provide financial independence.

Emotional and Psychological Consequences

Stress, Anxiety, and Fear Around Money: Sarah's broken money relationship breeds constant stress and anxiety about her finances. The worry about debts and an uncertain financial future weighs heavily on her, impacting her mental health and manifesting as physical symptoms like insomnia and stress-related ailments.

Strained Relationships and Conflicts: Financial pressures could strain Sarah's relationships with partners or collaborators. Disagreements over money management, coupled with her secretive spending habits, foster resentment and mistrust among loved ones, potentially leading to deeper relational rifts.

Low Self-Esteem and Lack of Confidence: Repeated financial missteps erode Sarah's self-esteem, locking her in a self-perpetuating cycle of doubt and financial paralysis. Her perceived inability to handle business finances may prevent her from seeking necessary help or pursuing potential investors.

Understanding the depth and breadth of these consequences illustrates why repairing a broken money relationship is not just beneficial but essential for a healthier, more secure life. This section sets the stage for the transformative strategies that follow, aimed at mending the fiscal fractures and paving the way toward a renewed and empowering money relationship for Sarah and readers alike.

3. Understanding What Shapes Your Relationship with Money

The Forces That Mold Your Monetary Mindset

Why do some people enjoy a positive relationship with money, while others struggle with financial stress, overspending, or a scarcity mindset? The factors that shape an individual's unique relationship with money can be broadly categorized into two main groups: internal factors and external factors. The complex interplay between these internal and external influences determines how someone perceives, values, and interacts with money throughout their life.

Internal Factors Shaping Your Money Relationship

Internal factors originate from within the individual – their thoughts, beliefs, experiences, and core psychology. These factors shape a person's inner world and deeply influence their attitudes, emotions, and behaviors when it comes to money matters.

Money Mindset

A person's financial mindset – their fundamental beliefs and attitudes about money – drives their approach to earning, spending, saving, and investing. For instance, those with an abundance mindset view money as a resource to be leveraged and multiplied, embracing opportunities with optimism. In contrast, individuals with a scarcity mindset see money as a finite asset, often feeling the need to hoard and protect their resources due to fear of loss. These mindsets are deeply influenced by other internal elements such as core beliefs, life experiences, and character.

Personality Traits

Innate personality traits play a principal part in shaping financial behaviors and attitudes toward money. For instance, individuals with high impulsivity and low self-control may struggle with overspending and poor financial planning. Those who are naturally risk-averse might avoid investing or entrepreneurial pursuits. Conscientiousness and discipline are traits often linked with positive financial outcomes, like consistent saving and budgeting.

Personal Values and Goals

The values a person holds dear and the life goals they've set for themselves heavily influence their money priorities and choices. If someone highly values financial security, they may prioritize saving and low-risk investments. In contrast, adventure and life experiences may be more valuable to a free spirit who spends liberally on travel. When personal values align with financial decisions, money management becomes much easier.

Family Upbringing and Culture

For many people, their relationship with money is deeply rooted in childhood experiences and family dynamics. Those raised in low-income households might develop a scarcity mindset or struggle with providing for their own needs as adults. Conversely, children from affluent families may have an unhealthy sense of entitlement or lack financial discipline. Cultural attitudes also play a role – some cultures encourage conspicuous consumption as a status symbol, while others promote frugality.

Financial Knowledge and Self-Awareness

An individual's level of financial literacy and understanding of money management principles is another key internal factor. Those with minimal financial education may make poor investment choices, carry heavy debt burdens, or lack a coherent plan for achieving financial wellness. On the other hand, developing financial self-awareness through education can lead to more intentional and productive money habits.

Understanding these internal factors offers invaluable awareness into the complexities of financial behaviors and finding strategies for fostering a healthier, more productive relationship with money. By addressing these foundational aspects, individuals can reshape their financial destinies, transforming their approach to money from one of stress and limitation to one of empowerment and abundance.

External Factors Influencing Money Relationships

While internal factors originate within the individual's psychology, external circumstances represent outside forces and realities that have a profound impact on shaping money mindsets and behaviors – for better or worse.

Life Experiences and Events

Significant life events, whether they are positive or negative, can dramatically alter one's financial trajectory and attitudes toward money. Experiencing a severe financial crisis like bankruptcy or job loss might trigger a strong desire for security, leading to aggressive saving or conservative investment strategies. Conversely, positive events such as receiving a substantial inheritance or achieving entrepreneurial success might foster a mindset of wealth accumulation and a sense of financial abundance.

Financial Education and Literacy Programs

Access to quality financial education, literacy programs, and resources plays a pivotal role in developing knowledge and skills for managing money effectively. From school curricula teaching basic money principles to workplace seminars on investing and retirement planning, these external educational forces help individuals build their financial knowledge foundation.

Income Level and Economic Status

An individual's economic status and level of income greatly influence their relationship with money. Those experiencing poverty may face constant financial strain, often leading to a scarcity mindset and short-term decision-making. At the opposite end of the spectrum, the ultra-wealthy, with resources far exceeding their personal needs, might adopt a different set of financial behaviors, such as engaging in philanthropy or exploring unique investment opportunities, reflecting diverse attitudes toward money.

Societal and Cultural Influences

The culture and society in which an individual is immersed from an early age significantly mold their perceptions and attitudes about money. Consumerism, heavily promoted through media and advertising, often encourages spending beyond one's means, linking self-worth to financial success. In contrast, cultural values that emphasize simplicity and modesty can mitigate materialistic tendencies. The prevalent social mindset of keeping up with the Joneses further influences financial behaviors, pushing individuals toward lifestyle inflation and competitive spending.

The Connection Between Internal and External Factors

It is important to note that while it's practical to distinguish between internal and external factors, in reality, these elements are closely interconnected, often influencing each other in a dynamic feedback loop that evolves over time. For instance, being raised in an affluent family might initially foster a sense of financial security and independence (an external factor), which shapes a confident and possibly spendthrift money mindset (internal factor). However, if that individual later faces significant financial setbacks, such as unexpected market losses or business failures, these new external challenges could profoundly reshape their internal views on money, potentially fostering a more cautious or conservative financial approach.

Through these examples, we see how external realities continuously interact with and redefine internal beliefs, mindsets, and values, illustrating the complex, intertwined nature of factors that shape one's financial life. This continuous interaction ensures that an individual's relationship with money remains a dynamic and evolving aspect of their life, influenced by both personal experiences and broader societal conditions.

4. Healing Your Money Relationship: Shifting Mindsets and Building Healthy Habits

How to Improve Your Relationship with Money: Forging a Path to Financial Fulfillments

At the heart of mending your relationship with money lies the dual process of transforming your mindsets about finance and enhancing awareness around your financial behaviors. This journey involves identifying the deeply ingrained "money scripts" that have shaped your attitudes and actions, and consciously replacing them with empowering new perspectives and habits.

Identifying Your Money Scripts and Beliefs

Money scripts are the underlying beliefs, attitudes, and narratives that we hold about money, often formed in childhood and reinforced throughout our lives.

These beliefs can be both conscious and subconscious, profoundly influencing our financial decisions and behaviors.

To start the process of identifying your money scripts, reflect on the messages you received about money growing up. What did your parents or caregivers teach you, either directly or indirectly, about money's purpose, acquisition, and management? Were there any limiting beliefs or fears instilled in you, such as "money doesn't grow on trees" or "rich people are greedy"?

Additionally, consider the cultural and societal influences that have shaped your money mindset. Certain cultures may emphasize saving and frugality, while others may promote conspicuous consumption or status-seeking through material possessions.

Once you've identified your money scripts, challenge them objectively. Are these beliefs truly serving you, or are they holding you back from achieving financial freedom and prosperity?

Developing Money Awareness and Mindfulness

Cultivating money awareness and mindfulness involves bringing a heightened level of consciousness to your financial thoughts, feelings, and actions. This practice allows you to observe your money habits with curiosity and non-judgment, ultimately empowering you to make more intentional and aligned choices.

Start by tracking your spending and savings patterns. Notice where your money is going and observe the emotions and triggers that accompany your financial decisions. Are there certain situations or emotional states that tend to lead to overspending or impulse purchases?

Building Healthy Money Behaviors and Habits

As you gain awareness and insight into your money mindsets and patterns, you can begin to implement new, healthier behaviors and habits around money. This process involves actively rewriting your money scripts and establishing routines that support your financial well-being.

Plan your spending according to your values and priorities. Rather than viewing a budget as a restrictive tool, reframe it as a conscious way of aligning your spending with your goals and aspirations.

Develop a savings habit by setting aside and automatically transferring a fixed monthly amount into an assigned account. Celebrate small wins and consistently reinforce these positive behaviors through affirmations and rewards.

Seek out financial education and resources to enhance your money management skills. Learn finance concepts like "compound interest" and investment approaches. The know-hows can help you make better decisions.

Creating a Positive Money Mindset

Shifting your money mindset from scarcity to abundance is a crucial step in healing your relationship with money. This involves cultivating gratitude for what you have, while simultaneously opening yourself up to the flow of prosperity and abundance.

Practice affirmations and visualizations that reinforce a positive money mindset and to rewire your subconscious beliefs.

Engage in activities that nurture a sense of abundance, such as creating a vision board or keeping a gratitude journal focused on your financial blessings. Celebrate your wins, no matter how small, and allow yourself to experience the joy and freedom that comes with a healthy money relationship.

Nurturing Money Confidence and Using a Money Compass

As you improve your relationship with money, it's also important to nurture your confidence and self-belief. Remind yourself that you have the power to transform your financial reality and create the life you desire.

Surround yourself with supportive individuals who share your commitment to financial well-being. Join communities, forums, or accountability groups to share and exchange ideas, and receive encouragement and motivation.

In subsequent chapters, we'll explore the concept of a "money compass" – a personalized financial road map that will serve as your guide on this transformative journey. This compass will help you stay aligned with your values, priorities, and objectives, ensuring that your newfound money mindsets and habits propel you toward true financial freedom and prosperity.

Healing your money relationship is ongoing. You'll need patience, kindness to yourself, and the ability to adapt to changing circumstances. By shifting your mindsets, developing awareness, and cultivating healthy habits, you can break free from the chains of a broken money relationship and clear the way for a life of financial abundance and fulfillment.

5. Conclusion

In this chapter, we've ventured deep into understanding the complexities of our relationship with money, examining both the internal and external forces that shape our financial lives. Through identifying detrimental money scripts, embracing mindfulness, and fostering healthy financial habits, we pave the way toward not just repairing but thriving in our financial interactions.

Chapter Takeaways

Recognize Your Money Scripts: Unearth the underlying beliefs that guide your financial behaviors. Understanding these foundational scripts is critical for initiating profound changes in your financial life.

Cultivate Financial Mindfulness: Enhance awareness of your spending, saving, and emotional triggers around money. This mindful approach allows for more deliberate and aligned financial decisions.

Adopt Healthy Financial Practices: Transition toward positive financial habits by setting realistic budgets, saving diligently, and investing wisely, all aligned with your personal values and long-term goals.

Shift Toward an Abundance Mindset: Move from scarcity to abundance by practicing gratitude and visualizing financial success. This shift is essential for attracting and maintaining wealth.

Build Financial Education: Continuously seek knowledge about financial management to empower your decisions and enhance your financial literacy.

Foster Supportive Relationships: Surround yourself with a community that supports your financial growth. Sharing your journey with others can provide encouragement, new insights, and motivation.

Remember, healing your relationship with money is ongoing and needs your commitment, self-awareness, and a proactive stance toward personal growth. Embrace the journey, and let the insights from this chapter guide you to a financially abundant and fulfilling life.

Appendix

Money Mindset Makeover

Imagine transforming the way you think about money – shifting from old, limiting beliefs to a fresh, empowering perspective. That's what a Money Mindset Makeover is all about. It's about ditching the negative attitudes that hold you back from earning more, saving better, and enjoying financial freedom.

Why Your Mindset Matters

Your relationship with money doesn't just influence your bank balance – it shapes every financial decision you make. Often, this mindset stems from deep-rooted beliefs instilled during childhood, shaped by phrases like "Money doesn't grow on trees" or "We're not the rich type." Such statements, though meant to instill caution, can plant a seed of perpetual scarcity in your mind.

A Money Mindset Makeover walks you through identifying and challenging these kinds of limiting beliefs. It helps you replace them with more positive, abundant ways of thinking about money. You'll learn to identify the negative beliefs that have quietly directed your financial decisions and how to challenge them effectively. It's about replacing the notion of scarcity with abundance and transforming anxiety into action.

What Is Money Mindset?

Money is more than just currency – it's a reflection of our deeply held beliefs, values, and emotions. Our relationship with money is shaped by our "money mindset," which is the foundation of how we think, feel, and behave when it comes to financial matters. Whether we realize it or not, our money mindset profoundly influences our ability to earn, manage, and grow wealth.

At its core, a money mindset is the lens through which we perceive and interact with money. It encompasses our attitudes, beliefs, and habits related to earning, spending, saving, investing, and managing our finances. Some people have a scarcity mindset, believing that money is scarce and that they must constantly worry about not having enough. Others have an abundance mindset, seeing money as a tool for creating freedom, opportunity, and fulfillment.

Why Your Money Mindset Matters

Understanding and cultivating a healthy money mindset is crucial because it impacts every aspect of our financial lives. Our mindset shapes our spending habits, our ability to stick to a budget, our willingness to take calculated risks, and our capacity to build long-term wealth. Individuals with a positive money mindset are more likely to make empowered financial decisions, while those with a negative mindset often struggle with overspending, debt, and a lack of financial security.

Your Money Mindset and Your Relationship with Money

Your mindset around money is like an invisible script that influences every financial decision you make. This script is written from childhood experiences, cultural conditioning, past traumas, and deeply held beliefs – both conscious and unconscious.

Let's say, you were brought up in an environment where money was a source of anxiety or conflict, you might unconsciously adopt a scarcity mindset – a deep-rooted belief that there will never be enough, leading you to cling tightly to what you have, out of fear. This mindset is what causes some people to be fearful about spending or avoid investing, forever caught in a self-perpetuating cycle of financial scarcity.

On the flip side, you may link money to feelings of unworthiness or shame – perhaps due to parental struggles or societal messages – you might find yourself underpricing your skills at work or overspending to fill an emotional void. These actions often stem from a fear of success or failure, which can sabotage financial growth and lead to a cycle of dissatisfaction.

Breaking Free from Negative Money Mindsets

Fear often underlies many people's dysfunctional money patterns – whether it's a fear of success (causing you to self-sabotage whenever you start making more money), or a fear of failure (paralyzing you from taking financial risks that could lead to breakthroughs). These fears fuel cycles of playing small, staying broke, and feeling unfulfilled.

Our relationships with money can also be complicated by emotional undercurrents. For some, money might symbolize power and control, a view often shaped by experiences of deprivation or manipulation in childhood. For others, money might evoke shame, guilt, or anxiety – emotions rooted in negative experiences around financial desires during formative years.

The first step toward change is awareness. Recognizing these deeply ingrained beliefs and emotional responses allows us to challenge and dismantle their influence over our financial lives. By confronting these hidden scripts, we can start to rewrite our financial futures, moving from subconscious sabotage to conscious prosperity.

The Nature of Money Mindsets

At the heart of every financial decision lies a person's money mindset – this is the lens through which we view our financial lives. It shapes our beliefs, values, emotions, and behaviors related to earning, spending, saving, and investing.

Common Positive Money Mindsets:

- *Abundance Mindset:* Believing in endless opportunities for wealth, fostering an optimistic outlook on financial growth.

- *Growth Mindset:* Committing to lifelong learning and improvement in financial affairs, recognizing that skills and understanding can always be expanded.

- *Delayed Gratification:* Choosing to prioritize long-term financial rewards over immediate pleasures, a key to building sustainable wealth.

- *Calculated Risk-Taking:* Willingness to embrace well-thought-out risks that can lead to greater financial rewards.

- *Financial Empowerment:* Feeling confident and in control of financial decisions, steering one's financial journey actively.

Common Negative Money Mindsets:

- *Scarcity Mindset:* The belief that money is limited, fostering a sense of perpetual insufficiency and fear of running out.

- *Fear and Avoidance:* Experiencing anxiety about financial matters, often avoiding necessary financial decisions or discussions.

- *Impulse Spending:* The tendency to make spontaneous purchases that exceed one's budget and undermine financial goals.

- *Entitlement Mindset:* Expecting wealth to come without personal effort, often leading to frustration and passive financial behavior.

- *Financial Disempowerment:* Feeling a lack of control over one's financial future, which can lead to despair and passivity in financial planning.

The Impact of Beliefs, Values, and Emotions

Our beliefs about money – whether it is a source of security, freedom, or anxiety – directly influence our financial decisions and actions. If you view money as a tool for freedom and security, your decisions are likely made for your financial well-being. On the other hand, if money is a constant source of anxiety, you might find yourself avoiding necessary financial planning or impulsively spending as a way to alleviate stress.

Values also play a crucial role. If you value experiences over material goods, you might choose to spend on travel rather than luxury items. Similarly, valuing financial independence may drive you to save and invest more aggressively.

Emotions are equally influential. People who associate money with positive feelings like empowerment and opportunity are generally more proactive about financial planning and confident in their decisions. Or, those who link money to negative emotions like fear or guilt may develop harmful financial habits such as overspending or extreme frugality.

Ultimately, our money mindset shapes our financial decisions and outcomes. A positive, growth-oriented mindset can propel us toward financial freedom and wealth-building, while a negative, limiting mindset can hold us back and perpetuate a cycle of financial struggle.

Origins of Money Mindsets

Our money mindsets – how we view and interact with money – are shaped by a complex mix of personal experiences, cultural influences, and societal norms. Understanding where these beliefs come from can help us reshape them into a more positive financial identity.

How Family Shapes Our Financial Life

From a young age, our home environment sets the stage for our future relationship with money. If you grew up in a home where money was discussed openly and managed wisely, you're likely to have a confident and proactive approach to financial matters. On the other hand, if money was a source of constant stress or conflict, you might carry negative associations with it into adulthood.

The financial habits modeled by our parents and caregivers are incredibly impactful. For example, children exposed to a scarcity mindset may grow up feeling that money is always limited, whereas those who see their parents handle money with an abundance mindset might learn to view money as a tool for creating opportunities.

Society's Impact on Our Money Beliefs

Our cultural backgrounds and the societal norms we've been exposed to can profoundly shape our money mindset. Diverse cultures may have varying attitudes toward wealth, saving, spending, and financial risk-taking, which can be passed down through generations.

In some societies, wealth and financial success may be celebrated and encouraged, while in others, there may be a stigma or discomfort associated with open discussions about money. These cultural influences can shape our beliefs about the role of money in our lives and our willingness to pursue financial growth.

Major Events That Mold Our Money Mindset

Experiencing financial hardship, such as unemployment, bankruptcy, or emergency bills, may reinforce a scarcity mindset or create fear and anxiety around money, while successfully paying off debt, receiving a windfall, or achieving financial independence can foster a sense of abundance and empowerment.

Personal experiences with money management, whether successful investments or business failures, also leave a lasting impression on our financial outlook. These experiences can either bolster our confidence in financial matters or make us wary of similar endeavors in the future.

How Education and Careers Shape Our Financial Views

Formal financial education, whether through schooling, workshops, or mentorship, gives you the knowledge and tools to cultivate a more positive and empowered relationship with money. A lack of financial literacy or exposure to healthy money management practices can reinforce negative or limiting beliefs.

Our careers also influence our financial attitudes. Different industries and professional cultures have varying norms around pay, growth opportunities, and risk, which can affect how we view our own financial prospects and security.

The Influence of Social Circles and Media on Our Finances

The media we consume and the people we surround ourselves with can also shape our money mindset. Popular culture, advertising, and social media often portray certain lifestyles and attitudes toward money, which can unconsciously influence our beliefs and behaviors.

Similarly, the spending habits and financial attitudes of our friends, family, and colleagues can create a "peer ripple effect," where we may feel pressure to align our spending or saving habits with those around us, even if they are not aligned with our true values or financial goals.

By dissecting these influences, we can begin to untangle the roots of our financial behaviors and reconstruct a healthier, more empowering money mindset. Awareness is the first step toward cultivating a more positive and empowering relationship with money.

The Impact of Money Mindsets on Financial Well-Being

Your money mindset has a profound impact on your financial future, shaping your spending habits, ability to save and invest, and build long-term wealth. Let's look at common financial mindsets and explore practical strategies to shift these perspectives toward a more positive and productive approach.

Overspending and Impulse-Buying Tendencies

- Problem: Those with a scarcity mindset or lacking financial self-control often struggle with overspending and impulse buying. This behavior is typically a response to fear of not having enough, leading to temporary relief through shopping.

- Counter Strategy: Cultivate mindfulness in spending by pausing before making purchases to assess whether it's a need or a want. Implement a waiting period for all non-essential buys, say 48 hours, to help curb impulse spending. Additionally, include in your expenses "treats" to satisfy spending urges without breaking the bank.

Lack of Financial Planning and Goal Setting

- Problem: A negative mindset may hinder individuals from engaging in financial planning and setting achievable goals. Those who feel overwhelmed by financial planning or believe they will never accumulate enough wealth may avoid planning altogether.

- Counter Strategy: Start small by setting short-term goals that are easy to achieve to build confidence. Use simple budgeting ways to track your finances and get a clear picture of where money goes. Engaging a financial advisor for initial guidance or attending financial literacy workshops can also provide structure and motivation.

Aversion to Investing or Taking Calculated Risks

- Problem: Individuals with a fear-driven mindset may view investing as too risky or feel too intimidated to engage in it due to a perceived lack of knowledge or resources.

- Counter Strategy: Educate yourself on the basics of investing through online courses, books, or workshops. Start with investments that have lower risk, such as bonds, and then slowly move into investments with higher risk. If you are unsure, seek advice from professionals to tailor an investment strategy that suits your comfort level and financial goals.

Struggles with Debt Management

- Problem: Negative money mindsets can lead to poor debt management, where individuals may accumulate debt to sustain a lifestyle beyond their means or view debt as a necessary evil without proper strategies to manage it.

- Counter Strategy: Tackle debt with a structure and strategies to settle as much and as soon as possible. Commit to not taking on new debts and focus on debt repayment. Financial counseling can also offer personalized strategies and support.

Failure to Build Emergency Funds and Save for the Future

- Problem: Saving for emergencies and future needs is often overlooked by those who do not see the immediate benefit or who are overly optimistic about future prospects without realistic planning.

- Counter Strategy: Automatically divert a part of your earnings into a banking account through direct deposit to build an emergency fund. Set realistic saving goals for the future, like retirement or children's education, and visualize the benefits to stay motivated. Educate yourself on the importance of compound interest and how saving now benefits you exponentially in the future.

Each of these counter strategies involves taking proactive steps to understand and adjust your financial behaviors. By identifying the roots of your current money mindset, you can begin to make better, conscious decisions for your healthier finances. Remember, shifting your mindset isn't just about changing how you think; it's about transforming how you act with your money day to day.

Cultivating a Healthy Money Mindset

Beginning the journey to a healthy money mindset is an adventure of self-awareness, self-reflection, and personal growth. It requires a willingness to identify and challenge limiting beliefs, reframe our relationship with money, and embrace a mindset that promotes abundance, prosperity, and financial empowerment.

Identifying Limiting Beliefs and Negative Patterns

1. To kickstart this transformation, the first step is to dig deep and identify any limiting beliefs or negative patterns that hold you back financially.

2. Reflect on your current thoughts, feelings, and behaviors about money.

3. Consider the beliefs or associations you hold around wealth, success, and financial security.

4. Do you feel anxious, fearful, or tend to avoid financial decisions?

5. Are there recurring behaviors like overspending or delaying financial planning that obstruct your financial growth?

Practical Steps:

- Keep a journal for one month where you note your spending habits, feelings about transactions, and any moments you avoid dealing with your finances.

- Review this journal to identify patterns and beliefs influencing your behavior.

When you know your limiting beliefs and negative patterns, you can start to challenge and reframe them.

Reframing Money Beliefs and Cultivating a Growth Mindset

Transforming your money beliefs involves actively replacing negative or limiting thoughts with more positive and empowering ones. This process can be facilitated through the use of affirmations, visualization exercises, and conscious effort to shift our internal dialogue.

For example, if you hold a belief that money is scarce or difficult to obtain, challenge that belief by affirming abundance and focusing on the numerous opportunities for wealth creation that exist. If you struggle with a fear of taking financial risks, reframe that fear as an opportunity for growth and potential reward.

Cultivating a growth mindset is also essential. This involves embracing a commitment to continuous learning and personal development in financial matters. Seek out educational resources, attend workshops or seminars, and surround yourself with individuals who embody a positive and empowered money mindset.

Developing a Positive and Empowering Relationship with Money

As you work to reframe your beliefs and cultivate a growth mindset, it's important to actively develop a positive and empowering relationship with money. This involves shifting your perspective from one of scarcity or fear to one of abundance and opportunity.

1. Begin to view money as a tool for creating freedom, security, and fulfillment – not as an end goal in itself. Recognize that money is a renewable resource and that there are always opportunities to generate more through hard work, creativity, and strategic financial decisions.

2. Embrace the mindset that you are on top of your finances and you can create the life and financial well-being you desire. Let go of any feelings of powerlessness or victimhood and take ownership of your financial decisions and outcomes.

Setting Realistic Financial Goals and Actionable Plans

With a positive and empowered money mindset in place, you can begin to set realistic financial objectives and construct actionable plans. Begin by defining what you want currently and also in the years to come. It can be something simple like saving for unexpected events, or paying off debt, or achieving financial independence.

Anatomize your objectives into small and achievable tasks and create a detailed plan of action. Decide the amount to save or invest every month and identify any lifestyle adjustments or income-generating opportunities that may be necessary to support your goals.

Celebrating Small Wins to Stay Motivated

Maintain a healthy money mindset as often as possible. It's important to stay motivated and keep the momentum going by celebrating your achievements, big or small.

Regularly reflect on your progress and the positive shifts in your relationship with money. Share your successes with supportive friends or communities and allow these wins to fuel your continued growth and commitment to financial empowerment.

Embracing a healthy money mindset is a transformative measure that needs commitment, self-awareness, and a willingness to challenge limiting beliefs. By cultivating a positive and empowered relationship with money, you unlock the potential for true financial freedom, security, and abundance.

Conclusion

Our relationship with money is deeply rooted in our beliefs, values, and emotional associations; it is a reflection of our money mindset. We've explored the profound impact that our money mindset can have on our financial well-being, shaping our spending habits, ability to save and invest, and capacity to build long-term wealth.

We've delved into the range of factors that contribute to the development of our money mindset, from childhood experiences and family influences to cultural conditioning and personal experiences. Understanding these origins is the first step in identifying and addressing any limiting beliefs or negative patterns that may be holding us back from financial success.

However, our money mindset is not set in stone, we have the ability to reshape it. This transformation involves:

- Reframing Our Beliefs: Challenge existing assumptions about money. If you've held onto the belief that "money is bad" consider reframing it to "money is a tool for doing good." This shift can open up new ways of thinking about wealth and what it can achieve.

- Cultivating Growth: Choose a growth-oriented mindset toward finances. Take every hurdle as a chance to learn and grow rather than obstacles that feel insurmountable.

- Building Positive Financial Relationships: Develop a relationship with money that is based on empowerment rather than fear or stress. Begin to see money as a tool that can help achieve your dreams rather than a necessary evil or a source of constant worry.

The journey toward a healthy money mindset is an ongoing process of self-awareness, self-reflection, and personal growth. It requires a willingness to confront our fears, overcome obstacles, and consistently take action toward our financial objectives.

Practical Tips for Maintaining Momentum:

- Set Clear, Achievable Goals: Break your financial goals into manageable steps. If you want to save up to buy a house, start by saving a small part of your earnings each month and gradually increase it.

- Have Friends Who Are Positive: Hang around people who are good at managing their finances. Their positive attitudes can influence and inspire your own financial behaviors.

- Stay Motivated Through Challenges: Financial journeys aren't linear. They come with ups and downs. Maintaining motivation through difficulties is crucial. Regularly remind yourself of why you started and the benefits you stand to gain.

Renovate Your Money Mindset: A Step-by-Step Guide

Just like renovating a home, revamping your outdated money mindset takes some hard work – but the result is worth it! Get ready to knock down those financially limiting beliefs and construct an all-new abundant mindset from the foundation up.

Step 1: Demolition Day

- Objective: Begin by tearing down the old, shaky beliefs that are the foundation of your current money mindset.

- Visualization: Imagine your limiting beliefs as a dilapidated house that's ready for demolition.

- Action: Write down every negative belief you have about money – things you learned as a kid or picked up along the way.

- Outcome: Just as a wrecking ball smashes old walls, visually demolish these beliefs. Picture clearing the lot to prepare for new construction, where each belief written is a brick removed from the old structure.

Step 2: Rebuild from the Ground Up

- Objective: Construct a new, robust foundation based on abundance and prosperity.

- Visualization: Think of your ability to attract wealth like a rainwater collection system. Replace the old, leaky system with new, efficient technology.

- Action: Every day, affirm positive beliefs about money. Examples include "I am worthy of wealth" and "There is enough for everyone."

- Outcome: Visualize these affirmations as rainwater filling your new, expansive storage tanks, symbolizing an overflowing abundance.

Step 3: Interior Decorating

- Objective: With a solid foundation, it's time to decorate your mindset to welcome and nurture wealth.

- Visualization: Imagine your mindset is a home. Replace old, unwelcoming mats that say "Lack" with ones that invite abundance.

- Action: Engage in behaviors that reflect an abundant life. This could be treating yourself to a small luxury or investing in something that adds value to your life.

- Outcome: Picture yourself rolling out a red carpet for wealth, creating an environment where prosperity is not just a visitor but a valued resident.

Step 4: Routine Upkeep

- Objective: Maintain your new mindset just as you would keep up a home after renovations.

- Visualization: See yourself regularly tidying and maintaining your house, to keep it in top condition.

- Action: Whenever you catch yourself slipping back into old habits or beliefs, consciously replace them with your new, abundant perspectives.

- Outcome: Regular maintenance stops small issues from becoming big problems and ensures that your mindset remains conducive to wealth.

Whenever you notice an old belief pattern creeping back, promptly prune it away with your new abundant perspectives. With consistent maintenance, wealth gains can flourish.

The more you clean out the cobwebs, the clearer it becomes to understand and apply these concepts to your own "money mindset renovation." A hands-on, step-by-step analogy makes the self-work feel completely doable. So dust off those metaphorical tool belts – your new abundant home awaits!

Chapter
Thirteen

Unhealthy Money Habits Are Keeping You Broke

UNHEALTHY MONEY HABITS ARE KEEPING YOU BROKE

Unmasking the Myths That Bind Your Wallet

How many times have you heard that more money would solve all your problems? Or perhaps you've clung to the belief that living debt-free is the only path to true financial freedom? These widespread financial myths, ingrained in our culture and conversations, subtly shape our behaviors and often, to our detriment.

In this chapter, we tackle the folklore of finance – the myths that have not only misled generations, but also perpetuated a cycle of unhealthy money habits. It's time to challenge the misconceptions that keep us from realizing our financial potential and replace them with truths that empower us.

Financial myths do more than misinform; they misdirect our financial trajectories. Believing that "once broke, always broke," can trap us in a state of despair, inhibiting proactive financial planning. Or the misconception that "you have to choose between making money and doing what you love" might lead you to undervalue your worth or overlook fulfilling opportunities that could also enhance your financial stability.

As we dissect each myth, ask yourself: What myths have I accepted as truth? How have they shaped my financial decisions? This chapter will not only reveal the reality behind these financial fables but also arm you with the knowledge to forge healthier habits. Here's what we'll dismantle together:

The Permanence of Poverty: Unpacking the belief that past financial struggles dictate a permanent economic status.

The Debt Dilemma: Rethinking the notion that all debt is dangerous, and understanding when it can actually be a leverage tool.

Income vs. Impact: Challenging the false dichotomy between earning money and pursuing passion.

Taking Control: Strategies for a healthier financial future

By the end of this chapter, you won't just question these beliefs; you'll have replaced them with strategies that foster a more truthful and productive relationship with money. Ready to turn the page on these myths and rewrite your financial story?

Let's begin by uncovering the truths that will set the foundation for your financial liberation.

1. The Path to Healthy Money Relationships

Build a Lifelong Bond with your Finances for Peace, Prosperity, and Freedom

What Good Money Relationships Look Like

A healthy relationship with money is rooted in intentionality, balance, and purpose. It's about aligning your financial behaviors with your deepest values and long-term objectives, steering clear of impulsive financial decisions. People who foster a positive money mindset consistently demonstrate habits and attitudes that secure a stable financial future.

Intentional Money Behaviors

Those in tune with their finances operate from an intentional, proactive mindset rather than being reactive to circumstance. Their money habits are purposeful, not haphazard, and include:

- *Budgeting:* Creating monthly budgets that allocate funds toward financial priorities like paying down debts, contributing to savings goals, tithing/ charitable giving, and quality experiences, while still allowing reasonable splurges. Budgets serve as a road map for conscious spending.

- *Tracking Expenses:* Consistently tracking or recording all expenses to retain full clarity over monthly cash inflows/outflows. This spotlights areas for potential cutbacks and illuminates any "money leaks" going toward non-essentials.

- *Paying Yourself First:* Making automatic transfers from each paycheck into dedicated savings, investing, and retirement accounts before spending on anything else. This enforces paying yourself and your future first.

- *Living Within Your Means:* Intentionally spending below what you earn, avoiding the trap of lifestyle inflation which leads to being cash-poor despite apparent wealth.

- *Proactive Financial Planning:* Taking a long-term, strategic view by meeting annually with financial advisors to discuss tax optimization strategies, reviewing investments, insurance coverage, estate planning, gifting, and updating financial plans as circumstances shift.

Their intentional habits ensure their day-to-day financial dealings are oriented around eventual life goals and value-alignment instead of aimless consumption or crisis reactions.

Balanced Money Attitudes

Those with healthy money dynamics also exude more balanced perspectives and priorities around wealth:

- *Defining Wealth Beyond Just Dollars:* They see wealth not just as financial accumulation but as quality of life, including fulfilling relationships, meaningful work, and personal growth. Money is just a tool, not their sole measure of prosperity.

- *Valuing Simplicity and Contentment:* There is a strong preference for simplicity and making do with "enough" rather than endlessly chasing for more.

- *Giving and Generosity Mindsets:* Instead of hoarding wealth, there's an eagerness to share it through charitable giving, impact investing, profit-sharing models for employees, scholarships, and supporting community initiatives.

- *Patience with Compounding:* They appreciate the slow and steady growth of disciplined saving and investing, understanding that true wealth builds over time.

By not viewing money as their sole source of happiness or status, they make room for richer life experiences, relationships, and societal contributions.

Action Point: Start a savings challenge today. Save a small, manageable amount daily or weekly, no matter how small, to build a habit and a cushion.

Positive/Empowering Money Relationship	Negative/Broken Money Relationship
Spends mindfully while allowing reasonable splurges	Chronic over-spending, can't stick to a budget
Consistent saving/investing toward goals	Little to no savings, living paycheck to paycheck
Calm, open attitude about discussing finances	Avoids/feels anxious discussing money
Actively manages money in an organized way	Chaotic, disorganized money management
Feels confident about managing money	Feels unsure and anxious at the thought of managing money
Views money as a tool for prosperity and security	Views money with a scarcity mindset, a source of stress and fear
Open to learning about financial skills/advice	Resistant to financial education and guidance

Emotionally Intelligent Money Reactions

Those with a sound financial mindset display emotional intelligence, particularly during tough times:

- *Resilience During Hardships:* They remain resourceful and solution-oriented when emergencies or income fluctuations inevitably strike. Rather than panicking or despairing, resilient people seek options and contingency plans to weather turbulence.

- *Accountability Over Blame:* They take responsibility for their financial state, learning from missteps instead of blaming external circumstances.

- *Reasoned Analysis Amid Scarcity Fears:* Faced with financial fears, they rely on factual analysis and sensible planning instead of making panic-driven decisions.

- *Letting Go of Entitlement:* They ground their lifestyle in gratitude and purposeful living, not entitlement or superficial success.

Overall, people with high financial emotional intelligence confront financial challenges directly with reasoned clarity and adaptability. They avoid knee-jerk reactions, resist making decisions driven by fear, and do not give in to a sense of entitlement, even in times of setbacks.

Those who have developed empowered relationships with money demonstrate behaviors that are deliberate and aligned with their core values and life goals, rather than being sporadic or off-the-cuff. They approach wealth with a balanced perspective, viewing it as a tool for achieving broader life goals.

In times of difficulty, their emotional intelligence steers them toward resilient and thoughtful strategies for recovery, avoiding impulsive or fear-based reactions. They place a strong emphasis on continuous financial learning, seeing it as vital to their growth. Their financial dealings are conducted with transparency and integrity toward themselves and their close ones. And they are proactive about their financial future, engaging in meticulous planning and regular reviews of their financial plans.

2. Your Relationship with Money Myths Debunked

Shattering the Illusions: The Truth Behind Financial Fallacies

As we work to improve our relationships with money, it's vital to proactively identify and release any lingering limiting beliefs or societal myths still obscuring your ability to create wealth. Here are some of the most common financial fables to watch out for:

Reflect on these myths and consider if they've influenced your financial decisions.

Myth: Once Broke, Always Broke

This defeating belief suggests that if you've ever struggled with money or experienced poorness, you're destined to remain in that financial state permanently. It robs you of hope for positive change.

Truth: While past struggles can create self-reinforcing negative patterns, they don't have to become a life sentence. By actively improving your financial mindset, habits, and skills, you can overcome these barriers. Consistent effort creates new results over time.

Action Point: Start a savings challenge today. Save a small, manageable amount daily or weekly, no matter how small, to build a habit and a cushion.

Myth: Financial Problems Are Solely External

This view blames all of your money issues on forces entirely out of your control – economic conditions, employment situations, investments gone wrong, etc. It denies your ability to steer your own outcomes.

Truth: While external factors matter, you are the principal architect of your financial realities based on your personal money behaviors, skills, and energy around wealth. Owning empowers positive change.

Action Point: Check your monthly spending and find at least two expenses you can control or reduce. Take action within the next week to adjust these expenses.

Myth: Financial Problems Are Unchangeable

This pessimistic outlook frames your financial station in life as hopelessly set in stone with no chance of improvement. It keeps you stuck by describing a fixed state.

Truth: Life is constantly moving and changing – including your finances. With intention and action, you can absolutely transform your circumstances and relationship with money over time.

Action Point: Set one financial goal that challenges your current situation. Outline ways to achieve the goal and start with the first step immediately.

Myth: Debt is Inescapable

This belief portrays debt as a permanent trap, suggesting that once you fall into debt, escape is impossible.

Truth: While some debt, like mortgages, can be part of a healthy financial strategy, you can break free from high-interest debt through disciplined planning and smart financial strategies. View debt as a temporary challenge, not a life sentence.

Action Point: List all your debts in order of interest rate. Make an extra payment, even if small, toward the debt with the highest rate today. Find a cheaper option for high-interest loans.

Myth: You Have to Choose Between Money or Meaning

This belief sets up only two choices, that you can either be wealthy or live a life with purpose and positive impact, but not have both simultaneously. It creates an illusion of having to sacrifice one for the other.

Truth: It's entirely possible to build wealth while also aligning that prosperity with your values and making a difference. Many of history's most successful entrepreneurs and investors have also been incredible philanthropists. Don't let this myth limit your thinking.

> *Action Point:* Reflect on what gives your life meaning and how you can align your finances with this purpose. Make one financial decision this month that supports this personal mission, such as investing in a course or donating to a cause you care about.

Having addressed these financial myths and the truths that counter them, the next step is to apply this knowledge. Each action point provided is designed to help you practically engage with and overcome these misconceptions. From initiating savings challenges to reevaluating your spending habits, setting realistic goals, strategically managing debt, and aligning your finances with your values – each action is a step toward clearer financial understanding and control.

We encourage you to implement these steps diligently and monitor your progress. Financial improvement is an iterative process that benefits from persistent effort and ongoing evaluation. Use the insights gained here as tools to build a stronger financial foundation. Start with the actions outlined, and slowly expand your efforts as you feel more assured.

3. Money Matters of the Heart: Navigating the Financial Dynamics of Your Relationships

How Your Relationship with Money Shapes Your Closest Ties and Influences Everyday Interactions

From romance to family, careers to self-worth, your financial attitude speaks volumes about the bonds you build. Money can't buy happiness, but it undeniably influences the quality of our relationships. This section explores how deeply your financial situation is intertwined with your connections to others and even yourself, shaping choices, setting boundaries, and acting as a filter for compatibility. Let's examine the profound impact of your "money mindset" on your life's relationships.

Romantic Relationships

The Financial Balancing Act

In romantic relationships, money often acts as both a foundation and a potential fault line. Whether you're a thrifty saver or embrace a more carefree spending style, your spending habits shape your relationship with your partner. Misalignments in financial priorities can spark conflicts, as seen when impulsive purchases clash with a partner's goal of saving. To foster harmony, consider establishing regular "financial date nights" where both partners are open to discuss money goals and spending strategies, turning potential conflicts into cooperative planning.

Financial Date Night Guide

Objective: Strengthen financial communication between partners and align on financial goals.

Frequency: Monthly or quarterly discussions.

Checklist of Topics:

- Review of current financial status (e.g., savings, debts).

- Discussion of what you want to achieve over time.

- Budget review and adjustment based on recent spending.

- Planning for large upcoming expenditures (e.g., vacations, home improvements).

- Personal spending allowances and rules.

Tips for a Productive Conversation:

- Schedule the conversation at a time when both partners are relaxed.

- Start with positive financial achievements since the last meeting.

- Use supportive language, avoiding blame.

- Set actionable goals together and agree on steps to achieve them.

Family Relationships

Family Fractures: The Influence of Money Mindsets on Family Bonds

Money can either strengthen or strain family bonds. Issues like inheritance disputes or differing views on financial support can create lasting rifts. Proactive communication is key – setting clear financial boundaries and expectations can prevent many conflicts. Organizing family meetings to discuss financial matters transparently can help ensure that everyone's expectations and contributions are aligned, thereby fostering a supportive family environment.

Family Financial Meeting Template

Objective: Facilitate open and effective financial discussions among family members.

Preparation Steps:

- Put together all the documents (bank statements, bills, investment summaries).
- Each member lists their financial concerns and goals.

Sample Agenda:

- Review of the family budget and recent spending.
- Discussion on large upcoming expenses (education, vacations).
- Allocation of financial responsibilities (who pays what bills).
- Setting or reviewing long-term financial goals (college funds, retirement savings).

Guidelines for Mediation:

- Allow each member to express their views without interruption.

- Focus on solutions rather than problems.

- Agree to revisit unresolved issues at the next meeting.

Friendships

Maintaining Connections Across Financial Divides

Economic differences can strain even the strongest friendships, particularly if financial disparities limit shared activities. To maintain these important connections, be open about your financial boundaries and suggest diverse activities that accommodate all budgets. This openness ensures that friendships can thrive based on mutual respect and understanding, rather than financial capacities.

Budget-Friendly Activity Planner

Objective: Maintain a vibrant social life across different financial situations.

Activity Ideas:

- Outdoor activities like hiking, biking, or picnics.

- Potluck dinners where each friend brings a dish.

- Game nights at home with board games or video games.

- Community events like free concerts or local festivals.

Planning Tips:

- Rotate the choice of activity among friends to ensure variety.

- Be upfront about costs when planning, providing a range of options.

- Encourage honesty about financial comfort levels without judgment.

Professional Work Relationships

Creating Equity at Work

In the workplace, perceptions of financial inequality can lead to jealousy and competition. To mitigate these issues, advocate for transparent policies regarding compensation and promotion. Encouraging a culture of openness and fairness in financial dealings at work can promote a more collaborative and supportive professional environment.

 **Compensation Transparency Framework**

Objective: Build trust through clarity on compensation practices.

Steps for HR/Management:

- Regularly update and distribute a clear compensation structure.

- Organize informational sessions on how salaries and bonuses are determined.

- Provide anonymous suggestion boxes for employees to voice concerns or suggestions.

Prepare specific questions about compensation before meetings

- Request regular reviews or feedback sessions to discuss performance and compensation.

- Use resources like industry salary surveys to understand fair market compensation.

Social Relationships

The Social Tapestry: Money Mindset Influence on Societal Ties

Social circles often reflect socioeconomic status, but expanding your network beyond economic boundaries can enrich your social life. Participate in activities that require more time than money, such as volunteering or joining interest groups, to meet a diverse range of people and form relationships based on shared interests, not financial status.

 **Inclusive Social Event Guide**

Objective: Design social events that are welcoming to people from all financial backgrounds.

Event Ideas:

- Community service projects that focus on giving back rather than spending.

- Cultural nights where guests share music, art, or food from their backgrounds.

- Sports events, like a community soccer game or a frisbee match.

Organization Tips:

- Clearly communicate that financial contributions are optional.

- Provide options for participation that don't require financial expenditure.

- Foster an atmosphere of inclusion by highlighting the value of each person's contribution, regardless of its financial nature.

Recognizing and addressing the influence of money on relationships is crucial. By adopting strategies that promote financial transparency and understanding, you can improve not only your economic well-being but also your interpersonal relationships. Continuously engage in discussions about money matters to cultivate an environment of respect and mutual support across all areas of your life.

4. The Deeper Meaning of Money: Perspectives for a Harmonious Relationship

Reflecting on Cultural Conditioning

From a young age, we are conditioned to chase after money and material wealth as primary symbols of success and pathways to fulfillment. Yet, many who achieve great financial prosperity find themselves paradoxically unfulfilled. Why is that? Have you ever felt that no matter how much you earn, true happiness remains elusive?

Money as a Means, Not an End

At its core, money is inherently neutral – it is a resource and tool that can be wielded for positive or negative ends. A harmonious relationship with money begins by shifting our perspectives away from seeing it as the end goal, and toward understanding its deeper meaning as a facilitator for personal growth, freedom, and creating a life aligned with our deepest values.

Whether we are raised with financial scarcity or abundance, many of us unconsciously internalize the belief that more money will allow us to achieve freedom, security, and lasting happiness. We think, "If only I could make X amount of money, then I could quit my unfulfilling job, travel the world, or never worry about finances again."

Understanding Money's Limited Role in Achieving Happiness

While having sufficient financial resources is advantageous for increasing our range of opportunities in life, a wealth of research demonstrates that money alone does not lead to greater well-being or life satisfaction beyond a certain baseline level. A ground-breaking study by Princeton researchers found that although life evaluation rises with annual income, there is no further progress beyond an annual income of $75,000.

Essentially, money can alleviate some of the misery and stress that poverty and lack of access to basic needs brings but beyond a moderate level of financial means, additional income has a decreasing impact on our day-to-day happiness and quality of life. So, if money alone doesn't bring the profound sense of flourishing we crave, what is the deeper meaning and purpose of pursuing financial prosperity? Used with intentionality, money can be a powerful tool to facilitate experiences, opportunities, and positive impact – but only if we don't treat it as the final destination.

Exercise: Assess your current financial goals and how they relate to your personal happiness. Are there goals driven purely by financial gain that might be redirected toward more fulfilling endeavors?

The Freedom Money Can Provide

One of the most compelling aspects of having sufficient financial resources is the freedom and autonomy it can provide. When we aren't constantly struggling to make ends meet or stuck in a career that slowly dampens our spirit due to lack of other options, we gain agency over how we spend our limited lives.

With enough money for a reasonable lifestyle, we become empowered to invest in personal growth and exploration through education, skill development, travel, and new experiences that expand our awareness.

We gain the freedom to take calculated career risks to follow our intrinsic callings, whether that's pursuing entrepreneurship, creative expression, research and innovation, or transition into more purposeful work. Our options multiply when we aren't solely bound by the restraints of making money for survival.

In addition, having enough financial means opens up greater freedom to contribute our time, energy, and money toward causes and initiatives that are meaningful to us and can positively impact the world.

At its highest vision, having a harmonious relationship with money and welcoming enough of its flow into our lives grants us the liberty to fully self-actualize and leave a positive legacy – a freedom that transcends purely materialistic motivations.

How could greater financial freedom help you pursue a life more aligned with your values?

Redefining Success Beyond Financial Wealth

Our typical cultural notions around success are tied to net worth and accumulating wealth. However, true success might better be defined by the richness of our relationships, our contributions to society, and our ability to find joy in simple experiences.

For example, what about the value we place on the richness of our relationships? Our curiosity, creativity, and persistent pursuit of growth? Our positive impact on communities, causes, and future generations? Our ability to find joy through simple experiences and express gratitude for what we already have?

When our vision is consumption and wealth-obsessed, we inadvertently disregard the nuances of what makes a life truly well-lived. We may sacrifice family, integrity, personal well-being, and concern for social and environmental consequences in pursuit of endless money-making.

Developing a harmonious relationship with money requires redefining the criteria for what we view as "success." Real success might better be defined in our ability to align our financial goals with sources of deeper purpose and meaning beyond just personal material gain.

Money as a Tool for Personal Growth

From this expansive view of success, we can utilize money as a powerful tool to guide our personal evolution. With financial resources comes increased access to education, development opportunities, resources for healing and well-being, and the gift of more quality time to dedicate toward rewarding pursuits.

At its highest expression, cultivated wealth serves our awakening – fueling us to grow beyond our limiting beliefs, to deepen our presence and service, and ultimately, to positively impact the collective consciousness. An abundance of money then is not just a means for acquiring toys and status symbols, but a profound vehicle for actualizing our fullest human potential.

In essence, money serves its highest purpose when viewed through the lens of consciousness evolution: As a resource for fueling our individual and collective awakening, instead of perpetuating ignorance and suffering through mindless hoarding or misuse.

Integrating these harmonious perspectives allows us to experience the freedom of money rather than its imprisoning potential. In doing so, we unlock wealth as a catalyst for the full blossoming of our humanity – our creativity, service, integrity, wisdom, and positive impact.

5. Transforming Fiscal Fears into Financial Empowerment

Turning Money Worries into Wealth Opportunities

Introduction: The Impact of Your Financial Attitude

Often, we're taught to see money as the ultimate measure of success and a key to happiness. However, Emma's journey illustrates a different truth. Emma had climbed to impressive heights in her job, earning more than she had ever imagined. Yet, despite her sizeable income and luxurious lifestyle, she felt a persistent sense of emptiness. This prompted her to explore how her beliefs about money might be influencing her overall satisfaction with life.

Understanding the Power of Mindset

Our financial reality is deeply shaped by our beliefs. Negative thoughts such as "I cannot be rich" or "money is bad" can create a barrier to achieving true financial well-being. Emma realized that her discomfort with wealth was rooted in her childhood, where money was always seen as a source of conflict. She began to rewrite her financial narrative, replacing old fears with new, empowering beliefs, learning to view money as a tool for doing good and achieving personal growth.

From Scarcity to Abundance

One of the most pervasive and damaging money mindsets is a scarcity mentality – the belief that there will never be enough money or resources. Emma once took the view that there is always a shortage of things, afraid that everything could run out. This fear made her miss out on opportunities to grow her wealth. She adopted positive affirmations like "there is always more where that came from," which shifted her focus from fear to possibility. This mental switch encouraged her to make smarter investment decisions and explore avenues for passive income, understanding that resources were not limited but plentiful. From this mindset of plenty, you open yourself up to pursue ambitious financial goals, invest boldly, and develop sources of passive income and residual revenue streams.

Turn Self-Doubt into Confidence

Another prevalent negative money mindset is being rife with self-doubt and a perceived lack of capability around financial matters. "I'll never be good with numbers," "investing seems too complicated," or "I always make poor money choices" are all examples of this disempowering inner critic arising. These beliefs foster inaction, financial paralysis, and avoidance of taking control of your money situation.

Lacking confidence in financial matters, Emma initially felt overwhelmed by investment options and financial planning. She committed to educating herself, starting with basic budgeting and gradually tackling more complex financial strategies. As her knowledge grew, so did her confidence, which she reinforced by repeating, "Each step I take in learning finances proves my capability."

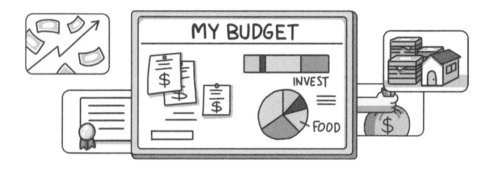

Cultivating Patience to Discipline

In our current era of instant gratification and easy debt, many people struggle with an impatience mindset, prioritizing immediate desires and impulse purchases over sustainable, long-term financial habits. This short-sighted view can lead to cycles of overspending, credit card debt, and a lack of forward progress on financial goals like saving, investing, and building wealth.

Used to the immediate gratification of impulse buys, Emma learned the hard way that such habits undermine long-term financial stability. She began visualizing her future self, enjoying the benefits of disciplined savings and smart spending.

Imagining her more secure future helped her prioritize her financial actions today, reducing frivolous expenditures in favor of significant, long-term goals.

Reframing this mindset requires developing greater self-discipline, delaying gratification, and considering the future rewards of your actions today. Visualize your future self, grateful for the building of habits like consistent budgeting, aggressive saving, and avoiding needless consumer debt and impatient purchases.

Overcoming Entitlement with Gratitude

For those on the opposite end of the spectrum, feelings of entitlement and expectation around money can severely limit financial potential. In place of this entitled perspective, cultivate an abundance mindset rooted in hard work, resourcefulness, and an attitude of gratitude for opportunities and anything you've earned yourself. Express daily gratitude for what you have while also motivating yourself by envisioning ambitious stretch goals to create even greater abundance. Mantras like "My work ethic, creativity and effort allow me to thrive" and "I have enough for my needs, and more is on its way" reinforce this positive shift.

Foster Empowering New Beliefs

Ultimately, the process of transforming negative mindsets into positive ones takes consistent, diligent practice – just as reframing any deeply-ingrained habit requires dedication. Spend time each day in meditation or quiet reflection and monitor your stream of thoughts around money. When a limiting belief arises, consciously stop that thought pattern and replace it with an affirmation or new empowering belief about your relationship with money.

For example, if you catch yourself thinking "I'm terrible with managing money," interject with a new belief like "I am learning and applying smart money habits every day." Or when feelings of scarcity creep in with thoughts like "I'll never get out of debt," reframe it as "My income continues to rise, and debt is leaving my life for good." Over time, as you reinforce these new positive mindsets about money, they'll become automatic default patterns in your brain.

Support Your New Money Mindsets

In addition to the internal work of reframing your thoughts, you can fortify these new positive belief systems by incorporating practices and habits that support and align with your desired money mindset. To reinforce her new mindset, Emma made practical changes in her daily life. She kept a journal where she noted positive financial updates, big or small, to remind herself of the abundance around her. She also established regular intervals to review and adjust her financial plan, ensuring it aligned with her evolving goals.

Affirmations and visualization exercises can also be powerful tools for solidifying new empowering money mindsets. Engage all your senses by imagining in vivid detail the life you'll manifest by adopting an abundance perspective, a spirit of generosity, patience for the wealth-building process, and radical responsibility for your financial future.

Of course, mindset alone is not enough – you must combine your reframed internal beliefs with consistent action steps and proven financial management strategies. However, when you operate from a foundation of positive and empowering money mindsets, you'll have the motivation, resilience, and perspective to more effectively implement wealth-building systems in your life.

Money Mindsets Are Not Stagnant

It's also important to understand that our mindsets around money are not stagnant, inflexible states. We have not only the ability, but the necessity of regularly assessing, releasing, and upgrading our money mindsets as we progress through different life stages and levels of income and net worth. The limiting beliefs and attitudes that may have served you at one point could eventually become hindrances to further evolution.

For instance, a scarcity mindset rooted in avoiding all investment risk may help you initially build a modest nest egg through aggressive saving habits. However, that same fear-based mentality could prevent you from ever growing that modest savings into long-term wealth through investing, business ownership, or passive income streams. At that stage, you'd need to adopt a more opportunistic abundance mindset focused on calculated intelligent risks and managing the upside.

Embrace the Truth: Your Mindset Matters

Our relationship with money is deeply intertwined with our relationship to ourselves. The negative or positive mindsets we hold about wealth and our perceived self-worth are reflections of the same beliefs. True transformation happens on both a mindset and a self-actualization level to unlock financial abundance.

Like Emma, we can see that our beliefs about money evolve. By continually reassessing and adjusting our financial mindsets, we embrace the opportunity for growth and improvement. Through self-awareness, education, and a shift in perspective, we can transform our relationship with money from one of stress and restriction to one of empowerment and freedom. Start small, think big, and remember, the journey to financial freedom begins with a single positive shift in thought.

6. Conclusion

Embracing a Life of Perpetual Prosperity

Throughout this chapter, we've explored how our relationship with money extends far beyond just the numbers in our bank accounts. Our financial realities are deeply intertwined with our mindsets, emotions, core beliefs, and how we invest our energy. Having a broken, disempowered relationship with money doesn't just keep us broke financially – it restricts the full experience of freedom, peace, and thriving in all aspects of our lives.

Key Lessons and Insights

Some of the core lessons and insights we've covered include:

- Our societal programming often instills dysfunctional patterns like scarcity thinking and tying our self-worth to our net worth.

- Early experiences shape deep neural grooves that drive our unconscious financial behaviors as adults.

- Emotions such as shame, guilt, and fear frequently underpin limiting money beliefs and habits.

- Viewing money as either "good" or "bad" fosters an unhealthy relationship where we inadvertently attract what we inwardly resist.

- Awareness of our incoherent thoughts and feelings toward money helps us correct our course toward wealth.

- Healing core wounds and realigning our financial goals with our true values is crucial in transforming our money relationship.

Each of these lessons reinforces that our financial difficulties reflect deeper, unaddressed areas within ourselves. Financial struggle often mirrors the parts of us that remain unintegrated, holding back our overall potential. Having a broken money relationship keeps us spiritually, emotionally, psychologically, and energetically "broke" in ways that sabotage our wholeness and potential. Which is why evolving our relationship with money is about far more than just acquiring wealth.

Ongoing Self-Work and Commitment

Enhancing our relationship with money is a continuous journey of inner exploration. It's not about a single moment of realization but a lifelong practice of self-awareness, curiosity, and a willingness to confront and release our limitations. As we peel back layers of old stories and self-destructive patterns, new layers emerge, each requiring integration and healing. This ongoing process is the essence of personal growth, enabling us to embody the fullest expression of ourselves. Money, in this context, serves as a powerful catalyst, illuminating our hidden crevices and accelerating our journey toward self-actualization.

Embracing this journey with radical self-responsibility and treating it as a sacred privilege allows our relationship with money to transform into one of our greatest strengths. With intention and compassion, we can reshape our financial mindsets and habits into forces that attract and maintain a life rich with joy and abundance.

To support this transformation, consider starting a daily practice where you reflect on your financial decisions and how they align with your emotional state. Keep a journal to track these reflections and rejoice with every advancement that you make. Regularly set aside time to check in and make changes to your financial plan to keep up with your evolving goals and values.

Ultimately, money is just a tool, but when wielded with wisdom and clarity, it can enrich our lives immensely. By committing to a deeper understanding and more conscious handling of our finances, we invite not only material wealth but also a profound sense of personal fulfillment and freedom.

Chapter
Fourteen

Lacking a Financial Road Map Is Keeping You Broke

LACKING A FINANCIAL ROAD MAP IS KEEPING YOU BROKE

In life, we all have dreams, aspirations, and goals that we strive to achieve. From getting a home, getting married, having kids to enjoying a comfortable retirement, you need to plan and work toward achieving them. Imagine a financial road map as your personal guidebook, detailing every twist and turn on the path to these aspirations. It doesn't just chart the course – it lights the way, ensuring each step you take moves you closer to your goals, not further away.

Take Javier, a creative graphic designer with a flair for vibrant colors but a faint grasp of numbers. At 30, his dreams were as vivid as his designs – traveling the world, buying a studio, and financial freedom by 50. Yet, with every paycheck, he found himself in a recurring loop of short-term gratifications – tech gadgets, impromptu trips with friends, and lavish dinners. Without a map to navigate his finances, Javier saw his dreams blur with each swipe of his credit card.

With a financial road map, you know how to prioritize your goals, save, invest, and better manage your finances. Throughout this chapter, we will help you understand what this road map is about and its importance in achieving your life goals. We will delve into the standard financial road map template, a general framework for common life events and milestones.

By the end of this chapter, you will have a deep understanding of the financial road map concept and the tools to personalize your road map to fit your life aspirations.

1. What's a Money Road Map and Why Should You Care?

What Is a Financial Road Map?

Think of a financial road map as your personal finance GPS. It's a detailed, customized plan that not only charts your current financial position but also outlines where you want to be and the best routes to get there. It's a guide for you to manage finances effectively and work toward all your desired financial milestones with clarity and precision. With the road map, you can stay focused, make informed financial decisions, and track your progress along the way. Without one, you can get lost and run out of money.

Key Functions of a Financial Road Map

Tracking Your Spending: Knowing Where Every Dollar Goes

Tracking where you spend can give you an idea why you have very little savings. It's like taking a snapshot of all your spending and commitments – you see exactly where every dollar goes. By watching your expenses closely, you can avert overspending.

Budgeting: Assigning Roles to Your Money

Budgeting is about giving every dollar a purpose before it even lands in your wallet. Whether it's for essentials like rent and groceries or fun stuff like nights out, a good budget helps spread out your earnings efficiently over all your spending needs. Think of it as casting your money in specific roles – some funds are earmarked for living expenses, some for savings, and the rest for entertainment. Expense management isn't about restrictions. It's about mindful spending with accountability, ensuring you don't live beyond your means.

Saving for Goals: Reserving Funds for Your Dreams

Ever dreamt of lounging on a tropical beach or owning a cozy cottage? A financial road map helps you turn that "wish" into a "reality" by setting and saving for specific goals. It helps you decide how much to save regularly to fund your ambitions, whether it's a vacation next winter or a future home.

Benefits of Having a Financial Road Map

- **Direction and Clarity:** Just as a GPS navigates you to your destination without getting lost, a financial road map offers a clear path to your financial goals. It shows you where to cut expenses and how to allocate more to your priorities like saving for a home.

- **Motivation and Accountability:** With a road map, you see your progress, stay on track, and resist the temptation to spend impulsively. It's akin to having a fitness coach who keeps you motivated to stick with your exercise routine.

- **Reduced Stress:** Money issues are a major stressor for many. A clear financial plan reduces anxiety by providing a structured approach to managing your money. Knowing your financial actions are aligned with your goals can help you sleep better, freeing you from constant worry about your finances.

A financial road map is not only a tool; it's your money co-pilot. It brings clarity, drives you to make purposeful spending choices aligned with your personal values and goals, and cultivates a sense of security, and provides peace of mind. By following this navigator, you ensure that each financial decision moves you closer to a future where your financial worries are minimized and your dreams are maximized.

2. The Perils of Lacking a Financial Road Map

Not having a financial road map isn't just inconvenient; it can set you up for some severe financial setbacks. Let's explore some of the risks that come from navigating your financial journey without a clear map:

Reactive versus Proactive Management: Without a road map, you're likely to find yourself constantly reacting to financial problems as they pop up. This can prevent you from taking strategic, proactive steps toward your long-term financial goals, leaving you always a step behind in your finances.

Directionless Spending: It's easy to lose your way without a compass. Similarly, without a financial road map, you may drift aimlessly, vulnerable to impulsive purchases and poor investment decisions that can derail your financial plans.

Living Paycheck to Paycheck: Lacking a plan often leads to spending everything you earn as soon as it hits your account, leaving nothing for savings. This cycle is precarious, making it tough to manage unexpected expenses or emergencies.

Accumulating Debt: Without a disciplined financial plan, spending can easily outpace income, leading to unnecessary use of credit. This habit can spiral into a daunting debt trap, compounded by rising interest charges that can choke your financial freedom.

Failure to Plan for Life Events: Significant events like buying a house, starting a family, or retiring require intricate planning. Without a road map, you risk being financially unprepared for these life milestones, which could put your dreams out of reach.

Vulnerability to Uncertainties: Life is unpredictable. A robust financial road map includes safeguards for unforeseen events like job loss or emergencies. Without it, you're left exposed, potentially jeopardizing your financial stability.

Increased Stress and Anxiety: The absence of a clear financial plan can amplify stress and anxiety over money. It's tough to feel secure when you're unsure about your financial standing and future, impacting not just your peace of mind but also your quality of life.

Lack of Accountability and Motivation: A good financial road map is about tracking progress and celebrating financial milestones. Without it, staying disciplined and motivated can be challenging.

Missing Opportunities: A thoughtful financial road map helps you spot and seize opportunities – be it investments, tax savings, or ways to earn more. Without one, these chances might pass you by unnoticed.

Financial Insecurity: Ultimately, the lack of a financial road map makes it difficult to navigate through life's storms or to plan confidently for the future.

The absence of this crucial planning tool can leave you reacting to financial emergencies rather than preparing for them, leading to aimless spending and trapping you in a perpetual cycle of debt. It can prevent you from preparing for sudden life changes and opportunities, increasing your financial stress and potentially compromising your long-term security. By understanding these risks, the value of a detailed and proactive financial plan becomes clear, highlighting the need for a road map that not only secures your present but also paves the way to a stable and fulfilling financial future.

3. The Financial Road Map: A Standard Template

The Foundation of a Financial Road Map: Goals, Plans, and Safety Nets

At its core, your financial road map is all about you and what you want in life. At the heart of all financial road maps are three core components: financial goals, financial plans, and financial safety nets.

Financial Goals: Setting Your Destination

Think of financial goals as destinations along your financial journey. They are specific targets or milestones that you aim to achieve within a defined time frame. They give you purpose, direction, and motivation, helping you focus your efforts and allocate resources effectively. Therefore, having clearly defined and specific money objectives is important. Here's how to think about them:

- **Short-term Goals** (1–3 years): Examples include savings for unexpected events, debt reduction or deposit for a house.

- **Medium-term Goals** (3–7 years): These may include starting a family, funding a kid's education, purchase of a vacation property, or achieving a specific investment portfolio value.

- **Long-term Goals** (7+ years): Common long-term goals include retirement planning, achieving financial independence, and retiring early.

Financial Plans: Mapping Your Route

Once you know your destinations, you need a clear route to get there. This is your financial plan – a comprehensive strategy encompassing all aspects of your financial life. A financial plan should include details of your financial life, budgeting, saving, investing, debt management, tax planning, and risk management.

- **Budgeting and Expense Management:** At the core of any financial plan is good budgetary know-how; know where you spend, and having allocations for savings, investments, and debt repayment is crucial for achieving your financial goals.

- **Saving and Investment Strategies:** Your money plan should include specific strategies for building wealth through savings and investments. This may involve contributing to tax-advantaged retirement accounts, and diversified investments.

- **Debt Management and Elimination:** Effective debt management is essential for financial stability and progress. Your financial plan should outline strategies to settle all the debts and avoiding the accumulation of new ones.

Financial Safety Nets: Securing Your Journey

No journey is without its bumps, and financial journeys are no different. That's where safety nets come in. They ensure you can continue toward your goals, even when unexpected challenges arise:

Emergency Funds and Liquid Savings: It's important to have the cash to cover for emergencies such as accidents, illnesses, home repairs, and unemployment. It is recommended to save up to six months of expenditures in a liquid, easily accessible account.

Insurance Coverage: Insurance is another essential safety net that protects you and your loved ones from potential risks and liabilities. This may include protection against death, illnessses, and house damage, among others. Ensure that your insurance coverage is adequate and tailored to your specific needs.

Diversified Investments: Don't put all your eggs into one basket. Diversify your investment portfolio to smoothen fluctuations. By doing so, you won't be overdependent on the performance of a single investment.

Backup Plans: Having plan B involves expecting challenges or setbacks that could derail your financial plans. This may include creating a plan for job loss, disability, or other life-altering events, ensuring that you have the resources and strategies in place to weather such storms.

Characteristics of Financial Goals, Plans, and Safety Nets

Understanding the essential attributes of financial goals, plans, and safety nets can enhance their effectiveness. Here's how to build these components effectively:

Financial Goals

Specific and Measurable: Well-defined financial goals should be specific and measurable, leaving no room for ambiguity. Clearly state the desired outcome, the amount of money needed, and the time frame for achievement.

Realistic and Achievable: While it's essential to set ambitious goals, they should also be reasonable and attainable based on your present situation, earnings, and resources. Unattainable objectives are bothersome and discouraging, hindering your progress.

Time-Bound and Prioritized: Each financial goal should have a specific timeline or deadline associated with it. Additionally, prioritizing your goals based on their potential financial impact guides you to divide up your resources adeptly while staying focused on what matters most.

Financial Plans

Comprehensive and Holistic: An effective financial plan should take a comprehensive and holistic approach, addressing budgeting, savings, investing, loan management, tax planning, and risk management.

Flexible and Adaptable: Life is unpredictable. Your financial plan needs to be adjustable to changing events. Regular reviews and changes should be built into the plan to ensure its continued relevance and effectiveness.

Money Safety Nets

Adequate and Appropriate Coverage: Your financial safety nets, such as insurance policies and emergency funds, should provide adequate coverage and protection developed on your detailed needs and position. Insufficient coverage can leave you vulnerable to significant financial setbacks.

Diversified and Risk-Managed: Just as with your investments, your safety nets should be diversified and risk-managed. This may involve having multiple insurance policies or spreading your emergency fund across different accounts to mitigate the impact of potential risks.

Accessible and Liquid When Needed: In times of emergency or unexpected events, your safety nets should be easily accessible and liquid. You'll need the cash to make payments. If you don't have the cash-in-hand, you may need to borrow, which could lead to financial strains.

Factors That Influence Individual Road Maps

- **Lifestyle:** An individual's desired lifestyle, such as the choice to remain single or have children, can significantly impact their financial road map. Those who prioritize a more minimalist lifestyle may have different financial goals and strategies compared to those who desire a more extravagant standard of living.

- **Values and Priorities:** Personal values and priorities play a crucial role in shaping one's financial road map. For example, some individuals may prioritize financial independence or early retirement, while others may place greater emphasis on philanthropic endeavors or leaving a legacy.

- **Career Path:** The chosen career path can also influence the financial road map. Entrepreneurs and small business owners may have different financial goals and challenges compared to those in traditional employment. Similarly, individuals pursuing advanced degrees or specialized professions may have unique financial considerations.

Customizing Your Financial Road Map

The standard financial road map serves as a basic framework, yet it's important to adjust it to reflect individual circumstances, values, and aspirations. No two financial journeys are the same, and your road map should be as individual as you are.

Example of the Different Routes and Road Maps

Single versus Married/Partnered: The financial road map for a single individual may differ significantly from that of a married or partnered couple. Singles may have more flexibility in allocating resources toward personal goals, such as travel or early retirement, while couples may need to consider joint financial obligations, such as shared living expenses and family planning.

Entrepreneurship versus Traditional Employment: Entrepreneurs and small business owners often face unique financial challenges and opportunities. Their road map may involve securing funding, managing cash flow, and navigating the complexities of self-employment taxes and benefits. In contrast, those in traditional employment may have a more predictable income stream and access to employer-sponsored retirement plans.

Advanced Education or Professional Degrees: Individuals pursuing advanced degrees or specialized professions may need to account for everything becoming more expensive. Their financial road map may involve strategies for managing student loan debt and planning for potential income increases associated with their chosen field.

Prioritizing Financial Independence or Early Retirement: Some individuals may prioritize achieving financial independence or retiring early, which uses different saving and investing strategies, and managing expenses. Their financial road map may involve aggressive wealth-building strategies, such as maximizing retirement account contributions and pursuing passive income streams.

Aligning Your Road Map with Personal Values and Goals: Customizing your financial road map is not just about adapting to individual circumstances; it's about orienting your financial strategies with your personal values and life goals. Additionally, your financial road map should reflect your broader life aspirations. If travel and exploration are important to you, your road map may involve budgeting for frequent trips or even planning for extended periods of travel during retirement.

Reevaluating and Adjusting Your Road Map

Remember, a financial road map isn't set in stone. As your life evolves – perhaps with a career change, marriage, or the arrival of a new family member – so should your financial strategies. Regularly revisiting and tweaking your road map ensures it stays aligned with your current needs and future aspirations.

Potential Setbacks and Pitfalls

Even the best-laid plans can face hurdles. Understanding these potential challenges and their root causes can help you anticipate and mitigate their impact on your financial road map.

Challenges Related to Financial Goals:

- *Unrealistic or Vague Goals:* Goals that are too ambitious or not clearly defined often result in disheartenment and loss of direction. Make sure your objectives are realistic and precisely articulated to keep you motivated and on track.

- *Lack of Prioritization and Focus:* Spreading your resources too thin across multiple goals can dilute your efforts. Focus on prioritizing your objectives developed based on their importance and immediacy.

- *Rigidity in Goals:* Life's unpredictable nature requires flexibility in your goals. Adjust them as your personal and financial circumstances evolve to keep them relevant and attainable.

Challenges Related to Financial Plans:

- *Inadequate Budgeting:* A poorly managed budget can lead to overspending and accumulating debt. Keep a disciplined track of your spending to be sure that it is in line with your money objectives.

- *Inconsistent Saving and Investing:* Regular saving and prudent investing are pillars of financial growth. Avoid procrastination and stay committed to your investment strategies to build and maintain wealth.

- *Poor Debt Management:* Efficiently working out your borrowings is important for your financial health. Develop a strategic plan for debt repayment to avoid overwhelming financial burdens.

Challenges Related to Financial Safety Nets:

- *Insufficient Emergency Funds:* An inadequate emergency fund can leave you financially vulnerable during unexpected events. Aim to maintain a fund that covers 3–6 months of living expenses.

- *Lack of Adequate Insurance:* Underinsuring yourself or your assets can lead to significant financial exposure during emergencies. Regularly review your insurance needs to ensure you have comprehensive coverage.

- *Poor Investment Diversification:* Overexposure to a single investment type or market can risk significant losses. Diversify your portfolio to mitigate risks and protect your assets from market volatilities.

The Certainties and Uncertainties in Every Financial Plan

Financial planning is an ongoing journey that adapts to life's varying phases, reflecting both predictable and unforeseen changes.

Certainties:

- **Life Events:** There are certain life events that are relatively predictable and can be planned for, such as education expenses, buying a home, retirement, and end-of-life planning. These events have a significant financial impact and require proactive planning and saving.

- **Fixed Expenses:** Certain expenses are relatively fixed and predictable, such as lease or housing loan payments, accommodation expenses, insurance contributions, and credit payments. Budgeting and allocating funds for these expenses is a certainty in financial planning.

- **Retirement Needs:** While the exact amount needed for retirement may vary, the need for retirement planning is a certainty for most individuals. Calculating retirement expenses, saving, and investing for retirement are essential components of financial planning.

Uncertainties:

- **Economic Conditions:** Economic factors such as inflation, market fluctuations, interest rates, and job security can impact financial plans in unpredictable ways.

- **Health and Medical Expenses:** Unexpected illnesses, accidents, or medical emergencies can arise, leading to significant and unforeseen expenses.

- **Life Events:** While some life events are predictable, others, such as unemployment, separation, or the loss of a loved one, can disrupt financial plans unexpectedly.

- **Longevity:** The exact duration of retirement and associated expenses can be uncertain, as life expectancy varies from individual to individual.

Must-Have Financial Safety Nets

Safety nets are plan B (or C or D) put in place before you need them. They provide financial security against life's curveballs, unexpected expenses and the retirement years when you don't have income. Instead of waiting to react to these needs when they arise, it's better to be proactive and prepare for them. These are some common must-have financial safety nets at every milestone of your financial journey.

Food, Shelter, and Health Safety Nets

This is your basic survival kit; money stashed away, a house to stay in, food to eat, and the ability to handle any medical needs. This changes with the life stages over time.

Emergency Fund

This is your rainy day stash to cover life's curveballs. From a small expense of a flat tire, leaky roof, or sudden job loss – this fund buffers finances needed in times of emergencies.

Life and Disability Insurance

Life insurance ensures your family is financially secure if you pass away unexpectedly. Disability insurance replaces part of your income if you can't work due to an injury or illness.

Retirement Fund

This one is in preparation for your golden years. It's important because you will stop working and not have any source of income in retirement. This fund must be sizeable enough to ensure you'll have enough financial resources to live comfortably until life ends.

4. Financial Road Map Myths and Misconceptions

As we've seen many times in the journey of personal finance management, several myths and misconceptions can steer you off course. Here, we debunk some of the most common fallacies to help ensure your financial road map remains clear and effective.

Myth: "I'll Worry About It Later"

One of the most pervasive myths is the belief that financial planning can be put off until a later stage in life. Especially in the younger years, we often fall into the trap of thinking that we have plenty of time to start saving or investing. However, the reality is that starting earlier allows more time for your investments to grow.

Myth: "One Size Fits All"

Another common misconception is that everyone bases their financial plans on one template. In reality, each individual's financial road map should be tailored to their unique circumstances, goals, risk tolerance, and values. Some things may work for one person but may not work for another. You have to create your own plan that aligns with your specific needs and aspirations. If you try to fit into someone else's plan, you might end up lost and frustrated, no different from not having a road map.

Myth: "Set It and Forget It"

Another myth is the belief that once you've created a financial plan, you can simply set it and leave it there. Over time, all your plans will come good. Financial plans can become outdated and ineffective over time because life is dynamic, and your financial road map needs to be regularly reviewed and adjusted to account for changes in your circumstances, goals, or the economic environment.

Dispelling these myths is important. Starting early, tailoring your plan to your unique circumstances, and regularly updating your strategy, are important must-dos for successful financial journeys. Don't let misconceptions steer you off course; instead, navigate your financial landscape with informed confidence and precision.

5. Getting Down to Work: Creating Your Financial Road Map

Crafting a financial road map is a proactive step toward securing your financial future. Here's a progressive guide to set up your financial road map.

The Step-by-Step Guide

Step 1: Assess your finances

Be honest with yourself when you assess your financial situation. This will provide a baseline from which to build your road map and identify areas that need improvement or attention.

- **Understand Your Income, Expenses, and Net Worth:** Being clear on what you earn and spend is crucial.

- **Identify Financial Strengths, Weaknesses, and Goals:** This helps you understand what you're doing well and where you may need to make adjustments.

- **Use Practical Exercises and Worksheets:** These tools can simplify the complex task of financial evaluation and make it manageable.

Step 2: Define Your Life Goals and Priorities

Knowing what you want to achieve in life and ranking them by importance based on your desired outcomes and values, is the bedrock of your financial road map.

- **Set Targets Across Stages of Life:** Short, medium, and long-term goals each play a unique role in your financial plan.

- **Prioritize According to Your Values:** Align your financial objectives with what matters most to you.

Step 3: Set Specific Financial Goals

Transform your life goals into actionable financial targets that are precise, quantifiable, and attainable. These goals will guide your financial decisions and measure your progress.

Step 4: Develop a Budget and Savings Plan

Create a comprehensive financial plan that outlines strategies for budgeting, saving, investing, debt management, tax planning, and risk management. This plan should be made for you, to fit your situation.

- **Create a Realistic and Sustainable Budget:** Tailor your budget to reflect your financial assessment and goals.

- **Devise Strategies for Reducing Expenses and Increasing Savings:** Effective money management strategies are essential for financial growth.

Step 5: Implement Safety Nets and Contingency Plans

Protect yourself and your financial plan against life's uncertainties by establishing strong safety nets.

- **Emergency Funds and Insurance Policies:** These are crucial for managing unexpected expenses and financial shocks.

- **Contingency Plans:** Prepare for the unexpected to ensure your road map remains viable under different circumstances.

Step 6: Check In to Calibrate Road Map

A money road map is dynamic, not static. Regular revisions are necessary to adapt to life changes and economic shifts.

- **Schedule Regular Reviews:** Make it a habit to assess and adjust your financial plan to stay aligned with your evolving goals and circumstances.

Your Finances to Meet Those Goals

Plans will only remain plans without outcomes if we don't work on them. To fund these goals and safety nets, you need a solid financial foundation:

Budgeting and Expense Tracking

You need a budget to allocate accordingly to meet these goals. Know how much of your income is spent on what items every month. It's a filter to catch the money leaks before they turn into huge financial sinkholes.

Debt Management (Paying Off High-Interest Loans/Credit Cards)

High-interest rate debts are financial sinkholes, taking up all your financial resources and making it harder to save for your goals. Paying them down as early as possible frees up cash for savings.

Building Good Credit

Keeping good credit scores proves your good financial standing to unlock better loan interest rates and terms that will help in your wealth building. Keeping a good financial reputation by exhibiting good financial practicies and spending within your means will open doors and opportunities down the road.

The Safety Nets in Place

Think of safety nets as handlebars that keep you stable through life's bumpy financial terrain, while your goals are your dreams of the life you envision to live. If you don't have safety nets in place, life's curveballs can derail your plans and dreams.

Plans to Achieve Your Goals

This involves budgeting, saving, debt repayment strategies, and investment planning. Here is a guide for achieving your financial goals:

Step 1: Set Up Clear Goals

What are your goals? Dream a little, what does your ideal life look like? The more specific you can be, the better you can plan. Whether it's buying a home, retiring early, traveling the world, or simply feeling financially secure, be clear on what you're working toward.

Step 2: Make a Game Plan

With the visions of your ideal life, now it's time to map out your game plan for reaching those goals. This involves looking at the cold hard numbers:

- How much will you need for that down payment?

- What does your monthly retirement budget look like?

- Get specific about how much you'll need to save and by when.

Step 3: Budget Like a Champ

List out your income sources, then all your expenses – rent, groceries, gas, Netflix, etc. Categorize and prioritize where your money needs to go first. This gives you an idea of how much you can spend every month.

Step 4: Treat Debt Like Your Worst Enemy

Every dollar going toward interest is a dollar not working toward your goals. Plan to pay down high-interest debts like credit cards. The sooner you neutralize debt, the sooner you can focus on saving more for your goals.

Step 5: Cut Costs and Increase Earnings

Find ways to trim your spending and subscriptions, shop smartly and avoid unproductive debts. Every bit of savings gives you more to funnel toward your goals.

Step 6: Invest Wisely

Once you've built up some cash, it's time to put it to work through investing. Depending on your goals and timelines, diversify your investments into different types of assets. The key is having a long-term, disciplined strategy aligned with your goals.

Step 7: Check Your Progress Regularly

Don't just make plans and forget them. Review your plan, budget, and investment performance regularly. Adjust as needed to make sure you're still on track. Celebrating small wins along the way helps keep you motivated too!

Having a clear purpose and financial road map, you can slowly but surely make progress toward turning your financial goals into realities.

Keeping Track of Plans to Meet the Goals

Adapt as your life circumstances change. In reality, life isn't static – things are constantly changing and evolving. Your job situation, relationships, living situation, health, and priorities can all shift over time in ways you may not anticipate. As circumstances change around you, you will need to adjust to adapt to those changes. For example, if you start a family, you will have to add their financial needs to all your financial goals. The key is to build in regular check-ins to go over your budget, savings, investments, and overall progress toward your money goals. Don't just set it and forget it.

Each step on this road map not only moves you closer to your financial goals but also equips you with the tools and knowledge to navigate the financial landscape with confidence.

Conclusion: Navigating Your Financial Journey with Confidence

As we wrap up this chapter, let's reflect on the vital role a financial road map plays in your life. This road map is more than just a set of directions; it's your personal guide to financial well-being, helping you navigate through uncertainties with confidence and clarity.

Chapter Takeaways

Start Early, Start Now: Starting to plan early allows your money more time to grow. When you reinvest your gains, your investments compound and your money can grow even faster.

Customize Your Approach: There isn't one money road map template that fits everyone. Customize your road map according to your unique circumstances, goals, and dreams.

Stay Proactive and Adaptable: Adapt and keep it relevant and effective with changing times. Regular reviews and adjustments are essential.

By taking control of your finances today, you lay the groundwork for a more prosperous and stable tomorrow.

Take that first step today. Assess where you are, define where you want to be, and start mapping out your path. Use the recommendations in this chapter to guide you. And remember, the journey to financial security is ongoing – regular checks and adjustments will help ensure you remain on track.

Every step you take on this journey is a building block for your future. With each decision, each saving and each budget adjustment, you're not just planning – you're also acting toward a life of financial independence and security. Start small if you must, but start today.

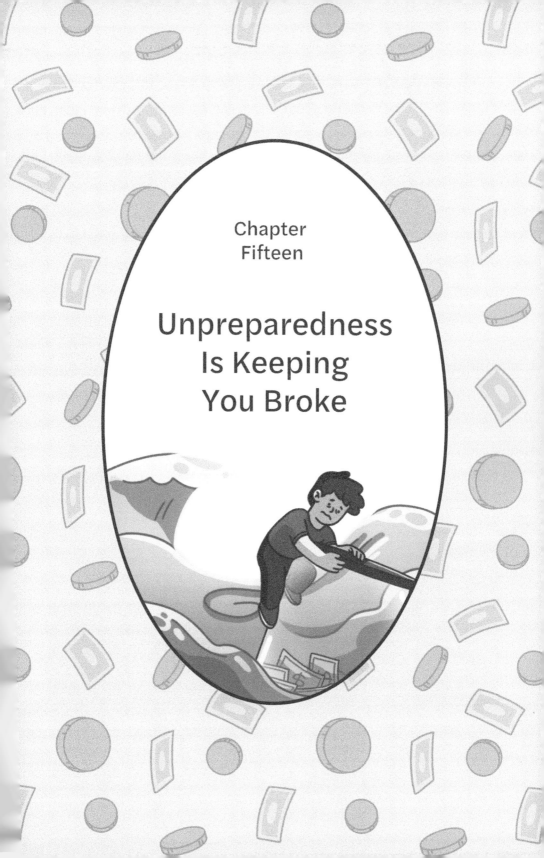

Chapter
Fifteen

Unpreparedness Is Keeping You Broke

UNPREPAREDNESS IS KEEPING YOU BROKE

If life has been uneventful lately, that should be a cause for celebration, right? While we crave excitement and thrill here and there, it's nice to appreciate ordinary days go by. The truth is, we rarely do. And when we do, it's usually because we find ourselves in situations we want to escape. Fast.

Mary lives a fairly exciting life as a media content producer. She travels a lot for work and makes more than enough money for her needs. Living her best life, she spends most of her earnings on experiences and shopping, believing she's only got one chance at life; parties, clothes, fancy meals, you name it. Everything was fine until she received the news that her mom was diagnosed with cancer. Mary's world came to a full stop. She was not expecting this. As the eldest child and the only one making a living, she knew she had to do something to help. Without her mom having health insurance and savings, and with steep medical bills to face and settle, Mary found herself in a tight spot, wishing she had considered this in her plans.

Unexpected events, emergencies, and curveballs – no matter how solid your financial road map is, these are things you cannot predict – but you can surely prepare for them!

In this chapter, we will show you how disregarding life's surprises can keep you from achieving your financial goals. Of course, we won't stop there! We'll also guide you on thoughtfully considering these possible bumps in your plans so you can deal with them as you tread the path of your financial journey.

1. Financial Curveballs: Life's Costly Surprises

Life will surprise you when you least expect it. You probably won't have any clue as to what curveball might come your way, so it's best to familiarize yourself with some twists to your financial story.

We've listed a few sticky situations you (or your loved ones) might encounter and leave you empty-handed:

Unemployment or Pay Cut: Losing a job or getting hit by a pay cut can hurt right away and effectively start a financial domino effect. Without significant savings or side hustles as alternatives, you risk falling behind on bills, drowning in credit card debts, and damaging your credit score.

Emergency Home and Auto Repairs: Things that are one day fine can unexpectedly present problems that need fixing in our homes (roof, plumbing) or on the road (car accidents, engine breakdowns). Without a safety net or the right insurance, this can lead to expensive rehabilitation, medical bills, and financial strain.

Natural Disasters: Act of God events can cause significant property damage, leaving you with hefty repair bills or the entire cost of replacing belongings, if you're uninsured.

Medical Emergencies: Unexpectedly falling sick or injuring yourself in an accident can cost a lot, especially without good insurance. This can significantly impact your finances, potentially leading to medical debt, bankruptcy, or the depletion of your retirement savings. The same goes for when a medical emergency involves your dependents and other family members, especially if you are the breadwinner.

Disability or Long-Term Illness: Sudden illness or injury can sideline you from work, hurting your income and, in effect, your financial goals and your lifestyle. You might also need permanent support from your family members, not to mention more than enough savings to get you through therapy and healthcare maintenance. Disability insurance can help provide a monthly benefit if you can't work due to a covered disability.

Caring for Children and Elderly Loved Ones: Being stuck in the sandwich generation is financially draining. While it's a cultural norm in many families to care for your elderly parents or relatives while also caring for your own children, underestimating its impact on your finances can be a shock. Costs like medical care, assisted living, home modifications, education, and even relocation can leave you and your wallet drained. That's why planning ahead and sharing caregiving duties with siblings (if there are any) can help ease the burden.

Educational Costs for Children: Educational costs for academic and other extra-curricular activities are a known expense for families, but what is often not considered is the yearly rise in tuition and other school-related fees. This can easily eat away at your budget if you haven't planned for it.

Loss of a Loved One: A spouse or family member's passing is a significant loss that can be difficult both emotionally and financially. Apart from the terrible loss it brings, funeral expenses, outstanding debts, and potential loss of income can impact your finances, especially if there's no life insurance or estate planning. Those who were left behind may also face hardship if they were financially dependent on the loved one who passed on.

Changes in Relationship Dynamics: Life and relationships are bound to change one way or another. Whether navigating a divorce, welcoming a new addition to the family, or taking on caregiving responsibilities, your finances are bound to be affected. By planning ahead and talking things through, you can adjust your budget, manage expenses smoothly, and keep your financial goals on track, whatever your family situation may be.

2. The Truth About Life's Surprises

We know how important emergency planning is and that we don't want to get caught up in the middle of an unexpected event. But sometimes, there are things we believe to convince ourselves that we can do without until we need it.

Myth 1: "Unexpected events won't happen to me." We'd like to think that life is predictable. Well surprise, surprise: It's not! Life does not always go as planned and unexpected events turn up more times than we think. You can lose your job, get into a nasty accident, or have your car break down in the middle of the freeway – these can impact your finances and derail your goals, especially if you're unprepared. When you prepare for the worst by building an emergency fund or getting yourself insured, you take charge of your financial future.

Myth 2: "My savings are enough to cover any emergency." It's great that you've been saving up. Still, your savings shouldn't be taking the hit for when life surprises you with unexpected events. Most times, they can be pretty expensive like a major car repair or a medical diagnosis that will need ongoing healthcare management – things that might be more than what your savings can handle. That's why having a fund solely for emergencies is an ideal safety net.

Myth 3: "An emergency fund can wait." Life is not a series you watch on your phone with a handy pause button. Preparing for events you cannot predict is something you can't afford to delay. Sometimes, all it takes is one emergency for your financial dreams to crumble so it's best to set aside some savings for these emergencies. Think of it as an investment you make for peace of mind.

3. Building Your Financial Fortress: Preparation Tips

No matter what curveballs come your way, no amount of planning can fully prepare you for them all. By having savings to deal with them, you can safeguard yourself against these events, softening the blows on your finances.

Build an Emergency Fund: Save change to three to six months of your expenses to cover unexpected events such as unemployment, accidents, and unexpected repair works for your home.

Set Up a Sinking Fund: If you have money kept for emergencies, also save for expenses you do expect, like timed and expected repair, maintenance, and replacements – much like your car's preventive maintenance. A sinking fund also covers planned expenses such as a weekend getaway or even a wedding!

Get Yourself Insured: Protect yourself and your loved ones from life's unwanted surprises with a well-chosen insurance plan. Consider disability, death, property damage, and similar events. Compare plans to find a comprehensive coverage that is not only a bang for your buck, but one that also suits your needs the best.

Reduce Debt: Settle loans and credit card due dates on time, and make sure not to take out any more unnecessary loans. Make repayment your top priority and use strategies like the debt snowball or debt avalanche method.

Create Multiple Income Streams: If your time and energy allow it, look for a side hustle, make sound investments, or generate passive income. Having more than one revenue stream can make you resilient and your finances rock solid.

Begin Estate Planning: Draft a written will and detail how you want your estate to be managed in the event of incapacity or death. Update these documents regularly to reflect any changes in your circumstances or preferences.

Post-It.

Debt Snowball Method: This method focuses on tackling smaller debts first before leveling up to the next bigger one. As you celebrate every debt paid as a win, you keep at it and build momentum until all debts are cleared.

Debt Avalanche Method: Contrary to the snowball method, this repayment strategy tackles the most expensive debt, the highest interest one, before moving on to the next one with the highest interest rate to save on charges in the long term.

4. Financial Resilience: The Power of Preparedness

Preparedness empowers you to navigate unexpected events in all aspects. Early and thorough preparation helps you deal with emergencies without risking your finances. The goal is to be financially resilient. How do we do that?

Let's examine the tips we shared earlier more closely, focusing on how they can build resilience in us.

Put Your Eggs in Multiple Baskets

 Having multiple sources of income is an essential strategy to protect yourself and your family. These money streams should be independent of each other so that when one takes a hit, the other can quickly respond. Here are ways various income channels can help:

Eliminates Single Income Dependency: Relying solely on a day job or business can make individuals vulnerable to financial setbacks in case of unemployment, a pay cut, or a closure. By having additional income streams, you will always have an alternative source of money.

Helps Weather Economic Storms: Mixed-income sources may perform differently during economic downturns or market fluctuations. For example, revenue from houses or spaces you rent may remain relatively stable even when you suffer a pay cut.

Cushions Against Job Loss: Maybe you get laid off. If you have other income streams, they can be your financial safety net while finding a new job. You can also monetize your hobbies and skills by doing side hustles or freelancing to help cover expenses during periods of unemployment.

Cut Down on Debt

Less debt means less stress for you; that's why it's important to clear as much debt as you can. Settling your debts helps you build financial resilience as it:

Lessens Financial Obligations: Slashing your debt frees up more breathing room in your budget. You'll worry less about the money you owe, and there will be more cash available for your other expenses like groceries, bills, and even your emergency fund! You have more control over your finances when you have less debt.

Lowers Interest Payments: Debt usually comes with interest. It is like quicksand that traps you deeper and deeper the more money you owe – it traps you with more and more interest, making it harder for you to work your way out. By reducing debt, you slash the interest you pay, saving money in the long term.

Boosts Credit Score: Paying down debt shows your creditworthiness, which improves your credit scores. This opens you up to better deals on loans and credit cards, like lower interest rates and higher credit limits.

Reduces Stress and Anxiety: The more debt you have, the more anxious you get, causing your stress levels to shoot through the roof. Cutting down your debt can help relieve this financial pressure-induced anxiety, giving you peace of mind.

Increases Financial Flexibility: Less debt gives you more wiggle room in your budget. With fewer debts to pay, you're more free to pursue your financial goals.

Protects Against Income Loss: Imagine losing your job or shutting down your business with debts to pay. It's a financial nightmare. That's why it's wise to cut down on your debts, so in tough times, the blow won't hurt so bad. You can even use your savings from debt repayment to get you through your recovery period.

Start Estate Planning

Part of your financial road map should include estate planning documents. These legal documents serve as a guide on what happens to your stuff after you're gone: they usually outline how you want your money, properties, and possessions handled. These documents ensure your wishes are communicated, respected, and followed while also protecting your loved ones left behind, avoiding any family squabbles in the future. Some common estate planning documents include:

Last Will and Testament (Will): A will is a legal document that outlines how a person's assets and properties should be distributed after their death. It allows you to specify beneficiaries, designate guardians you trust for your kids, set up a trust fund to provide financial support for them until they reach adulthood, name an executor (someone to oversee the distribution of assets), and address other wishes such as funeral arrangements.

Revocable Living Trust: Like a vault, it holds your assets for safekeeping while you're alive and able, and provides instructions for their distribution upon your passing. It avoids probate or a lengthy court process and keeps things under wraps. The good thing is that you can control it while you're alive and name someone you trust for when you pass on later.

Living Will (Advance Directive): Think of it as your voice when you can't speak. This lets your loved ones' doctors know how you want to be treated medically in the event you are too sick to tell them yourself. It serves as a guide on what treatments you will allow (or not), especially in tough situations like deciding on whether to put you on life support, artificial nutrition, or to pull the plug. A living will helps ensure your desires are expressed and respected while taking the burden of making difficult decisions off your loved ones.

Durable Power of Attorney: It lets you appoint someone you trust to manage your finances and make medical decisions for you when you are unable to. For example, if a person suffers a severe injury in an accident, their designated agent can continue to pay for bills, manage investments, and handle other financial matters according to their wishes.

Beneficiary Designations: These are instructions on what to do with some of your accounts, like retirement funds or life insurance, when you're gone – all without having to go to court. They are somewhat like a shortcut that lets you assign who receives your money after you pass on minus the hassle. A clear and comprehensive estate plan minimizes disputes within your family about who has a claim on your assets. This is especially helpful in ensuring a smoother inheritance distribution, avoiding expensive and lengthy legal battles.

Estate planning documents work to ensure your wishes are followed, assets are protected, and loved ones are cared and provided for even after you are gone. Consult a professional to help you create an estate plan tailored to your needs.

Post-It.

Probate: A court process that sorts out one's assets (money, property, belongings) and distributes them according to the law in the absence of a will. This process can take time and can also be part of public record.

5. Conclusion

Life is full of surprises; some are good and some are bad. Try as we can, predicting each one is futile, which makes financial preparedness our best bet in facing them. Not only do we protect ourselves and our savings from a possible financial crisis, but we also empower ourselves on how to confidently weather life's many storms.

Debunking myths like "Our savings can cover any emergencies," "Unexpected events won't happen to me," or "I can prepare for emergencies later" will help us begin our financial preparedness journey.

Important tasks include building a financial fortress against life's curveballs like prioritizing savings for the unexpected and planned purchases, getting insured, cutting back on debts, pursuing multiple sources of income, and sorting our affairs with estate planning. These are ways to protect us from the unexpected and keep us financially healthy.

Remember, a little effort goes a long way when it comes to preparing for our future. Readiness lets us control our money destiny, embracing the unexpected with a little less fear and a lot more confidence.

Bonus: To know more about easy ways to make your money work harder for you, our Appendix section has these covered and more! Oh, and don't forget to check out our emergency fund calculator, it's a great starting point to your financial preparedness journey.

CONCLUSION

Yay! You've made it here! Props to you!

By now, you may have realized that financial freedom does not depend solely on making more money. You haven't shattered a lot of myths to be stuck believing that, right? Yes, increasing your income is important, but it's only one part of the story.

Think of it like filling your water canteen to keep you hydrated while you tackle your financial road map. It's challenging because you only get to fill it up at rest stops where fresh water's available. Similarly, increasing income provides you with the security and ability to address unexpected needs. But just like a water bottle with holes in it, simply earning more won't guarantee a secure future if you're not keeping tabs on your spending. Managing your expenses plugs those leaks, making sure that the water you've worked so hard to accumulate stays in your hydration pack. You see, both strategies – earning more and spending wisely – are crucial for financial preparedness.

For many young people, planning for future finances feels like a chore. That's why we're so proud of you for taking the time to read this book and reaching this point! It's one step you've taken toward investing in your future and taking control of your financial well-being.

This just makes us all the more committed to push forth with our mission to empower everyone, especially young adults, to successfully manage their personal finances. Full steam ahead!

What you need to do now is to keep it up and be consistent. Developing good financial habits could seem daunting at first, but it's no more difficult than forming bad ones and trying to get out of them later. The key is to make sure you vibe with the right tribe who influence you positively, share your vision, and constantly encourage you to focus on the end goal: financial freedom! Eyes on the prize!

Speaking of vision, here's ours: A generation of financially empowered people, confidently taking control of their future! We at The Simple Sum want to equip you with the knowledge and tools you need to become financially disciplined, no matter what your situation may be. Because even when life throws you curveballs, the core principles of financial planning remain your constants on this journey.

Still, we want you to know that this is only a guide, not a rigid blueprint. Follow the pieces that apply to your unique situation and goals, and trust yourself that you can take charge of your finances.

We wish you the best of luck as you build and travel your financial road map!

Cheering you on,

The Simple Sum Team

P.S.
Come back anytime you need to check on something. That's what we're here for.

Find Us On:
🌐 thesimplesum.com
📷 instagram.com/thesimplesumsg/
📘 facebook.com/thesimplesumsg/
♪ tiktok.com/@thesimplesumsg
▶ youtube.com/@TheSimpleSum
✈ t.me/thesimplesum

INDEX